THE CHILDREN'S CHOIR

RUTH KREHBIEL JACOBS

The

Children's

Choir

AUGUSTANA PRESS   Rock Island, Illinois

THE CHILDREN'S CHOIR

Copyright, 1958, by

AUGUSTANA BOOK CONCERN

Library of Congress Catalog Card Number 57-12900

MT
88
.J17

Third Printing

[PRINTED
IN U·S·A·]

AUGUSTANA BOOK CONCERN
Printers and Binders
ROCK ISLAND, ILLINOIS
1960

Preface

THE STEADY GROWTH of children's choirs, both in numbers and in quality, is a strange enigma. Almost every condition under which they have taken root and flourished is unfriendly to them: comparatively few ministers recognize their value; professional church musicians are only superficially trained in their guidance; and religious education directors in general look on them with distrust. But in spite of these unfavorable circumstances, they steadily increase in numbers and in effectiveness.

Like Topsy, the children's choir movement "Just growed," without benefit of disciplined guidance. For the comparatively few experienced directors, trained in the techniques and psychology of teaching in general, and of music teaching in particular, there are many, many more, who because they play the piano a bit, or get along well with children, have been drafted into directing the children's choir. And they have had to carry on alone, creating their own methods and generating their own enthusiasm, without the encouragement of contact with others in the field. Until recently there was no medium for the exchange of ideas and experiences; nor any opportunity to measure one's achievements against a common standard.

It was to meet these needs, and to supply a sense of direction to the movement, that the Choristers' Guild was organized in 1949. From a very small beginning it has grown into a non-profit association with an interdenominational and international membership of educators, directors, and clergy, concerned that the children's choir should not degenerate into a popular fad, but become an increasingly purposeful implement for the cultivation of Christian character.

The more one works with children's choirs, the more one becomes convinced of the determining influence they can have on the church as well as on the children. In a good choir the child soon learns that each is responsible for the whole. And eventually he learns, too, to accept that responsibility. Since in singing, the carelessness of one child can cancel the concentrated efforts of the whole choir, it is of the greatest importance that children learn to give wholehearted co-operation, even at the cost of personal indulgence. They develop that quality not through generalized preachments, but by learning to practice it.

v

For the same reason, the choir is in a unique position to teach the meaning of worship. One cannot be responsible for the spirit of worship without oneself becoming responsive to that spirit. It is much easier to be conscious of being in the House of God when clothed in a churchly vestment, and responsible for leadership in the acts of worship, than when sitting half asleep in one of the pews.

With discrimination in the music used, the years in the children's choir provide the child with a wealth of religious truths, expressed with dignity and beauty, and easily remembered because of music's great power of recall.

The potential contribution of the children's choir is not limited to one area. It is a character-forming agency; it affords an unparalleled opportunity for the experience of true worship; it can supplement and extend the curriculum of the Church School. The honest director accepts responsibility for good music, good habits, sound religious education, and sincere worship. It is a program for which the director himself needs constant encouragement and renewal.

The *Choristers Guild Letters,* published monthly from September through June, are an attempt to meet that need. They come to the director each month with suggestions for materials and rehearsal procedures, disciplinary problems, administration, parental co-operation and the many other considerations that are determining factors in the success or failure of a choir program. But they also bring him the comforting consciousness that he is part of a great fellowship that shares his disappointments as well as his aspirations.

This book is an organized collection of the materials published in the *Choristers Guild Letters* from the first issue in September 1949 until June 1957.

Wherever possible, quotations were traced to their original source, and both author and publisher acknowledged.

But much of the material comes from the experience of the Guild members themselves. This volume is not the product of laboratory controlled tests, but rather the summary of the experiments, the flashes of inspiration, the ingenuity, the devoted steady effort of creative directors in churches of many denominations, in all parts of the country, working with children of varied cultural and economic backgrounds.

And it is to these generous collaborators that this book is gratefully dedicated.

August 4, 1957

RUTH KREHBIEL JACOBS

Contents

The Choristers' Guild

The Choristers' Guild is an organization dedicated to Christian character through children's choirs. It was started in 1949 to help church musicians with the many problems of maintaining a children's choir. The churches that expected an inclusive choir program were increasing; schools were graduating church music majors without training in children's choir techniques; and both churches and directors were at a loss as to objectives and methods.

Realizing the great potential influence of the children's choir movement, the Choristers' Guild has undertaken to give it purposeful leadership. Its program has come to include:

The *Choristers' Guild Letters,* published monthly (September to June), filled with suggestions and practical advice on the many subjects related to children's choir work, such as, discipline, organization, selection of music, rehearsal plans, hymn learning, parent co-operation, equipment, sight singing, tone, etc.

Better standards of achievement through the Guild Merit System.

Choristers' Guild chapters for the encouragement of local directors.

Progressive material for children's choir notebooks.

Short seminars in all parts of the country.

Summer schools.

Children's choir festivals.

It is our firm belief that the choir can be a profound factor in the

1

religious growth of children. It teaches them to give themselves wholeheartedly to group endeavor; it gives them happy associations with the church; it trains them in the fundamentals of leadership: regularity, loyalty, dependability, and idealism; it teaches them the great song literature of the church; it provides a satisfying means of self-expression; and through a responsible part in the service of worship, it opens the door to the experience of worship.

Furthermore, the children's choir bridges denominational differences, as it can be a means of tying together the far corners of the whole Christian world.

The children's choir is a powerful tool, and the Choristers' Guild is dedicated to its use in the intelligent shaping of worthy Christian leadership. Working together toward that objective are dedicated ministers, teachers, and musicians in all the states of the Union, and in many foreign countries. The directed efforts of a world-wide association can accomplish things that are impossible for an individual, or any number of unorganized individuals.

If the Choristers' Guild is to realize its full potential, it must appeal to the faith and the generosity of a large number of people. Each of us can help in our own way, with Contributing memberships, special gifts, and by interesting others in the movement.

GUILD MEMBERSHIP

Membership in the Choristers' Guild is open to all people interested in children's choirs, and their potential influence on Christian education. Annual dues are $4.00, which entitle one to receive the *Choristers' Guild Letters,* published from September to June.

Members who are actively in charge of a choir are encouraged to:
Reach as many children as possible.
Present worthy music, adequately prepared.
Encourage reverence.
Use the choir as a means of character development.
Make the choir a religious, artistic, educational and recreational influence in the lives of the children.
Support the purposes of the Choristers' Guild.

CONTRIBUTING MEMBERS

A gift of $10.00 a year makes one a Contributing Member. Both organizations and individuals may become Contributing Members.

2

The children's choir represents a tremendous character influence. It works with two of the greatest powers known: religion and music. It works through the strongest moral force known to society —the Christian Church. The Contributing Member has a keen awareness of his personal obligation to the present and the future, to others and to himself. Because of that awareness, he is constantly improving his methods, enlarging and deepening the meaning of the choir experience, and supporting the Choristers' Guild's efforts to knit together in one universal movement the scattered seeds of growth. It is the Contributing Member who will bring that goal in sight.

VOTING MEMBERS

Voting Members are those who have been Contributing Members for five successive years. They are entitled to attend the annual meeting, and to a voice in determining the policies of the Guild.

All memberships are annual, and run from September to September. The *Choristers' Guild Letters* are mailed to all members.

THE CHORISTERS' PIN

The Merit System

75 credits for 100% attendance at rehearsals and performances.
50 credits for 85% attendance at rehearsals and performances.
25 credits for a complete and neat notebook.
25 credits for 100% attendance at church school.
15 credits for 85% attendance at church school.
25 credits for good behavior.
> (It is suggested that a child be given a demerit, if he needs to be reprimanded. Ten demerits should disqualify him for these credits.)

15 credits for bringing a new member.
> (granted only if new member remains through the season; no more than 15 credits granted in any one year.)

This system is based on a nine months' season of regular weekly rehearsals. To earn a pin, a chorister must earn 100 credits during the year. The virtue of the system is that it is impossible to earn a pin without being regular, and it is also impossible to earn one by attendance only.

The Choristers' pin is the first year award in the Junior Choir.

Each successive year, the pin is returned to the Guild, to have a pearl set in it.

Upon graduation to the Junior High School Choir, the pin is returned to the Guild to have the guard attached.

CHORISTERS' GUILD CHAPTERS

With the increase in Guild members in various communities has come the formation of local chapters for mutual encouragement and more purposeful local action. That every chapter may honestly bear the name of the Choristers' Guild, and worthily serve its high purposes, the following conditions are required:

The official title shall be: The *(city or area)* Chapter, an Affiliate of the Choristers' Guild.

There shall be a minimum membership of five.

Every member must be a member of the national organization.

The Chapter shall promote an annual Children's Choir Festival.

At least four regular meetings shall be held annually.

An annual report of the Chapter's activities shall be sent to the Choristers' Guild headquarters.

The Chapter fulfilling these conditions shall be entitled to the use of the Choristers' Guild's copyrighted letterhead.

Suggested Subjects for Guild Chapter Meetings

September. On reaching the WHOLE church.
October. Making the home music-conscious.
November. Better rehearsal methods.
December. Teaching resources.
January. Providing for the changing voice crowd.
February. Our responsibility for worship habits.
March. A community-wide, interdenominational music program.
April. Symposium on new materials.
May. Plans for next season.

Organization

ESSENTIALS OF A WORTHY CHOIR SEASON

Ceremony of Choir Dedication
  to open the season.
A Thanksgiving project
  one that provides opportunity to show thanks by giving.
A Christmas celebration
  it should reflect the real, not the superficial, spirit of Christmas.
A Program underlining the meaning of Holy Week.
A Festival of the Singing Church,
  a culmination of a year of hymn study, with family participation;
  (to include a Family Night as well as the festival).
A Children's Choir Festival
  participating with other choirs of the community.
Two major study projects.
  (Hymns for the Festival of the Singing Church may be one.)
Service of Recognition
  to close the season;
  presentation of promotion certificates and Choristers' pins.

Additional Interests

Two or three unusual parties.
A trip in connection with one of the project studies.
A summer camp, during the vacation period.
  (May be held at the church, or some resort.)

DIRECTOR'S CODE TO ACHIEVEMENT

Avoid Trouble

Keep the age range in each group limited.

Four to six; seven and eight; nine to twelve; Junior High; High School.

Plan a full schedule of interesting events.

Keep the rehearsals full and varied.

Have a few basic rules, understood and accepted by all, including you.

Keep careful records—attendance and all requirements.

Win the Respect of the Children

Be fair, but firm.

Don't lose your temper.

Learn to know each child, his home, his interests, his personality.

Welcome and respect their confidences.

Show a real interest in their other activities.

Share the Responsibility

Plan, and work in co-operation with the minister and the religious education director.

Have a regular hymn study period with the children's departments of the Church School.

Keep the church informed on the activities of the choirs.

Organize a choir mothers' guild; give them specific responsibilities and authority.

Dignify the program with an annual Service of Dedication and of Recognition.

Reach Out

Co-operate with other denominations for a festival.

Start a Choristers' Guild chapter; share your ideas and your problems.

Visit some outstanding church; attend a seminar or summer school.

Map out a program of constructive reading for yourself.

Find some way to help make the Choristers' Guild financially secure.

Learn to Be

Patient, but persistent.

A steady worker whether things go well or not so well.

6

Openminded and openhearted.

Serious without being solemn.

Resourceful and imaginative.

Have Faith In

GOD, the children, the church, yourself.

and in

the responsibility of children's choirs to the future.

FOR A PROFITABLE SUMMER

Lay your plans for attracting new children to the choir.

Do something to increase your knowledge.

Select a dozen new anthems and memorize them, words and structure.

Read one or several books.

Attend Summer School.

Collect materials.

Illustrations for the bulletin board.

Interesting little designs to make the notebook pages attractive.

Make a collection of children's prayers.

Find some worth-while service project for next season.

Catch up on music.

Review your *Letters* for new music suggestions.

Write to the publishers for selected on-approval numbers.

Have the children help mend and file the music used this season.

Start a community-wide plan; invite directors to a meeting to consider:

A festival, and be prepared to make suggestions for music and organization.

A children's concert series.

(Perhaps you could sponsor a concert by the Columbus Boy Choir or some other well-known children's choir.)

A series of movie matinees for the children, using such films as Martin Luther, John Wesley, Prince Valiant, etc.

IN UNION IS STRENGTH

Your choir is a part of the total religious training program of your church, and your church is a part of your community. All three should profit from your efforts.

In making your plans for the choir, remember that you are working with formative human beings who:

Learn most easily whatever seems to them important.

Learn most quickly what is related to that which they already know.

Learn most willingly from someone they respect and admire.

Learn by doing.

Remember that the Church School is interested in the same children, and that if you work as a team, the impact of both is greater.

Remember that there are other directors in the community who need your help, and some who can help you. Jealous aloofness is an unworthy trait in one whose profession is character building.

In your year's program, consider all three: children, church, community.

GETTING STARTED

"How does one go about organizing a choir where there has never been one?"

It isn't easy, but with hard work and great enthusiasm it can be done in any church. Here is how it was done in one instance, as related by Fred Holler of Baton Rouge, Louisiana:

Announcement was made in the newspapers and in the church bulletins, in the church and in the Church School. The minister furnished the names of people who sang or who might know of singers. I began making calls; I called on 96 prospects, but it took twice that many calls to find them all at home.

As I approached the completion of my calling, I became increasingly enthusiastic about the large, fine choir we were going to have. Everyone was so glad we were to have a choir at last, and nearly all my prospects were interested in joining. I was elated, and told the minister that 55 people had definitely promised to be at rehearsal.

Friday night came: 7:30 was the hour. Arriving early was a middle-aged alto. At 7:30 there were five people present. I was disturbed, but did not allow the faithful to sense my dismay. Two men came in, both tenors. We began the rehearsal with eight people. A little later, one more alto came. A doctor came in quite late. We finally had a grand total of ten people—five sopranos, two altos, two tenors, and one bass. And 55 had definitely promised! I was disillusioned. Everyone had been so willing to have a choir (that is, if someone else did the work).

But by noon the next day I had recovered and was vigorously calling to find out why the miscreants had not appeared. This steady plugging produced results. The people began coming in from outside our church as well as from our own members. We worked hard at rehearsals. We had an ideal to fight for, and we won out.

And the moral of the tale is this:

He called on all prospects.

He didn't make the faithful suffer because of the unfaithful.

He worked with those present.

He recovered from his disappointment, and redoubled his efforts.

He had an ideal, and instilled an ideal.

And the work prospered. *It's bound to.*

WHAT'S IN A NAME?

There is so much variation in the use of choir names that they give no indication of the age range of the choir. Among our members, Carol Choir (for instance) is used for Preschool, Primary, Junior High girls, and High School choir. The only way we can avoid confusion is to refer, in this book, to the basic divisions in school and Church School.

Beginners: nursery and kindergarten; 4-5 years old.

Primary: first to third grades; 6-8 years old.

Junior: fourth to sixth grades; 9-12 years old.

Intermediate: seventh to ninth grades; 13-15 years old.

High School: tenth to twelfth grades; 16-18 years old.

Letter to Parents at Beginning of Choir Season

Date:

Dear Friends:

The Children's Choir will start a new season with its first rehearsal on ...., the .... of September, at ....o'clock.

We hope your child will want to attend, and are writing to make sure of your approval and co-operation.

Although the choir is for children only, we know that the entire family actually becomes a part of the organization.

Family interest helps the singer learn the hymns and anthems.

Family planning helps the choir member to be on time.

Family responsibility avoids plans that conflict with choir obligations.

Family co-operation helps the children develop pride in their choir, and loyalty to its goals.

Our choir is a member of the Choristers' Guild, a world-wide association; through its merit system your child may earn a Chorister's pin. These are to be awarded in a public ceremony at the close of the season. The merit system is outlined below. Study it carefully, and help your child to work at the top level of his ability.

The choir should be an important experience for your child; by working together, we can make it so. Will you both sign the pledge of membership, and bring it along to the first rehearsal.

Very sincerely yours,

. . . .

Choristers' Guild Merit System

75 credits for 100% attendance at rehearsals and performances.
50 credits for 85% attendance at rehearsals and performances.
25 credits for excellent deportment.
25 credits for a complete and neat notebook.
25 credits for 100% attendance at Church School.
15 credits for 85% attendance at Church School.
*15 credits for bringing a new member.

> * only if new member remains through the season. No more than 15 credits granted in any one year.

To qualify for a Chorister's pin, the chorister must earn a total of 100 credits during the season.

Pledge of Membership

As co-operating members of the . . . . choir, we agree:
To make every effort to be regular, dependable, co-operative and loyal.
To memorize all the required music.
To give advance notice in case of necessary absence.

Choir member . . . .

Parent . . . .

(A separate card to be enclosed in the letter.)

Letter to Parents at Close of Choir Season

Dear Choir Parents:

Many of your children have been members of the choirs for the past two years. It is with deep gratitude that all of us who work with the choirs say "thank you" for your co-operation and understanding.

Last year only the choir mothers evaluated the year's work, and in view of that evaluation planned for this year's choir activities.

But this year we want your reactions as parents. So we have prepared an evaluation sheet for you to check. You need not sign it, if you so prefer. But we want your honest opinion, mailed by March 6, and sent to the church, attention Choir Mothers.

On May 7, our fall plans will be made in view of your evaluation sheets. Please help us make a better choir program for the children of our community.

Please check Yes or No:

Does the music satisfy your child's ability?

Is enough time allowed to memorize the music?

Are you satisfied with the quality of performance?

Do you think the notebook is a help to your child?

Have the refreshments worked a hardship on you?

Do you think that having your child as a member of the choir has enriched his life and given him a fuller understanding of Christian fellowship?

With the same type of program in view for next year as we have had in the past, do you think your child will return to choir in the fall?

Could you assist in the work of the choirs by serving as a choir mother, or an accompanist?

Comment, please.

What do you feel that those of us who work with the youth choirs can do to make choir more interesting to the Junior High age level?

If the novelty of choir has worn thin for your child, what would you suggest that we as choir mothers do to help stimulate his interest?

Other comments:

This is a part of the evaluation program at the Carpinteria, California, Community Church, where John Imbach is pastor, and his wife has charge of the music. The church has a membership of 350. Seventy-three families are represented in the choirs, and fifty-two of the evaluation sheets were returned. A separate evaluation sheet was given to the boys and the girls in the Junior High choir.

At the Choir Mothers' Evaluation Luncheon, these responses are given careful consideration and help to determine the program for the following year.

On Recognition Sunday, the Choir Mothers were surprised by being presented Choristers' pins in recognition of their faithful service. Mrs. Imbach reports that they were even more proud of their insignia than the children.

SPRING HOUSECLEANING

The Oklahoma winds, warm weather, and school activities are taking their toll. The youth whose interest has been so high this year suddenly turns to thoughts of out-of-doors, baseball practice, and such. Then, too, the leaders are also aware that spring is here with its beckoning finger.

While planning the All-choir dinner, its decorations coming from hymns and anthems that we have studied during the year, and arranging the music for our fifth annual Festival of Choirs, there comes the thought that now is the time to evaluate the progress for the year. This includes materials used, methods of teaching, and how much we accomplished toward our goals for this year.

In order really to start at the beginning, I must examine first the materials that we used. What was the response from the choir members? Did we teach the materials outlined for the year in the most interesting way? Have I been able to inspire the leaders to greater effort and understanding? Had my choice of certain individuals to work with a certain age group been wise?

With the use of the broom, we should make our fall plans now.

This year we have had twenty-eight helpers to carry on a 12-choir system for 400 people, so my first objective for the fall school of choirs is to set up the faculty. What are the qualifications I seek in selecting the faculty? A love of children, the love of church and serving its program, and a love of good music. Without all three qualities, a person is never invited to join our leadership program.

It is like seeing old friends again to sit down and go through files of anthem materials, teaching methods, Sunday school literature, hymnbooks, public school music materials, books on youth choir organization and methods, this year's repertoire and goals, and catalogues of new materials. After consultation with the church staff about the church goals, I then proceed to adopt goals for the next season for the ministry of music, with the help of the above-mentioned materials. I set up the theme-of-the-month, hymn-of-the-month, orchestra project, special programs (Christmas, Youth and Men's Club

12

appearances, World Day of Prayer, Easter, Choir Festivals, etc.), mimeograph this outline, gather all the materials for each particular age group, help set up the outline for the coming year, select the songs and present the leaders with mimeographed sheets, so that lesson plans can be made for the year by June. In system there is comfort.

What does this do for your leaders? It gives them the necessary time to study and understand the materials they will be teaching. Can they vary the outline? Certainly; it occurs all the time. But the knowledge that we always have more material ready than we can possibly use gives them assurance. I meet individually with the leaders of each age group. A teachers' meeting is held once a month during the year, at which time I must give them new vision, new ideas, and get them to work a little harder. Who among us but pales a little at the thought of what can and should be accomplished with the youth in our churches compared with what we are doing?

It is true that spring has perhaps brought the yearning to be free of all responsibilities; but it also awakens in us the desire to get at the business of cleaning up the untidy corners and setting our "music house" in order again. So by July I must have our ministry of music program all set (not to stay that way, for children have the wonderful ability to make their presence felt in every room). But at least during July and August my wonderful leaders and I can think about the neatly planned program, and enlarge upon its outline for the enrichment of the lives of our choristers.

Contributed by William Lemonds, Westminster Presbyterian Church, Oklahoma City, Oklahoma.

THE MOTHERS' CHOIR GUILD

Of all the agencies in a church which aid in the development of a choir program, the Mothers' Choir Guild will perhaps be given first place. A properly organized guild can relieve the director of much responsibility and work, and allow his energies to be spent on the choristers and their spiritual and musical training.

Let us note some specific details of organizing such a group:

First, if it is possible to enlist the fathers of the children in our choirs, by all means we should do so, for their interest and support can be a most valuable aid on many occasions, and their good-will is an invaluable asset. In cases where this is possible, one might change the name to "Parents' Choir Guild" and proceed as usual with the organization, using as many fathers on as many committees as possible.

Probably the most successful pattern for organization will be a choir mother for each choir, with another mother (appointed by the director, preferably) to act as chairman of the Guild and be the link between the director and other choir mothers. The Guild would then be composed of a choir mother from each choir, the director, and a general chairman for the entire group.

This chairman should be a person with a good over-all picture of the choir program. She should be able to co-ordinate the work of all choirs with the other choir mothers, and aid the director in accomplishing the work as he has it outlined for the season.

It should be her responsibility to arrange all group meetings for the Guild, and keep the activities of the various choir programs before the mothers of the choristers. She should see that through the Guild all the things the director would like are accomplished through each choir.

She should be very tactful, affable, and popular, with a keen sense of humor. Intelligence and good judgment will be most helpful in the discharging of her duties, and through clever planning and engineering this very important person can attend to practically all the harrowing details which necessarily claim much of the director's time and energy in the season's work.

The director should have a definite plan of procedure for each choir. This should be outlined in advance of the beginning of the season, so that each choir mother may have definite instructions for her other mothers. When the director has such plans ready, it is a simple matter for the chairman then to call the first meeting of the Guild for the season, at which time the director explains what is expected from each choir for, shall we say, the first three months.

The director should outline the major projects for the year, involving the entire system; for example, combined choir programs at Christmas, Easter, and end of season. Possibly a hymn festival, or other such project, may be an additional activity involving all choirs. Dates should be announced at this meeting, if possible. The special features, prepared by individual choirs, should be announced at this meeting also, for in this way misunderstandings and much loss of time can be avoided, and the mothers can *know* what is expected of them. The director should be *definite* in giving instructions to the choir mothers, and a well chosen guild can alleviate almost all the unnecessary, but too often experienced painful ordeal of producing a season's work in a multiple choir program.

Probably two other such group meetings during the year will be

14

sufficient. However, some guilds have monthly meetings, and discuss the month's activities. This frequent meeting can very easily combine a social hour (luncheon, etc.) with a business meeting, and a congenial group can have a very profitable, as well as delightful, time. Many lasting friendships have been made in this way, and it is well worth one's giving this plan a trial.

Each choir mother in turn will need to have more or less the same qualifications suggested for the chairman. She will be responsible for organizing the mothers of her particular choir. She will appoint committees to care for certain phases of activities. The more mothers enlisted in the activities of the choristers, the more interest there will be in the choir.

The director might best determine the appointment of committees for which the mothers are best suited by having them fill out a questionnaire similar to the following:

Name _____

Address _____ Phone _____

Child's Name_____ Age__ Birthday_____
Mo. Day Yr.

There are many avenues of service for our parents in this organization. You can each be of great assistance to both your director and to the children. If you are willing to serve on any one or more committees, kindly check your choice in order of preference.

_____ *Clerical work* (typing, filing, etc.). Only occasionally will there be need of such help, but it can be of great assistance when needed.

_____ *Attendance records.* Weekly, monthly, and yearly records, attendance contest records, etc. *Very* important, and will require regular attendance at rehearsals.

_____ *Telephone.* Names of choir members will be divided into groups and telephone chairmen appointed for getting messages to choir members and their mothers.

_____ *Vestments.* Mothers are needed to keep vestments in good repair, and assist children in getting them on, and returned to proper place after being worn.

_____ *Transportation.* Possibly two or three times a year there may be needed the use of several cars for transporting the choir.

_____ *Hospitality.* A few social functions during the year will mean much in building and developing morale. Planning and executing parties and pleasant experiences for the group will be of great service.

15

_____ *Public performance.* At Christmas, Easter, and at other times, assistance may be needed in helping children get on and off the platform, etc. Just a bit of "mothering" in other words.

_____ *Librarian.* To assist in giving out, and returning to proper place, books, mimeographed material, etc.

_____ *Equipment.* Moving of tables, chairs, instruments, musical game materials, etc. (if these are used).

_____ *Miscellaneous.* From time to time there will be small needs not anticipated, and if you are willing to serve in the capacity where most needed, please check.

Thanks,

_____
Director

As one can readily see, a director who is fortunate enough to have a choir mother in each group who can and *will* discharge all the details through functioning committees, can almost shed the cares and worries which would otherwise make it almost impossible to produce a quality job. But with an efficient guild backing him, he can have opportunity to become a real specialist in his field, and devote his entire attention to the children and their musical and spiritual training. So often directors are so hampered by the heavy load of details involved in the development of a choir program that they necessarily have to spread themselves exceedingly thin in too many places to do all that must be done.

But the director must not only be a *good* director who knows how to *teach music;* he should be a good psychologist as well, for he will encounter many types of parents—many good ones, but also many "problem" parents. The choir mothers whose qualities are listed above, are exceptions, and are few and far between.

In most every group, one is apt to encounter some of the following problems:

The *unsympathetic parent*—one who is impatient, nags, and reprimands the child instead of encouraging him on his way in his musical and spiritual experience.

The *misguided parent*—one who is over-anxious and expects too rapid musical progress because of a lack of understanding of the natural limitations of the child, and the mental and technical problems facing the young child.

The *ignorant parent*—one who expects the child to do his assigned work voluntarily and often punishes him and distracts him in various ways. Without parental interest and encouragement, the average

16

chorister will not continue through the initial stages of choir work to the time when he can begin to enjoy singing and other musical activities.

The *indifferent parent*—one who is perhaps the most commonly encountered. The "catch-as-you-can" attitude is one of great seriousness and presents a problem for even the expert director-psychologist.

The *emotionally disturbed parent*—one who unconsciously creates a negative home environment, and is psychologically the underlying cause of a degree of failure in the child.

What then can we as directors do to alleviate the stress and strain caused by these "problem" parents?

Of first importance is the director's own attitude toward these parents. We must ourselves be tolerant, patient, kind, sympathetic, and objective before we can begin to help the parents of our choristers. We must possess a sincerely friendly attitude toward each parent, and avoid scorn; for the parent is not deliberately trying to make things difficult, but rather is acting unwittingly. We must always be diplomatic in our methods of approach, and avoid embarrassing situations.

If the director shows his parents that he is sincerely interested in them and their children, and presents them with very definite and rational plans to follow in assisting with the choir work at home, he is more apt to win easily the confidence and co-operation of his parents.

An active "parent-director" group is the most effective organization I can recommend for the well-being of a multiple choir musical program.

Contributed by Mrs. Haskell Boyter, Atlanta, Georgia.

Choir Mothers' Guild

The wise director is a good organizer. He lets others do what others can do just as well. He will certainly have a choir mothers' guild. There will be a co-ordinating chairman, and a chairman for each of the youth choirs. He will appoint these leaders carefully, for they must be people who know how to get things done, and how to win the effective co-operation of others.

Before the choir season begins, he will invite the mothers of all the choir children to a tea, at which the year's work for each choir will be outlined with definite dates for the major events. Every mother present will be given a mimeographed sheet on which to check the kind of assistance she prefers to give.

Those requiring regularity:

Attendance—care of all the records.
Vestments—their care, and getting them on and off the children.
Librarian—care and distribution of materials used in rehearsal.
Equipment—setting up the rehearsal room.

Those requiring occasional work:

Clerical—typing, mimeographing, etc.
Telephone—when parents or children need to be reached.
Transportation—for occasional trips or parties.
Recreation—planning several parties.
Public performance—extra help for vesting, etc.
Miscellaneous—small, unexpected needs.

Women will be assigned to committees according to their stated preference. With such an organization, the director needs to confer only with the choir chairman, or the co-ordinating chairman.

YOUR BEST FRIENDS

Of major importance for the smooth handling of a series of youth choirs is a well-organized, active Choir Mothers' and Fathers' Guild. (Who can suggest a good new name for such a group? How about "Choir Parents' Committee" or "Choir Mom and Dad Club"? Keep this in mind as you read the rest of this article.)

It may be that the idea of fathers in such a guild seems strange to you. Many Church Schools are finding that couples as teachers of children's classes are doing a much better job than either could do alone. They share the teaching, share keeping up the attendance, share the overseeing and controlling. It brings parents together in their church work. I believe choir directors can take a tip from the Church School and enlist the help of both fathers and mothers in the work of a guild. It is good for the choristers to know that both men and women are interested in the work of the choirs.

There should be an over-all head couple and an assistant head couple. These people do not need to have children in the choirs, but they should have a thorough understanding of the choir's work, aims, and above all, have a "way" with children.

From the personnel of each youth choir the head couples should find two couples who are parents of children in the choir, who would be responsible for that choir for the choral season.

The responsibility which these parent-couples take will vary according to the need of the choir and the desire of the director. Among the obligations I want them to assume are:

Assist in each rehearsal in the taking of attendance, help with wraps, doing some follow-up calling in case of absence or sickness, help make the choir room attractive with flowers, etc.

Take charge of fitting the vestments to the children, repair the vestments, see that the vestments are ready for them when the choir sings.

On singing days, help the children into their vestments, help them line up for processional, sit near them during services, compliment them when they have sung effectively and when their conduct has been commendable, and after service see that the vestments are put away properly. Dads can be a big help on these occasions.

I want the Choir Parents' Committee (or have you a better name by now?) to plan and carry out some parties or outings during the year. Some things which can be done are skating parties, hobby shows, fishing trips, boat trips, attendance at professional ball games, a musical movie, a concert, radio broadcast, a TV show, etc. The choir should have a few events of this nature each season and the "Choir Mom and Dad Club" (I think this name is best) can plan and carry out such events.

No matter by what name you call them, a group of parents with a love of the church, a love of children, and an earnest desire to help the music program, can make life easier for the director, and help the youth choirs function more effectively.

Contributed by Dr. Federal Lee Whittlesey, Highland Park Methodist Church, Dallas, Texas.

BOYS' CHOIRS—The number of requests for information on boy choir training indicates a rather general impression that a boy's voice must be trained differently from a girl's. This is an entirely mistaken impression. The manner of training in a professional boys' choir is naturally not the same as that in a volunteer children's choir. But good vocal training is the same for girls and for boys with unchanged voices. Anyone who can train a children's choir to sing with good tone can achieve the same vocal results with a choir of boys.

19

There is no rule of voice training that can be applied to the situation like a poultice, with guaranteed results. The only possible way to get the greatest beauty out of the boy's voice, is to study the child's voice in recordings, concerts, school choruses, rehearsals, books on boys' choir training, to keep the ears keenly alert, and so to develop discrimination in the quality of the boy's voice.

Father Finn, who spent his life in the tradition of the professional boys' choir, had very decided convictions on voice training, and created beautiful tone with his Paulist Choir. Herbert Hoffman, founder of the Columbus Boy Choir, produces exceptionally beautiful tone with his choir. He was educated as a director of adult choirs, and went into boys' choir work more or less by chance. The approach of these two men is entirely different. There is no one-and-only method guaranteed to produce results. But there is a rule: To produce good tone, the leader must be sensitive to vocal variations, and be intelligent.

With most of us, the question is not so much how to get tone, as how to interest and hold enough boys. Apparently some are finding the answer, because an increasing number of our members are reporting a boys' choir as a part of their choral organization. It would be good to hear from them how they manage to hold a boys' choir.

They would undoubtedly credit their success to a variety of circumstances, but I am quite certain that they are all enthusiastic, well-balanced, openminded, and positive but patient people. The boys probably treat them with a mixture of affectionate disrespect.

For those who have both the choir and the personality, but want some suggestions for improving their work, there is a book that may be helpful: *Training the Boy Chorister.* By T. Tertius Noble, G. Schirmer.

In selecting music for the boys' choir, a balanced diet would include:

Fun songs: such as rounds, cowboy songs, etc.

Sturdy, enduring hymns. Welsh tunes are particularly vigorous and singable.

Service music and chants found in the back of all fine hymnals. *Methodist Hymnal* has very inclusive service section.

Classics, such as, "If with all your hearts ye truly seek Him," (from Elijah).

Anthems that avoid the trite, commonplace, or over-sweet.

20

Statement of Purpose
Westminster Presbyterian Church, Oklahoma City, Oklahoma

OUR PURPOSE

Our purpose as we unite in Westminster is to become such complete disciples of Jesus Christ that we shall discover God's will for our lives, and do it.

Therefore, we commit ourselves to Christ, and purpose to acquire a dynamic faith through Christian experience, worship and study.

We dedicate our lives to the expression of this faith by word and deed, seeking to work with those of like purpose and inviting others to join us in building today for a Christian world.

Westminster Church has had a phenomenal growth, and has a spirit of friendliness and dedication that is unmistakable to even the casual visitor. Could it be because of this simple, honest statement of purpose and an honest effort to measure up to it?

It is not surprising that a church of this calibre should have a "Congregational Choir." The report has come to me that this choir, comprising the whole congregation, meets weekly to study and sing hymns. The minister highlights the meaning of the texts, and the minister of music, conducts their singing. It would seem that they had discovered the true purpose of church music.

Card File
Community Presbyterian Church

Mrs. Margaret Imbach, Carpinteria, California, has a card file of all her choir children, with the signature of the child and the parent under this statement: "I promise that I will attend all rehearsals of my choir (except when I am ill), and that I will make every effort to make my choir the best, by promptness at all rehearsals, and by learning my music.

Personal Calls

Soon after my return from that inspiring weekend in Des Moines, I began working on a chapter of the Choristers' Guild for the suburban area of Chicago. This last Sunday afternoon the first official meeting was held, with ten present. We plan to meet every other month, and our first project consists of having an all-day song fest and fellowship get-together for our choirs on a Saturday afternoon in

May at one of our neighboring forest preserves. *One of our plans for membership is to call personally on ministers in the area whose churches* were not represented on Sunday, and find out if they have active Junior choirs, and if not, whether they would be interested in having a representative attend our meetings, and thereby gain some knowledge of their workings, and perhaps thereby become inspired to start one. *Mrs. E. A. Kammerling, Bellwood, Illinois.*

A Three-point Plan

It is self-evident that the music and religious education programs of the church should work hand in hand; but we have been more slow to recognize the advantage of parental co-operation. It is easy to bemoan the indifference of parents. It is not easy to hold the interest of the children without parental co-operation, but it can be done. But it is the three-point plan—parent, teacher, and director together—that wins the day.

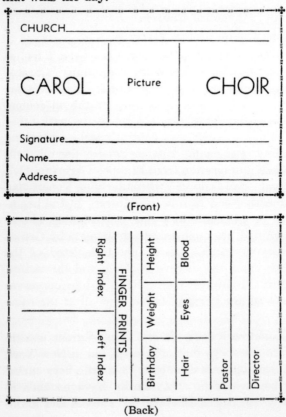

(Front)

(Back)

FINGER PRINTS

Richard Oglesby, who helps with the boys' choir, thought up this card. He will take the boys to the police station to be fingerprinted. I have not thought of anything to equal it for the girls, and I don't know what they'll say when they know about it. Guess we will have to t a k e them to Hollywood for a screen test. *Dorothy Woods, Atlanta, Georgia.*

It Works Both Ways
First Methodist Church, Santa Barbara, California

The Junior Department of our Church School has not been noted for its singing. Last spring I began going into the Department for a ten-minute period of hymn study, not only singing, but learning to understand the hymns. I found that many of the children could not even read the text, much less understand it (*Hymns for Junior Worship*, Westminster Press). The response seemed meager, but this fall the children are beginning to sing with evident enjoyment, and when I call for favorite hymns hands fly up all over the room, and the number of voluntary recruits for the Junior Choir is steadily growing. With the Primary Department, the system is worked in reverse. The very large Primary Choir learns the songs found in their study material, and so give wings to the singing of the whole Department.

An Ecumenical Church
American Church, Caracas, Venezuela

Whenever anyone asks me to tell about my work here, I feel at a loss to picture it to those who do not know the community. Caracas has the largest American colony outside the United States (some 5,000), and the majority of them are brought here by the oil companies. Some of the American business men are connected with other companies, but the oil refineries color and control nearly everything in the city and the communities in the interior where the oil wells are. Further, there is much immigration from Europe: Germany, Holland, France, England, Spain, and Italy. So the underlying Venezuelan culture is colored by American and European cultures. In the beginning of this immigration, people came to a raw, uncultivated, almost cultureless country, which had been oppressed for 40 years by Gomez and, never aggressive or resourceful, were almost depleted of the ability for progress. Then came the discovery of oil, and the radical changes it brought with it. Highways, traffic lights, water conservation systems, telephones—all are being installed, and all at the same time.

Caracas is a city of contradictions. It is a city of great wealth, and abject poverty. There are shops that are unequaled in New York for splendor; and in the evenings you can always see little boys curled up sleeping in the big bay windows. They really have no beds to sleep in. Whole hills in Caracas are inhabited by natives and immigrants who live in shacks that have no floor, water, or light. If they have one bed in a family of six, they are considered rich.

All of this is a background for the American Church. It is inter-denominational, and because the services are in English, the congregation is composed largely of Europeans and Americans. We hear much of the ecumenical church these days; I find it refreshing to be in the midst of one which works so admirably.

The American Church was founded in 1940 with a congregation of 70, and now numbers 600. I have never seen a church so full of children. If ever a church needed a choir program, it is this one. The church has grown rapidly in a material way, with a more than usually weak spiritual underpinning. There is constant fluctuation in the congregation because of the traveling and entertaining that is demanded of the young executives. This has its effect on the community at large, on family life, and on the church.

You can see what effect this fluctuation has on the building of a stable choir program. Because the parents fluctuate, the children do, too. The children also suffer from too many advantages. The two country clubs take much of their time, and because the climate is inordinately fair, swimming, riding, tennis, golf, are a constant call. The call of the church must be strong enough to overcome this materialism and instability. RUTH PARKHURST

Fall Presentation
Central Presbyterian Church, Atlanta, Georgia

We find it best to present pins in the fall at the first Church Night Supper of the season. It brings all the old children back for the beginning of the new season, heightens interest of the whole congregation, and presents choir goals and purposes in the best way I know. In addition, we can keep our records right to the end of the season, June first, and then have time in the summer to check them, order the pins, and be ready for fall. REV. HUBERT TAYLOR

Five Year Plan
St. Paul's Methodist Church, Cedar Rapids, Iowa

We have a five-year program of special objectives for our music. The first year's special effort is to make more effective and worshipful the music of the worship service. The second year stresses music in Christian education. The third features children's choirs, the fourth will be music and the family. The major attention in the fifth year will be on monthly vesper festivals. BROOKES DAVIS

24

Little Church with Large Vision

First Methodist Church, Devine, Texas

My contact with you last summer during the clinic in James Berry's church was such a wonderful inspiration, and an experience for which I am deeply grateful. I told you how we had left the full-time ministry of music to enter full-time ministry of the Word, and what a rewarding experience it has been.

Our choir system in this tiny town has been the "shot-in-the-arm" which our very dead little church needed. In all the years that we served large churches all over the United States we have never had the complete response that has come from this congregation. Parents and children are living in a state of eager anticipation from one rehearsal to the next. You see, in a large city church, choir is just another activity. In this community it has become the top interest. Oh yes, there are active garden clubs, PTA, Boy Scouts, Girl Scouts, piano lessons, etc., but our congregation has been made aware in a vital way of what it means to serve God through worship. As I so often tell our people, there is no other way in the world, except in the choir, that a child may actually serve in the worship services.

We are exceedingly proud of these children, because there is absolutely no music in the school system, except a High School band. When we started in September, 1954, no more than ten children could match a pitch, much less carry a tune. This year the Junior girls sang "Come unto Him," and the Junior boys sang "He shall feed His flock," in our Messiah program and, furthermore, their tone was excellent. We are now doing a bit of part work with good results. It is a matter of "want to."

You should see these children work; and their attendance is a miracle to behold. No one—just no one—ever misses choir unless he is ill; and we never tell them they can't be excused. On choir enrollment day parents and children come together in the sanctuary, and we explain what it means to be a good choir member. If parents and children are not willing to put service to Christ and His Church ahead of everything else, we ask them not to enroll. Dental appointments, parties, shopping trips are not excuses. No child ever is to say, "May I be excused for this or that." If he does, he is reminded that at the first of the choir year he pledged himself for one hour a week to rehearse for his own betterment, and for God's service. He did not pledge to us, but to Christ, and now he is to go apart and take it up

25

with Christ as to where he should be—shopping in San Antonio, or at rehearsal.

Regularity of attendance solves its own problems. There has been much illness in our part of the country due to dryness and dust, and yet our percentage is 97%. We consider that good. Our church has had the honor to be asked to sing for the Annual Conference this year, and since we are almost the smallest full-time charge in southwest Texas (more than 500 churches), we are proud of our people.

I made the requirements for pins in our groups a little stiffer than you suggested. They received only twenty points for notebooks and only ten for a new member. However, they were given additional points for being able to sing each anthem individually the week following the performance. This last month they have been required to sing individually against a harmonizing part which I would sing. We are not awarding any pins in the High School Choir, nor in either of the baby choirs. However, the promise of these pins has kept the Carol, Crusader, and Celestial choirs digging like beavers.

I won't go on any more with this chitchat; just thought I'd tell you that in the rural church there is a field white unto harvest for the presentation of musical and spiritual values. This summer we are giving a clinic for rural churches to show a choir program and its usefulness, plus a completely different method of organization than is used in the large church where a full-time minister of music is employed. Let me know what the new fees are, as I wouldn't be without my membership. Our choirs are also interested in becoming contributing members. They are proud of their connection with the Guild, and look forward to news from other churches.

MRS. DUANE SPENCER

26

A Vacation Singing School for Primary and Junior boys and girls will be held the week of June 11 to 17. The school will meet every morning from 9 to 11:30, and will include a worship period in the chapel, vocal instruction, rhythm drill, note reading and writing, hymn singing, and a story period. A talent show will be staged on Friday. Parents are invited to this and the final hymn sing. All boys and girls are invited to enroll, whether they are choir members or not. Choristers, invite your non-choir friends to come with you.

FOSTER HOTCHKISS

27

The Country Church That Made Good

Federated Church of Sandwich, Illinois. Population, 2,900; membership, 300.
Reverend Robert Frerichs, Minister; Mrs. Frerichs, minister of music.

The original Junior Choir, including boys and girls from fourth through eighth grades, in two years outgrew its choir loft. The obvious solution was to organize a Junior High Choir. When it became clear that it would mean an end to the large losses of young people during the critical Junior High and High School years, and would mean a significant strengthening of the spiritual, educational, evangelistic, and fellowship program of the church, a complete graded choir program was undertaken. It was carefully integrated with the Church School and youth fellowship programs, and was to continue on a high spiritual and musical level.

The Music Committee, responsible for the music activities of the church, helped organize Junior and Junior High mothers' groups, which are essential to a program of this sort. They provide help every Sunday for robing, keep robes clean and mended, furnish treats, and help constructively to maintain high morale and loyalty among the children.

Music training is a part of the program of the Cradle Roll, Preschool and Kindergarten departments. In the Primary Department, preparation is made for promotion into the Junior Department, and into leadership, as a choir member, in the public worship of the church. Some of the hymns, the Lord's Prayer, and other parts of the church's worship are a part of the learning program. On Rally Sunday, the new Junior Choir, including fourth to sixth grade children, makes its first appearance each year.

In the Junior Choir, the children learn simple anthems during the first part of the year; then, for the Christmas concert and later, they begin to sing anthems with descants, or two-part anthems. At the end of three years in the Junior Choir, the children graduate to Junior High Choir, where two-and three-part music is used almost entirely, and where special opportunities are presented for more talented singers. The Junior High Sextet is a select group which sings three part girls' music and, of course, has an extra hour of rehearsal and more numbers to prepare.

The rehearsal of the Junior High Choir is held as part of the three-hour Sunday evening program for Junior Highs, beginning at 5 p.m. with an hour of musical work. Then comes supper, served in rotation by the mothers of the children in the Junior High Fellowship.

28

After supper, under the guidance of their sponsors, the group has its business meeting, frequent programs, and a social hour with adjournment at 8 o'clock.

Graduation from Junior High marks the entry of most of the young people into the Senior Choir, and into the special high school groups, which include the famous Federated Girls' Octet, and the Boys' Chorus. For girls, membership in the Octet marks the highest honor in the musical program. This group, entered only by tryouts, and open only to girls in the music program, meets every Monday night for an hour's rehearsal, and is always in demand for special concerts and other appearances. This year, as well as last year, the Octet has made tours of churches in Illinois and Iowa.

The Boys' Double Quartette, begun two years ago, has already appeared in several of the Octet concerts, and sung often in church services. Open to all High School boys, it rehearses for an hour every Sunday morning. All of this is in addition to the work of the Senior Choir, for membership and faithful attendance in the choir are required for membership in both honor groups. Altogether the Senior Choir has twenty-two high school age members.

The Senior Choir, in addition to its leadership of the worship services, presents annually at least two concerts. The Christmas concert is given jointly by all the groups. At Easter, the Senior Choir presents the annual Messiah concert, and usually shares with the other choirs an all-request concert in the spring, or presents one of the great oratorios. There are forty-three members in the Senior Choir, more than half of whom take free voice lessons with Mrs. Frerichs, and are frequently used as soloists. The Senior Choir is not just for High School students; it points with pride to its three generations of Potters, Mrs. Eva Potter, her son Glendon, an outstanding baritone soloist, and his son Donald, a sophomore in High School, all regular members of the choir. The balance of young and mature voices has been found to provide the best possible results for church choral singing.

When the program had increased to somewhat near its present strength, the leadership program was started. The six young people for whom the church provided organ lessons are now available for accompanying, for special work, and to relieve the regular organist. Mrs. Frerichs taught five girls in the basic procedures of conducting and choral management. These young people are now conducting most of the choral groups under the supervision of the minister of music.

The church, because it appreciates its musical leadership, has for the past six years given children in its music program the gift of a week at camp, provided they have met the high requirements of the choir program. Every summer, forty to fifty girls and boys with their leaders have six days at the Federated Music Camp, with the expenses paid by the church. At camp, classes are held in creative music and worship for the children, while the High School young people act as counsellors and are trained in Christian leadership.

After the first four years of this expanded program, the church has answered its original question, "Can it be done?" with an enthusiastic affirmative. Church school attendance has increased 100% and because the teachers wanted more time, the hour of the Church School was put at 9:30 instead of 10. Attendance is always good, for the goal of the choir members is attendance at church school, church, and rehearsal, at least 90% of the time. The two youth fellowships—Junior High, and High School—each meet for a three-hour program of worship, food, and fellowship on Sunday evenings during the church year. Many new families have been attracted to the church by its program for children and youth, although strict rules forbid the enrolling of choir members who are related to other churches in the community. The greatest value to the church lies not alone in the quality and beauty of its music, but much more in the long and fine training its children receive in responsible leadership, Christian education, and in service to the church. Experience is continually teaching that children who grow up in the music and educational programs of a church which requires high standards of them are members who take their church very seriously and are active leaders in its work.

Condensation of a report by Rev. Frerichs, who is now director of the Rural Church program of the American Baptist Convention.

Practical Ideas

North Glendale Methodist Church, Glendale, California

If I were to pick out some specialties of our youth choir program (three choirs totaling 143 members from grades four to twelve—each a mixed group), they would probably line up as follows:

Careful attention to promotion and publicity within the church itself and the community, climaxing this year with a picture of our youth choirs massed in the form of a cross, filling the chancel and extending down the center aisle, the News-Press photographer taking the picture from the balcony. It was used on the cover of the *Glendale News-Press* weekly magazine the day before Easter, because our church holds Easter services of general interest to the public in the civic auditorium each year.

A fine choir guild of twenty members, with one—college trained in home economics—in charge of food for the three choirs. She either takes full charge of suppers, picnics, etc., or plans, shops, and directs the mothers from the particular choir involved, without actually going into the kitchen. The High School Choir and Choir Guild served an all-church dinner in January, featuring singing waiters.

Service projects for the two older choirs—singing at inter-racial churches and community houses, and at Boys' Home chapel services.

Fast-moving rehearsal for the youngest choir, using many ideas from the Guild *Letters*. Five mothers are in attendance; two serve punch and cookies, and three help in the rehearsal room. Our accompanist supervises fifteen minutes of ball playing in the gym before all line up for refreshments. The play and children's magazines help to keep things under control while the children are arriving from their various schools.

Three cookie cans are taken home by the children in alphabetical order. Colored "cut-out" notes and this verse identify the can:

"O mother dear, it is your turn to fill the cookie can
With cookies not too large or small, from stove or kitchen pan.
So fill it to the very top, and put the lid on tight!
The Descant Choir will sing its thanks with fervor and delight."

This week we had a backwards rehearsal. We have a definite rehearsal order, starting with an opening prayer, ending with a closing hymn, and generally an instrumental solo (prearranged by the choir mother) in the middle. When we are reading new numbers, the accompanist takes the sopranos to an adjoining room for about ten minutes' work, while I take the altos. We sing much during the first

31

two-thirds of the rehearsal and then have a study project, announcements, etc. At any rate, we went through things from ten to one, and had time left over, because they were so alert and fascinated.

For a special Easter rehearsal I sent this jingle to the children: "Easter is coming . . . and so are you, to the Auditorium, 'Of course you knew,' Six-fifteen Saturday right in your chair, ready to sing. All must be there. Sunday I'll see you in vestments like new, at 8:15 sharp at the stage door. . . . Adieu." Whenever I want to be sure to get the attention of every one, I say it in verse.

I was glad to read the account of the experience with the balky youth choir. Certainly the business of gaining the co-operation of the high school choir is a serious one. The over-all program for the teen-agers in the church has to be good, and co-ordinated with their choir life, for the choir to be a success. A monthly cabinet meeting (brief) is helping in my choir.

LOUISE WHITMAN

Definite Choir Goals

Boston Avenue Methodist Church, Tulsa, Oklahoma

Our youth choirs have definite goals for 1954-55, the first of these being the building of eternal values into the life of each child.

First, to teach basic beliefs through music, and to use music as a means of religious education.

Second, to teach reverence and worship. The children are taught the significance of the various parts of the worship service, the meaning of the appointments in the sanctuary, and how to conduct themselves at worship.

Third, to teach correct basic habits in singing. Good posture, deep breathing, ease in singing, and correct pronunciation are stressed in rehearsal.

Fourth, to attempt to bring the child to a place of musical competence. Supplementing the training the child receives elsewhere, the elements of musical notation and sight reading are taught.

Fifth, to train the child in self-discipline and co-operation. In a choir all must work together for the good of a worthy cause. This takes self-control, faithfulness, and submission to appointed leadership.

Sixth, to teach the great hymns and anthems of the church. An effort is made to teach music that they will grow into, not music that they will outgrow.

32

Seventh, to prepare and present music for occasional services and special music programs, through which the congregation may worship God.

MARVIN REECHER

Student Teachers
Johnson Bible College, Kimberlin Heights, Tennessee

Last year was my first in teaching a class in graded choir methods. The first semester we studied methods and learned many songs. One requirement was to read the Choristers' Guild *Letters* placed in the library.

The second semester we organized an experimental choir (ages six through ten). The girls had the experience of helping organize and maintain the interest of a choir. They learned from experience many things I could never have taught them. After each rehearsal we discussed ways of improving the rehearsal and the presentation of the songs. As the children arrived, one girl met them at the door, two checked attendance, one girl played the piano, and another took over as soon as five or six arrived, singing review songs, until time for rehearsal to begin. We had a short devotional at each rehearsal. The children particularly enjoyed the short chalk talks which some of the girls presented.

MRS. CLARK ROWLAND

Membership Certificates
First Baptist Church, Toledo, Ohio

I had a problem this year because nearly all of the children qualified for a pin, and I was afraid the few who did not would feel very much left out at the presentation service. Therefore I had certificates made, so everyone would get something. I had them rolled and tied with a red ribbon. Each member stood as his name was called, and received the certificate from the minister's hand. It took about 10 minutes for the comments and the presentation of eighty-nine certificates. I mentioned, at a given time, that all those whose names were hereafter called would receive pins, and the pins were sent by mail with a congratulatory note. The children were pleased and many told me their certificates were framed and hanging on their walls. There is no substitute for the Choristers' pin, but the two can go together, I believe, with little extra expense.

IRENE SIEBENS

33

Work Camps in India
Kodaikanal, South India

Work camp was so popular last year that there was a great demand among the students for another this year. For a week six of our High School students and six Indian young people worked side by side at the job of laying the foundation for a small hostel on a Christian youth conference ground, digging, piling in rocks, screening sand, mixing and pouring cement, raising huge stone pillars, cleaning and stacking tile, and mixing plain mud. After the camp, three of us teachers had almost three weeks of adventure in Assam, the most northeastern state in India, which borders on such forbidden lands as Bhutan, Tibet, and even China itself.

As for the borders, you are kept at a safe distance—100 miles or more. They take no chances. Within its borders is Cherraponge, the wettest place in the world with an average rainfall of between 400 and 600 inches.

The "College in Bamboo" is a miracle of faith, and the product of 100 years of Christian missions in this area. Now in its infancy, Union Christian College represents ten or twelve of the Christian hill tribes. Mr. Pugh, himself of the Khasi tribe, gave up prominent educational positions elsewhere to serve his own people as president. Staff and students housed in bamboo huts are now seeing the erection of their first permanent building.

At Jorhat we marveled at the ever-expanding medical work, and the boundless energy of Dr. and Mrs. Hasselblad. Besides looking after the hospital, T. B. sanatorium, and leprosarium, this man of inexhaustible energy finds time before dawn to care for the medical needs of the people of several large tea gardens, and preach the gospel on Sunday. They have also undertaken to keep an eye on the medical work in Manipur, where missionary work had to be discontinued. To this center we "jeeped" 200 miles through the hills with Mrs. Hasselblad.

At Imphal, the capital of Manipur, we were thrilled by a wedding procession, a band leading, and the wedding party following on a lumbering elephant, coins flying in all directions to the mob on the street below. And to climax it all, colorful Manipur dancing in costume was arranged for a visiting high official, and we were invited to witness it. Trekking for three days over thirty miles of beautiful cultivated Sikkim hills brought us to the famed smallest capital in the world, Gangtok. The school nurse and I left Pedong, last Indian outpost, at daybreak with two Lepsha boys carrying our huge bedroll and a provision basket. Dropping down thousands of feet on the dusty cobblestone road to the river, and then climbing out of the canyon again on the other side, spending the night in Dak bungalows— that and an ever-changing view describes our trek.

Expecting to stay two days in Gangtok, our permit was extended to seven, so that we might attend the famous Lama dances at the monastery. But more thrilling to us were the mule caravans coming and going over the steep zigzag mountain trails, bringing in Tibetan wool, or carrying out cases of tea and other supplies. They were picturesque—the leaders gaily decorated with colorful masks. Red pompons dangled from their necks encircled by a collar of bells. As they went swinging along, you could hear the muleteer coming along behind, wearing heavy boots, a long black robe, fastened at the waist with a girdle, and a fur lined hat, singing and calling to his animals above the continuous sound of the bells.

The scenery, too, is beautiful on a clear day, with a whole range of snow-capped Himalayan peaks in view. One lone missionary woman, Miss Patterson from New Zealand, is allowed to remain in this buffer country to supervise the large girls' school—the only foreign resident in Sikkim.

Now once again back in Kodai, we are preparing for the arrival of our 250 students from Arabia, Thailand, Indonesia, Ceylon, Burma, and India. For another year we shall try to match the educational privileges and the home environment their parents could offer them, had they not chosen to "go into all the world and preach the gospel."

EMMA RUTH

Methods

LET'S LEARN FROM THE PUBLIC SCHOOLS

The other day I spent an hour in a second grade class. There were 42 children in the room; the teacher kept them calmly at work. I thought how distraught some of us would be to take care of that many second graders for just one hour; and this teacher has them six hours a day, five days a week. What is their secret?

For my special benefit, they started with a music lesson. The teacher very quietly, but with a tone of expectancy, told them to take their music books out of their desks and to find Page 42. "When you find the page, raise your hand." The book was *The American Singer,* Book II. The children followed the song while they listened to a recording of it. Then they sang it with the recording, and then without. It was evident that the teacher enjoyed the music; so did the children. Then the children wanted to sing some of their favorites. For some they used the books; others they acted out. The attitude was not learning, but enjoying. When the singing became somewhat raucous, they were reminded, in a soft voice to sing softly, and the next song was one that suggested gentleness.

The next lesson was spelling, and strips of paper were passed out to the children. Again, as soon as they had finished writing the word, they raised their hand. The lesson finished, the children automatically lined up single file around the room, and one by one filed past the teacher to have their papers corrected. For each one there was a word or a pat of commendation or encouragement. As each one went back to his desk, he began to study the poems neatly printed on the blackboard.

The poem for Mother's Day was a lesson in appreciation, family attitudes, spelling, reading, and writing—all at the same time; but to the children it was not a lesson at all, but just a poem that they were going to use when they were to make a beautiful Mother's Day card tomorrow.

There I reluctantly left them and went to the first grade room, where the children put on a movie for me that they had made themselves. The story was about three little goats who got into all kinds of trouble. The story unfolded itself on a long scroll that two boys transferred from one cardboard roller to another like a camera film. Each episode of the story, printed in large letters, was illustrated by drawings the children had made. The episodes were connected with songs that all the children sang. The story was read by individual children, each reading one episode. Now and then the children would turn around, to make sure that I was enjoying their movie as much as they were.

Wouldn't that be a wonderful way to teach Bible stories, or the history of the church, of the life of Christ, or any number of other study projects?

In the second grade room, I had learned a number of things: the value of a quiet voice, the time saved in making routine matter habitual (passing papers, correcting spelling, raising hand, etc.), and that the fine art of appreciation is caught, not taught.

If more of our rehearsals were conducted as these two classes were, and the parents were invited occasionally to a "Come, See," there would be less complaint about the lack of parental co-operation. Of that I am sure.

And if the rehearsal room were more attractive to the children, their parents would not have to insist on attendance. The school I visited is a very poor one, and there are no funds for extras, but the rooms had a number of pictures attractive to children, at eye level. There was a "science corner," and one space was devoted to an interest in reading. There was a small shelf of loan books, and on the wall there was a colored paper pocket for each child with his name on it. Some were filled with bright colored paper markers; each bore the name of a book the child had read. Some pockets were full, others had only one. The children were encouraged to tell to the class the story they had read. Just when the interest was keenest, the teacher would say, "Oh, you'd better not tell them any more—they may want to read the story themselves, and if you tell them more, it will spoil the surprise."

This same teacher has a large scrap book of poems she has collected. She calls it "The Highway of Magical Beauty," and the poems are classified under the headings: "Animals and Insects," "Mother Goose Rhymes," "Flowers and Trees," "Good Health and Safety," "Months—Special Days—Seasons," "Nice Manners and Things to Do," "Prayers and Lullabies," "Everyday Life—Play—Home—People," "Humor—Nonsense," "Miscellaneous." And she has a book of short stories, every one of which the children know and love. It is called *Favorite Stories*, by Cooper and put out by Southern Publishing Company of Dallas.

That morning I almost wished that I could be a child again, and go to school to that teacher, and in that room!

THE QUESTION BOX

Q. "This is my first position—a rather large church with great ambition musically, but not too much talent."

A. Well, sir, you are lucky. Think what it would be to work in a church with a lot of talent, but no ambition. The most helpful quality any church can offer its director is active interest.

Q. "I wonder how I really should direct the choir: sing with them, tap time, or what? I am a violinist; I do not have too strong a voice, and when more than ten youngsters get enthused, I get drowned out."

A. There are a lot of choirs that would sound much better, if they could drown out their directors. I suppose the besettingest of all besetting sins is to sing with the children's choir. They don't sing loudly enough to suit us, so we lift our voice, and the resultant tone is neither bird, beast, nor fish—nor music. Just how important are the motions that we make before the choir in the name of conducting—or how effective? The important thing is to establish good singing habits; and if one gets the results, the means used in getting them are likely to be valid.

Q. "We have them vocalize. This they do very well, but when they get on a real melody some of them seem to have trouble."

A. Don't we all! Sing do-re-mi-fa-sol-fa-mi-re-do on the syllable oo or oh. Now sing the phrase "Let us make the tones all round and bright." It is much harder to get uniform tone because there are

39

so many different vowel sounds, not to mention the consonants that must be sounded.

It does help, though, to use one sound as the pattern, and then immediately afterwards sing the words, trying to make them into as smooth a phrase as the one-sound phrase.

Q. "One of the things I want the children to get used to is singing with the organ."

A. The kind of organ tone used to accompany the children can make or break their singing. A heavy, tubby tone will drag them off pitch. Unrhythmic playing will do the same thing. It is better to use light, clear stops, and to keep either their melody or a contrasting one in the foreground, and the harmonies in the background. That kind of organ accompaniment will enhance the tone of a children's choir.

Q. "What do you advise on letting a youth choir sing regularly with an adult choir? It seems all I've ever heard is that it's not good. In my own judgment, I believe they would be imitating a tonal quality plus faults I'd rather they didn't hear."

A. What is the age of the Youth Choir? Do you direct both the Youth and the Adult Choir? If the Youth Choir is under High School age, it should be used with the adults only as a separate unit, as in descants or antiphonal numbers.

If of High School age, and there is a general shortage of singers, they could be used together. But the poor tone of the Adult Choir should be corrected, and the music used should not be taxing either in range or power.

Q. *"Should* children's choirs be used in the morning worship service? And if so, with any regularity? I feel that my children sing well and behave well in the service, that they have a right to sing, and need the additional incentive. My minister prefers that they sing in the evening service, or in more informal programs. He says that the ministers he has talked to support his view. But I feel that it takes the teeth out of the program to deprive them of this experience. What do you think?"

A. "Should Children's Choirs be used in the morning worship service?" The answer to that question depends altogether on the concept held by the minister and the minister of music. If the minister is thinking in terms of exploiting the children of the church, the answer is definitely NO. If the minister of music is thinking

40

in terms of "putting on a performance," the answer is definitely NO.

Personally, I feel that all of the services of the church should be pointed toward the entire family and should be a worship experience for all concerned. Therefore, I favor the use of children's choirs in all church services, though not for special music each Sunday. Their presence, if they are properly trained in reverence, can enrich the service even when they do not sing an anthem.

Every worship service needs to be properly balanced, just as every choral group needs to be properly balanced—music, scripture, prayers, and sermons all having their place in the service. If any one of these is too much in preponderance, the service loses balance. If the service is to provide a worship experience for all, all must participate. There is no place for the spectator in a Christian worship service.

The essential factor, then, is not whether the children shall sing morning or evening, but that they should be made to feel a part of the service and of the church, and not just to be put on display on special occasions."

Q. "How do I go about *directing* my Children's Choir?"

A. The concentration of attention, and the subtle phrasing and shadings possible with a good adult choir, only the overambitious would expect of a children's choir. But there are things the children can learn to do: watch the director; follow the tempo; respond to dynamic indications. But they must have practice. When an anthem is fairly well learned, have them stand and sing it as if in a concert, and offer a prize to the ones whose eyes never leave the director (a piece of candy is sufficient). Teach the choir the basic patterns of conducting, and let them use them while singing. Take some very familiar anthem, and conduct it with constant changes in tempo, daring the choir to be caught napping. Do the same with many changes in dynamics. With such stunts, they will find it fun to be responsive.

Q. "How much theory should there be in the Primary and Junior Choir?"

A. In the Primary Choir the children should learn the elements of music notation: note values, clefs, lines, and spaces. Simple rhythmic patterns should mean, "It sounds and feels like this." They can become very familiar with the first five tones of the scale, being able to sing the different intervals, and making up all kinds of tunes with them.

41

In the Junior Choir most of their theory will be the practical application of the knowledge they have gained; being able to clap the rhythm of new anthems; trying to read at sight some of the easier ones.

Q. "How shall I introduce theory when the choir includes all grades from the fourth to the tenth?"

A. That *is* a problem, and probably the best way is to make the theory a means to an immediate end. For instance, in introducing a new number, write the octave scale on the board in the key of the anthem. Have the children sing at sight the notes of the scale as you point to them; give them all kinds of intervals (never so difficult that they feel frustrated), and then point out the intervals of the melody of the anthem, first just as intervals, and then in the rhythm of the number. Then give them the music, and let them recognize it as the same they have been singing from the board. Do the same with the rhythmic pattern of new anthems. Write the rhythmic patterns (first few measures only) of several familiar numbers on the board. Let the choir clap, and identify them.

LEARNING IS FUN

The response the game ideas have produced in my grade school music classes amazes me. We have all had so much fun. And to top it off, the youngsters have learned more musical vocabulary in this one month than I was able last year to teach them in three. Why? First because, being fun, it was no longer a task, and open-hearted co-operation made learning easy. Second—more variety in class sessions keeps their interest high. Today we made up original songs about autumn, with a Dennison autumn-leaf sticker as a reward for each song in the first three grades. I am saving and mounting pictures suitable for original "song-stories." One of the most inspirational things you gave us in Portland was to insist that we not try to imitate someone else, but develop our own creative personalities as we grow as music directors.

HELEN KLEGER, Clatskanie, Oregon

Rehearsal Fun

Sometimes when you need to spark up a rehearsal or choir party, play the second or third phrase of a familiar hymn, and see who can name the hymn or repeat the words of the phrase played. It is not as easy as it sounds, but it is fun.

THE ETERNAL QUESTION—WHAT TO DO WITH MONOTONES

Possible reasons:

Some speech impediment: adenoids.

Inability to *hear* differences.

Lack of co-ordination.

Lack of tonal memory—unable to remember phrases.

Lack of experience—told they couldn't sing, and haven't tried.

Fear of ridicule.

Failure to find singing voice or head tone.

Treatment:

Distinguishing between tones very far apart.

Distinguishing between tones within an octave.

Let them sing a tone, and *you* match *theirs*.

Ask them to sing a different one, and you match again.

Sing a short phrase on his tone, and have him repeat it.

Combine sight with hearing, flight of steps, xylophone, etc.

Sing a fairly low tone, ask them to match it.

Let them imitate a fire siren (helps to break into head tone).

Call roll on musical phrases; they answer with same notes.

Example: Johnny Brown (mi do do).

In class:

Put them in front of and beside good singers.

Encourage others to help.

Let others sustain tones for them to match.

In songs, be sure they have the first tone right.

Be matter of fact about the situation.

YUM-YUM EXERCISES

In trying to solve a problem with our little twenty-member choir of fourth, fifth and sixth graders, I stumbled on a device which may be helpful to others, and pass it on gladly.

Although I needed a simple vocal exercise to open up sleepy voices, and get the sound coming up *out* of the back of the throat, I hesitated to talk about tone production, or create any self-consciousness, for fear of losing that most priceless ingredient of a children's choir, fresh spontaneity. Trying to use conventional mi-mi-mi-mi exercises would also certainly result in hilarity—they *are* ridiculous to the honest ear of a child. So I converted them to a form more acceptable, but just as effective as a tool, and now they ask for them.

I have the accompanist play an A major chord with e in the
soprano:

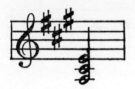

Then I ask, "Who likes apple?" and the choir sings:

Yum - yum - yum - yum - yum.

"Who likes blueberry?

Yum - yum - yum - yum - yum. . . .

"Who likes cherry?

Yum - yum - yum - yum - yum. . .

"Who likes chocolate?"

Yum - yum - yum - yum - yum. . .

Then, all together, (forgetting that some of us "can't" sing high E):

We love   pie! . . . .

Take one deep, long breath before starting, and sing slowly enough to get resonance on the m's. Result, a joyous voice-awakening and no snickering at the comical rituals of a grown-up world!

PHYLLIS EDELMAN, Hudson, Ohio

RECREATION FOR THE CHILDREN'S CHOIR

Are your choirs in a "rut"? Do they have the disease called "rut-itis"? This is a dread disease of many church activities. The cure for it is a varied program. One way to change the program is to be sure to have some recreation in it the year round. Not "wreck-reation." That's another disease of the average church. I have found a plan that works wonders. Not that I approve of awards and prizes, but a little life in the church in the way of parties won't hurt the active Christian.

Here is my secret: We have five choirs. After they have performed in a special program, or after they have inspired the morning congregation with a lovely anthem, or after they have served on a city-wide program, why not make the rehearsal different? Have a filmstrip, a party, a story hour, games, a good movie, and make it entertaining as well as informative. Most choir directors have very little time for parties with their choirs but if you keep an element of surprise in the background they will be there—and on time—for each rehearsal for fear they might miss something. Recreation is a fine way to put variation into the choir program.

You say "I don't have time to hunt for ideas." Bless your heart, you don't have to hunt. Just read on, and you will find out where to get ideas.

The National Recreation Association, New York City, has fine program material. Be sure to ask for their *Playground Guide for Summer.* It's grand.

Most University Extension Services have excellent monthly bulletins. They are used by 4H Club workers all over the world. West Virginia University at Morgantown, West Virginia would co-operate gladly.

Write to Reading, Pennsylvania, for their Recreational Bulletin. It's fifty cents a year, and you can't get more for the money anywhere, except in the Choristers' Guild *Letters.*

All of the following are from the Methodist Publishing House in Nashville (I am sure you have just as fine material in your own publishing house.):

Handy 1 and Handy 2. Lynn Rhorbough
Family Pleasure Chest. Helen and Larry Eisenburg
The Pleasure Chest. Helen and Larry Eisenburg
Skits and Stunts. Helen and Larry Eisenburg
Children's Party Book (fine). Helen and Larry Eisenburg
The End of Your Stunt Hunt. Helen and Larry Eisenburg
Promenade All. Helen and Larry Eisenburg
Lift Every Voice (a fun-song book)

Here are some themes for parties, which I will add for what they may be worth.

January: Winter Wonderland (tried it and it was successful).
February: Back in Grandmother's Days.
March: Irish Get-Together.
April: April Showers.
May: Here We Come A-Maying (Maypole dance and all; not for perfection, but for fun).
June: Teasers and Riddles (The Graduates' Party. Contests.)
July: Ye Old Swimming Hole (hot dogs, outdoor recreation).
August: Box Social.
September: School Days (Readin', Writin' and 'Rithmatic: Dunce Cap School).

46

October: The Ghost Roams.

November: The Indians Have Returned.

December: Keeping Christ in Christmas (filmstrip, "Joel's Gift," went over well this year. Carols, slides, etc., refreshments).   ALTA ICE

YOUTH LEADERSHIP

Barbara Tuttle reports on a Youth Welfare council meeting led by Ben Solomon, lecturer at New York University. "I went, hardly expecting that his recreational approach would apply to choir work, but it certainly did. I got so many helpful hints that I'm sending along an outline of his talk, thinking that you might like to get his book, *Leadership of Youth,* published by Youth Service, Inc., Putnam Valley, N. Y."

What Is a Leader?

A leader is a person who has *influence* with other people which causes them to:

1. Listen to you and agree on common goals.
2. Agree to follow you on your advice.
3. Go into action toward those goals.

Basic Aims of Youth Leadership:

1. Help them to become better men and women—very little relationship to skill.
2. Help combat pressures of vice, immorality.
3. Help to solve problems of each individual.
4. Emphasize fundamental values of particular activity.
5. Teach high standards of homemaking.

Qualifications of a Youth Leader:

1. Worthy of emulation by children—good citizen, right philosophy of life.
2. Sympathetic tolerance for children.
3. Knowledge of the basic values of your particular activity with proper emphasis on them. (However, do not rate skill higher than training.)
4. Skill in activity you're leading. (Not most important, however.)

47

Principles of Youth Leadership:

1. Do more than your job. Leadership starts where job ends.
2. Exercise power *with* people. Don't try to force.
3. Don't be satisfied with status quo. Try to lift ego.
4. Learn from failures and defeats. Don't rationalize—analyze.
5. A leader *is* his brother's keeper—he cares about individuals.
6. Advance your own field of work—make a contribution.
7. *Achieve*—the easiest way to defeat opposition.
8. Deserve and earn co-operation.
9. Develop leaders while leading.
10. Have ideals, and fight for them. Don't be impatient, but don't abandon ideals.
11. Radiate confidence and faith. When you are discouraged, don't let it show.
12. Never have hidden motives—that turns leader into dictator.
13. Rise above your own interests.
14. Always have time to listen to and consult with group.

Techniques:

1. Dare to pioneer, to experiment.
2. Make decisions. Let people know where you stand.
3. Have definite goals, and keep working toward them.
4. Be a spark plug—start good things going. Be a "social gardener," planting seed in fertile soil and nourishing it to fruition.
5. Start where *they* are, and by easy natural steps bring them up to where you want them. Don't negate them (unless what they're doing is actually unsafe).
6. Use food—not because they're hungry, but as social integration technique. For little girls—anything that makes them think they look prettier.)
7. Use gang leaders. Sell individuals the idea and the rest will follow. Go to them seeking advice, not telling them. Lead from behind. (If you can't reach the leader, try the second in command.)
8. Close the culture gap. Come down to their level—almost! Talk about the things they know. Don't overdress.
9. Use community leaders—service clubs, nationality groups, women's clubs, societies. (Leaders are not always officers.)
10. Use children's heroes, regardless of what kind they are.

48

11. Use the children's rules. Give them a chance to experience success.
12. Liaison with professional social workers in your area on problem cases.
13. Service the shy and unskilled 90%. They need you much more than the skilled 10%. "There are extraordinary possibilities in ordinary children." Fosdick.
14. Play is their world. Keep interest and fun uppermost.
15. Use the children's questions. They are open doors.
16. With teen-agers—glamor, dramatization, imagination.
17. Give pleasure and credit liberally. The more you divide it, the more it multiplies.
18. Anticipation is often enjoyed more than participation. Expand it.
19. Don't short-circuit experience. Don't give them all the answers. Let them find out for themselves.
20. Always remember that you are a professional. Don't let your glands take over! Problems are solved by thinking, not by losing control of yourself.
21. Remember that you are working with human beings, not with metal or wood.

Problem Cases:

Consider the environment. Work with *individual*:
1. Each case is different.
2. Choose right person to work with him.
3. Don't always use reason and logic. Work through emotions.
4. Understand child's vocabulary. They may mean something other than what they're saying.
5. Use doctor's approach—examine, diagnose, treat, *follow-up*.
6. Lead, help, but *don't judge*.
7. Service immediate needs. Make him feel wanted.
8. Convince him you're his friend.
9. Visit home, and school, and get picture of background.
10. Consult social agencies.

Girls are Different, Physically, Mentally, Emotionally.

Girls mature at different ages—plan activities accordingly. Their emotional cycle brings them ups and downs—expect them. Don't try to push. Girls worry more, are more restricted, more affected by home tensions and responsibilities. Be considerate.

General Suggestions:

1. Find a niche for everyone.
2. See that everyone experiences the thrill of success.
3. Use the margins (the spare moments) to get better acquainted.
4. Feel the pulse of the group. Ask leading questions. What do they like or dislike?
5. Strike while the iron is hot.
6. Speak constructively. Say nice things, or nothing at all.
7. Never show shock.
8. Keep a twinkle in your eye.

A YEAR'S PROGRAM

The serious interest in children's choirs is growing by leaps and bounds. Summer sessions in New York City; Lynchburg, Virginia; Green Lake, Wisconsin; and Lake Junaluska, North Carolina, have acquainted people from all corners of the country with the work of the Choristers' Guild. Churches are beginning to recognize the difference between good and indifferent leadership. Ministers are joining the Guild. The time for haphazard work is past. The price of effective choirs is planning and preparation. Start the new season with a plan for the year's program

A minimum program would include:
Choir dedication service.
Something special for Christmas and Easter.
Choir recognition. (A choir dinner at which all awards are presented.)
At least two study projects for the year.
Guided notebook work.
A program of training in music essentials.

CHOIR NOTEBOOKS

Suggested Contents:
Choristers' Pledge.
The Significance of Vestments.

The words and meaning of the congregational parts of the worship service:

> Lord's Prayer, Call to Worship, Doxology, Offertory, Gloria Patri, Benediction.

Hymn of the Month material.

The words of the songs the choir is to learn.

The Point System.

A collection of children's prayers.

The notebook should be brought to each rehearsal.

A star should be placed on each song learned, and each page completed.

The notebook should be handed in at the close of the season for judging.

It should be neat, and have all work completed, to merit the 25 points.

MAKE REHEARSALS COUNT

Start on the level of the children.

> Concentrate on one thing at a time.

> Make explanations clear and simple.

> Start where you left off at the last rehearsal.

A PROGRAM OF MUSIC EDUCATION IN THE CHURCH

By Mrs. Kathryn Hill Rawls
St. Luke's Methodist Church, Georgetown, Washington, D. C.

Rehearsal Times

Cherubs, 4 and 5 years old ....Saturday 1:30-2:15
Carol Choir, 6 to 9 ....Friday 3:30-4:15
Choristers, 9 to 14 ....Thursday 3:30-4:30
Chapel Choir, High School ....Sunday 5:30-6:15
Chancel Choir, Adults ....Thursday 8:00-9:30

Plan of Rehearsal (Carol and Choristers)

Doxology

Scripture Verse . . . Learn one a month.

Gloria

Roll Call: Imitate—word on given tones. First meeting—their names. Later—Alleluia, Hosanna, Hallelujah, three or four word phrase from one of the anthems.

Breathing Exercises: Inhale while I play 10 to 15 chords; exhale smoothly enough that a candle will not flicker.

Vocalizing: Scales up and down in different rhythms.

Always a tongue twister, such as, "Peter Piper picked a peck of pickled peppers."

Hymn Sing: Learning always a new one, and the three for the next service.

New Work: Learning by phrases and repetition, solos, and small groups.

Work Period: Rhythm or note values, etc.

Review: Songs learned at previous rehearsal.

Record of memory credits.

Benediction Song.

Cherub rehearsal is similar, but with longer work period. Note familiar rhythms, etc. I include the Jacque Dalcroze Eurythmics: clapping, walking, arms and feet in 2/4, 3/4, 4/4, 6/8.

I use and teach the Doxology and Gloria in the first lesson, and even the youngest learn the words. The Cherub and Carol Choirs memorize everything, and the Choristers usually do, though sometimes we are sparring for time as they sing at the 8:30 service on the third Sunday of every month.

My High School Choir sings at the 8:30 service on the fourth Sunday of the month; sing SAB, do many things with the Chancel Choir.

In order to provide a definite singing program, as a member of the Commission on Education, I work with the departments, and last year I initiated a monthly worship program in each department. The respective choir, in its vestments, is responsible for a specially prepared opening worship service. (Quite an event for the little ones, candles and all.)

In the Chorister and Carol Choirs I have a ten-minute period of instruction at each rehearsal. One month will be meters and note values; another, intervals and singing numbers to scales; another, memory work, etc. Two lessons will be instruction, the third a "spelling bee" on the work, and the fourth also a bee, with the winners in each row getting a little prize. They *love* that; no election ever had more excitement.

Each choir elects its officers in May for the next season. They may be nominated from those highest rating in attendance and conduct.

When a small child is a monotone or almost one, I let him appear in every performance, moving lips only. It's a game. I gave a special award last spring to a boy of 9 who was a "frog in a pond," and had

52

been a good sport for three years. Last spring he suddenly carried the tune perfectly. The musical roll call teaches them to listen, and listen to the others, and they are not about to miss an imitation.

As we all know, the young choirs are very uneven in their musical preparation. To try to remedy this, I have for the past three years offered a Vacation Singing School for the children of the Primary, Junior, and Intermediate departments, plus the Cherub Choir, during the last week of June, Monday through Friday from 9 to 11:30. This has been very popular, and most rewarding for the next year's work. The general plan included a half hour worship service and opening with candles, a vested group, and an older boy or girl as the minister, and instead of a sermon a religious "short" movie. (A member of our church owns Religious Films, Inc.)

Plan

9:00-9:25 Worship
    Candles—Silent Procession
    Doxology
    Psalm or verses
    Gloria
    Lord's Prayer
    Response
    Hymn
    Announcements
    Movie
    Closing Hymn used as
        recessional
    Choral Benediction

9:30
    Musical Roll Call
    Breathing exercises
    Vocalizing
    A Round

9:50
    All move to tables.

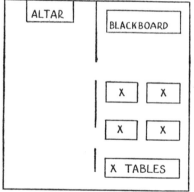

Room in two sections, divided by screens with cutouts of musical signs in bright colors.

Everyone provided with lined paper and pencils.
First Day: All musical signs, and note family.
Second Day: Note values in bars 4/4.
Third Day: Letters of treble staff, drill.
Fourth Day: Word spelling on staff.
Fifth Day: Original song, four phrases, words
    and music.

10:25

Assistant changes chairs in worship center to two rows along the long wall.

Screen in front of altar.

Eurythmics.

10:50

Story. I sit on a small chair in the middle of the circle.

First—Where music came from.

Second—The orchestra and its instruments.

Third—Mozart.

Fourth—Bach.

Fifth—A talent show (parents invited).

11:15

Hymn Sing (song sheets). Learn one new song.

11:30

Mizpah.

SUMMER CAMPS

The choir program does not need to stop with the close of the school year. In fact there are many churches where the best work of the choir can be accomplished during the summer, when there is more free time, and the program can be more extended and more informal. What might be an impossible undertaking for one church may be accomplished through the co-operation of several churches.

Summer camps can be carried out in the church building itself, or in co-operation with a community park, or even on the farm of some good friend. Much can be done with little, with the help of some ingenuity. The important thing is that the children learn something worth while, have fun in learning it, and have a chance to become aware of God's great nature.

Here is the chance to enjoy the wide range of teaching methods: films, music games, nature study, creative hobbies, comradeship, devotional services, plays, rehearsals, culminating in a public performance.

Of course it is work; but it is the kind of work that keeps the mind and body and spirit young.

Financing the Summer Camp

Albert McConnell of Central Reformed Church, Grand Rapids, maintains a summer choir camp. One of his means of financing it is an old-fashioned singing school. With an uninhibited song leader, box lunches, old custumes, square dances, a fiddle and a reed organ, the whole church can have a grand time together, and fill the choir camp bank.

Do you want an inexpensive book of games and stunts? Then send 30c to the Superintendent of Documents, U. S. Government Printing Office, Washington 25, D. C., and ask for a copy of *Handbook for Recreational Leaders.*

Three Simple Games Suitable for Rehearsal:
One child hums a line of a song, or claps the rhythm of a song; choir guesses name of song.

A child calls the name of another child, then repeats the words of one line of a hymn or anthem. If the child whose name is called can repeat the following line, he may choose another hymn for another child to guess.

If the children have been learning to recognize musical signs, they can make a "Do I Look Like This" game out of it. One child is chosen as the guesser; the other children decide on a musical sign, and the guesser must ask questions that can be answered by Yes or No, until he can draw the sign correctly on the blackboard.

Who knows any others?

Summer Vacation Is Just Around the Corner

What happens to your choir then? Do they scatter to the four winds, with the close of school? Do they roam the streets aimlessly? Or do they look forward to a choir camp?

Summer is the time to extend the rehearsal into a recreational period. Summer is the time to come closer to the children. Summer is the time for the strongest part of the choir experience.

Another and much more extended program is the Choir camp, one of the most successful of which is the one conducted in Southern California by the Board of Education of the Presbyterian Church. Last summer the Junior and Youth Choir camps were attended by more than seven hundred boys and girls of that area.

Miss Dorothy Arnim, Children's Division director for Southern California, is the guiding genius of the camps held at Pacific Palisades. The annual announcement folder gives the following pertinent information: date; cost; where to send registration.

Why Choir Camps?

Good Christian music is essential to Christian nurture. Good music enriches life. Good music enriches the church's program. A music program builds youth into the life of the church.

But choir camp programs are not all music. They have the richness of well-rounded Christian growth and fellowship which characterize all our Presbyterian camps and conferences.

Who Should Attend?

All members of children's and youth choirs. Any boy or girl of proper age who loves to sing and wants to learn to sing. The Junior camps are for those in the fifth and sixth grades. Youth camp is for the seventh grade and above, including High School.

Adult leaders of children's and youth choirs. Other adults who direct music in church schools or youth groups. Any adult who is interested in learning more about conducting, or who wishes to improve the music in the Christian education program of his church.

What Is the Program?

The theme this year is the church. Music and study will be built around the theme. The program majors in music—training in fundamentals and learning great music for the concert which climaxes each camp on Friday evening.

But there will be Bible study, hymnology, story telling, worship, films, recreation.

There will be fun, lots of fun, through well-directed play, on the grounds and at the beach. Most meaningful of all, perhaps, will be the fellowship of older and younger persons in the busy days of a wonderful week.

Leadership Classes

Classes in conducting, discussion of choir methods, program and repertoire, are held twice daily for those who come as leaders. Opportunity will be given to conduct rehearsals and selections in the camp concert for those interested.

Medical Blank

The usual medical certificate (to be mailed to delegates) will be required upon arrival at camp.

Program and Schedule

6:45	Rising Bell
7:45	Breakfast
8:10	Morning Devotions
9:00	Bible Classes (delegates)
	"Music in Worship" (adults)
9:35	First Class Period
10:10	Second Class Period
10:45	Third Class Period
11:20	Recess
11:40	Choir Rehearsal
12:30	Lunch
1:30	Rest Hour
2:30	Craft, Recreation, Swimming
4:45	Quiet Time (delegates)
	"Conducting" (adults)
5:30	Dinner
6:30	Vesper and Evening Program
8:30	Bed Time—Junior Camp
9:30	Bed Time—Youth Camp

Alternating sections of hymnology and recreation classes in music training. (placed beside 10:10–11:20)

Arrive? Leave?

Arrive Sunday afternoon between 3 and 5. Leave after concert Friday evening, or any time Saturday before 2 p.m.

What to Bring?

Ordinary clothing for the usual camp life; warm clothing for the rather cool evenings; a change of clothing for the Friday evening concert. Bring Bible, notebook and pencil, toilet articles, bathing suit, sleeping bag or blankets, sheets, pillow case, towels. Have linens and clothing marked for identification.

Leadership

A large, competent staff is provided for each choir camp, including a number of choir directors, teachers, and counselors. There will be an adult leader for each six or eight delegates.

Churches sending delegates are asked to provide an adult counselor for each ten delegates, either by sending a leader, or by paying board and room for a counselor recruited by the committee.

A counselors' Training Conference is held the 24 hours before camp begins. All counselors *must* attend.

57

Camp Counselors

A bulletin for the camp leaders gives clear instructions on organization, individual responsibilities, material to be used in the classes, class schedule, outline for cabin group devotions. The "Leads for Counselors" gives some notion of the details to be considered in planning a camp.

Being a leader in choir camp is a twenty-four-hour-a-day job. Each one is responsible for a group of children (those in his cabin) not only during the time they are in the cabin, but at other times. We are concerned for the welfare and happiness of each one during the entire week.

Our goal is the greatest possible good for each camper. Our concern is particularly for our own "little household," but we do feel ourselves a part of the whole camp and, therefore, have a concern for every child in camp.

We should know each child individually. Most likely you will be with children from your own church, but this doesn't mean you know much more about the children than their names. Learn about their families, their likes, their hobbies, their abilities. Show an interest in each. Try to help each at his point of need.

Counselors abide by the same rules as the campers. This means going to bed with the children both at rest period and bedtime. "Lights out" for children means the same for the counselors.

Check on physical needs of each child in your cabin. Check daily bowel movements; much of the ills during a week of camp stem from constipation. Check on cleanliness of body and clothes. Some children bring enough clean clothes to keep clean all week, but fail to use the clean clothes.

A nurse is provided in each camp. For any first aid or illness refer child to nurse.

Provide for quiet cabin entertainment. Leaders have found the value of providing books to read, quiet games, puzzles. Let's encourage the better type of reading by providing good children's books. No comic books! Plenty of them will show up with the children.

A piece of rope or clothesline is handy in providing a place to hang wet bathing suits.

Each counselor is asked to collect the money from each child and act as banker for his cabin. Each camper is allowed ten cents a day for candy or pop, *no more*. Some will want to spend some money on craft materials. Stores will be open only once during the day (after rest period).

58

Campers do not go off grounds. If there is shopping to be done, it can be done by a counselor, who *arranges with the dean* to make the trip to the village.

Counselors will be asked to fill in a registration form (to be given out at camp), listing each child in your group. Information asked for will be name of each camper in cabin, and his address, age, and church, and your own address and church.

All counselors are asked to observe the following rules for rest period: The first half-hour all must be on beds and absolutely quiet. No exceptions.

The last half-hour all must be quiet, but may read or write.

The last five minutes of the hour may be used for dressing for the beach.

Cabins must be cleaned before breakfast. This means:

Beds made.	Wet clothes and towels on line.
Floors swept.	Suitcases neat and closed.
Clothes hung up.	Papers picked up around cabin.

Inspection of camp is made each morning.

Evening prayer time. The end of the day in camp should close in prayer. Suggestions for this period are included in the bulletin.

Report any cabin repairs or need for supplies to the *dean* who in turn will report to the management. If you have a leaky faucet, need a light bulb, etc., report to the dean.

CRITERIA FOR THE SELECTION OF VOCAL MUSIC FOR CHILDREN

From "Keyboard, Jr."

Does the music set standards that the children can really meet?

(Are four-part arrangements left to the higher grades where they can really be sung?)

Are the arrangements suited to the elementary child's vocal capability, both as to range and key selection?

Does the book contain a goodly number of "common heritage" songs—those that are a part of every child's musical legacy?

Are new songs included to catch the interest and the imagination?

Are these new songs worth while? Do they add something to the child's musical education?

Are the words of the songs fitted to the child's vocabulary, and do they add to his understanding and interests?

Is there a good accompaniment? Is the music fairly easy to play?

A Teacher's Prayer

Lord, I thank Thee for a chance to work at a task which makes the hours so full. Let me use those hours to guide the precious lives entrusted to my daily care in ways of goodness. Help me to be calm in the face of disturbance, kind to all regardless of circumstance, tolerant when understanding is lacking, and faithful to duties great and small. I pray for the strength of mind and body to do what is expected of me without losing my willing spirit. Forgive the mistakes I made this day, and give me wisdom to correct them. In the name of the Great Teacher, I pray. Amen.

FRANCES H. BUTLER, Cooperstown, New York

FIRST STEPS IN SIGHT READING

Lesson One

From flash-cards acquaint the children with the notes and corresponding rests.

Divide the choir and see which side will recognize the most cards. (Call on the one who raises his hand first.)

Put the following chart on the board.

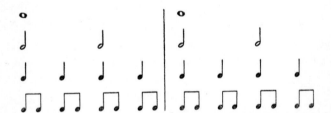

Have the children tap and count the notes while you point to them.

Let different children come to the board and tap with rhythm sticks.

Take four children at a time, each tapping one line.

Use drums, bells, rhythm sticks to keep separate lines distinct.

All the children count *all* the time.

60

Lesson Two

Bring a big round apple to class;

Have the note value outline (Lesson One) on the board.

Cut the apple in two—all clap second line, counting aloud.

Cut each half in two—all clap third line, counting aloud.

Cut each quarter in two—all clap fourth line, counting aloud.

Repeat procedure of Lesson One.

Explain time signature.

Upper number tells how many counts there are in a measure.

Lower number tells what kind of note gets a count.

Show flash cards of: $\frac{4}{4}$ $\frac{3}{4}$ $\frac{2}{4}$ $\frac{6}{4}$ $\frac{4}{2}$ $\frac{3}{2}$ $\frac{3}{8}$ $\frac{6}{8}$ $\frac{9}{8}$ time signatures.

Let each child explain the meaning of one signature by laying the right size and the right number of apple pieces in a row. (You will need two apples for 4/2 and 9/8 time.)

Write the following chart on the board:

Have one child arrange the apple segments, while another writes the right time signature before the measure.

Lesson Three

Review Lesson Two (without the apples).

Write a variety of 4/4 measures on the board (use notes and rests).

One child taps while all count.

Example: $\frac{4}{4}$ ♩ ♩ 𝄾 𝄾 one ,two, rest, rest.

Lesson Four

1. Explain dotted notes and tied notes. Use an apple again as illustration.

61

2. Flash cards: notes, rests, dotted notes, time signatures.

3. Write a series of simple measures on the board, using several tied and dotted notes. Let the class tap them (always counting) first individually, then together.

Lesson Five

Write the following series of 4/4 measures on the board:

Tap them while everyone counts.

Let children tap them with you.

Call on different children to tap one measure each.

Repeat the series, everyone tapping and counting.

Tap measures at random, and let a child point out the measure you are tapping.

Let one child tap a measure and another point it out.

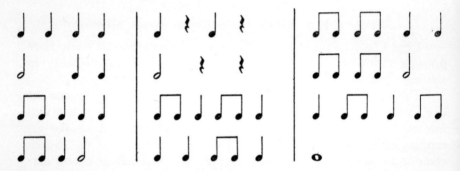

Lesson Six

Write the ascending scale in a variety of singable rhythmic patterns on the board. Let the children sing them, first in unison and then individually. When they can sing them with assurance, let one child tap one of the patterns, and another child point to the pattern being tapped.

Example:

Lesson Seven

Rhythms and Note Values for the Junior Choir

At the close of the rehearsal give each child a card with a simple rhythmic pattern on it, and a number. At the next rehearsal copy

62

the same patterns and their respective numbers on the board. Each child taps his rhythm. A prize to the one recognizing the largest number of patterns.

Lesson Eight

Signals society—One child taps a rhythm, second child imitates it. If right, he qualifies for membership in the Society, and gives a new signal to the next child.

If your children are familiar with the looks of some rhythmic patterns, instead of tapping out the answer, they may write it on the board.

MUSIC READING IN THE CHURCH JUNIOR CHOIR

By CARROLL A. RINEHART
Minister of Music, First Methodist Church, Tucson, Arizona

I have been so pleased with the type of experiences so many have presented through the Guild *Letters* that I feel a responsibility in sharing some of our rich experiences in children's choirs.

The particular program which I describe is a part of the one for our children's choir of the age group including grades three to six in our public schools. The grouping has been determined by the arrangement in our Church School. The music program of the church choir is an extension of the music program of the public schools carried over into sacred literature.

The reading program of the Tucson public schools is based upon recognition of basic tonal patterns. Each week an additional tonal pattern is found in a hymn or an anthem being studied, and that pattern is added to the "reading charts."

To explain more fully the program, this is how one tonal pattern was used in the choir. The hymn for one of the months was "The God of Abraham Praise." The children learned the song, discussed the meaning of the text, and sang it. The following week, the instructor, outlined the tonal pattern for that day on resonator bells. It was "mi, la ti, do, re me," or the opening phrase. The children were asked to identify it, which they did by saying, "The God of Abraham Praise."

The next step was to have a child come up and play "by ear" the pattern on the resonator bells. This is a very important step because it requires careful listening. All children were given an opportunity

63

during the next weeks to find the tonal pattern on the bells. The pattern was placed on a sheet of music manuscript tagboard and the music names (so-fa syllables and letter names) were identified. The third week the children were given a study sheet about the hymn for their notebooks. In addition to reading the history of the hymn, we studied a pattern which was put on the page, and space was provided for recognition of the same pattern in other music.

The instructor played "The Moldou"—Smetana—for the children while they discovered the same pattern was there but with a skipping rhythm. They counted the number of times that basic pattern was repeated, noting variations.

The fourth week they heard the same pattern again through listening to "Oh Vermeland, Thou Lovely," Swedish Folk Tune found in RCA Victor Education Album E-81 (Listening 5).

This pattern was added to those previously studied for the roll call. The director called roll by singing the name of the child to one of the patterns in their reading vocabulary. They respond by singing back the syllable names of the pattern.

The interesting thing about this new adventure into reading of music is the improvement in intonation. Through it the children have learned to listen and this carries over into their singing habits.

After about eight weeks of working by this method, and having discovered and worked through six patterns, the children "sight-read" David William's hymn-anthem on "Come Thou Long Expected Jesus." Only rarely did the director join them to keep them on the correct pitch. The joy of the work came as they finished the first verse and one wide-eyed girl, pleased with her efforts, beamed forth with the statement, "Why, I know this song!"

In using tonal patterns to establish a reading program the following steps are important:

1. Learn the song, the meaning of the text, and be familiar with it through the singing activity.
2. Identify by ear (by words, etc.) the tonal pattern to be studied. (Piano and resonator bells are good to isolate the pattern.)
3. Have the children put their fingers around the pattern being isolated.
4. Have a child find the pattern on the bells.
5. Put the pattern on chart and identify music names (syllables, numbers, or/and letter names).

6. Sing the music names.
7. Relate pattern to other music or in songs to follow.

WHAT IS A BOY?

Between the innocence of babyhood and the dignity of manhood we find a delightful creature called a boy. Boys come in assorted sizes, weights and colors, but all boys have the same creed: To enjoy every second of every minute of every hour of every day, and to protest with noise (their only weapon) when their last minute is finished and the adult male packs them off to bed at night.

Boys are found everywhere—on top of, underneath, inside of, climbing on, swinging from, running around, or jumping to. Mothers love them, little girls hate them, older sisters and brothers tolerate them, adults ignore them, and Heaven protects them. A boy is Truth with dirt on its face, Beauty with a cut on its finger, Wisdom with bubble gum in its hair, and the Hope of the future with a frog in its pocket.

When you are busy, a boy is an inconsiderate, bothersome, intruding jangle of noise. When you want him to make a good impression, his brain turns to jelly or else he becomes a savage, sadistic, jungle creature bent on destroying the world and himself with it.

A boy is a composite—he has the appetite of a horse, the digestion of a sword swallower, the energy of a pocket-size atomic bomb, the curiosity of a cat, the lungs of a dictator, the imagination of a Paul Bunyan, the shyness of a violet, the audacity of a steel trap, the enthusiasm of a fire cracker, and when he makes something he has five thumbs on each hand.

He likes ice cream, knives, saws, Christmas, comic books, the boy across the street, woods, water (in its natural habitat), large animals, Dad, trains, Saturday mornings, and fire engines. He is not much for Sunday School, company, schools, books without pictures, music lessons, neckties, barbers, girls, overcoats, adults, or bedtime.

Nobody else is so early to rise, or so late to supper. Nobody else gets so much fun out of trees, dogs, and breezes. Nobody else can cram into one pocket a rusty knife, a half-eaten apple, three feet of string, an empty Bull Durham sack, two gum drops, six cents, a sling shot, a chunk of unknown substance, and a genuine super-sonic code ring with a secret compartment.

A boy is a magical creature —you can lock him out of your work shop, but you can't lock him out of your heart. You can get him out of your study, but you can't get him out of your mind. Might as well give up—he is your captor, your jailer, your boss, and your m a s t e r—a freckled-face, pint-sized, cat-chasing bundle of noise. But when you come home at night with only the shattered pieces of your hopes and dreams, he can mend them like new with the magic words—"HI DAD!"

ALAN BECK

(Used by special permission of the New England Mutual Life Insurance Co.)

WHAT IS A GIRL?

Little girls are the nicest things that happen to people. They are born with a little bit of angel-shine about them, and though it wears thin sometimes, there is always enough left to lasso your heart—even when they are sitting in the mud, or crying temperamental tears, or parading up the street in mother's best clothes.

A little girl can be sweeter (and badder) often than anyone else in the world. She can jitter around and stomp, and make funny noises that frazzle your nerves, yet just when you open your mouth, she stands there demure with that special look in her eyes. A girl is Innocence playing in the mud, Beauty standing on its head, and Motherhood dragging a doll by the foot.

Girls are available in five colors—black,

white, red, yellow, or brown, yet Mother Nature always manages to select your favorite color when you place your order. They disprove the law of supply and demand—there are millions of little girls, but each is as precious as rubies.

God borrowed from many creatures to make a little girl. He used the song of a bird, the squeal of a pig, the stubbornness of a mule, the antics of a monkey, the spryness of a grasshopper, the curiosity of a cat, the speed of a gazelle, the slyness of a fox, the softness of a kitten, and to top it all off, He adds the mysterious mind of a woman.

A little girl likes new shoes, party dresses, small animals, first grade, noise makers, the girl next door, dolls, make-believe, dancing lessons, ice cream, kitchens, coloring books, make-up, cans of water, going visiting, tea parties, and one boy. She doesn't care too much for visitors, boys in general, large dogs, hand-me-downs, straight chairs, vegetables, snow suits, or staying in the front yard. She is loudest when you are thinking, the prettiest when she has provoked you, the busiest at bedtime, the quietest when you want to show her off, and the most flirtatious when she absolutely must not get the best of you again.

Who else can cause you more grief, joy, irritation, satisfaction, embarrassment, and genuine delight than this combination of Eve, Salome, Florence Nightingale? She can muss up your home, your hair, and your dignity—spend your money, your time and your temper—then just when your patience is ready to crack, her sunshine peeks through and you're lost again.

Yes, she is a nerve-wracking nuisance, just a noisy b u n d l e of mischief. But when your d r e a m s tumble down and the world is a mess—when it seems you are pretty much of a fool after all—she can make you a king, when she climbs on your knee and whispers, "I love you best of all!"

ALAN BECK

(Used by special permission of the New England Life Insurance Company.)

$\mathcal{D}$iscipline

CONSIDER THE CHILDREN

LOVE, ACCEPTANCE, SECURITY, PROTECTION, INDE-PENDENCE, FAITH, GUIDANCE, CONTROL. The National Association for Mental Health claims that all of these are necessary to every child for good mental health.

In all these areas, the minister of music can help to create an atmosphere conducive to mental and emotional health.

ACCEPTANCE. The director who thinks of behavior in terms of growth will have infinite patience and understanding. He will need to correct or punish, but the culprit will know that "he likes me in spite of the way I act."

SECURITY. The child needs to know that he is a vital part of the group; that he can count on his director in times of trouble.

PROTECTION. A child needs to be prepared for new and strange situations. He does not want to be made conspicuous by a blunder that could have been avoided.

INDEPENDENCE. He needs to know that the director has confidence in his ability to accept responsibility and to carry through.

FAITH. The relationships within the choir need to represent certain standards: fairness, consideration, honesty and self-control.

GUIDANCE. The child needs help in developing these qualities; and he needs *an example*.

CONTROL. He needs to know that there are limits of behavior

beyond which punishment is inevitable. Much as he will test the patience of the director, he wants to be sure that he can't get by with it.

No one can say how deep the influence of the choir will be on the child; but we do know that the choir that meets these basic needs will have to be under the guidance of one whose life exemplifies those qualities.

AUTHORITY WITH CHILDREN

Self-government with tenderness—here you have the condition of all authority over children. The child must discover in us no passion, no weakness of which he can make use; he must feel himself powerless to deceive or to trouble us; then he will recognize in us his natural superiors, and he will attach a special value to our kindness, because he will respect it. The child who can arouse in us anger or impatience or excitement feels himself stronger than we, and a child respects only strength.

The mother should consider herself as her child's sun, a changeless and ever radiant world whither the small restless creature, quick at tears and laughter, light, fickle, passionate, full of storms, may come for fresh stores of light, warmth, and electricity, of calm and of courage. The mother represents goodness, providence, law; that is, the divinity, under that form of it which is accessible to childhood. If she is passionate, she will inculcate in her child the idea of a capricious and despotic God.

The religion of a child depends on what its mother and father are, and not on what they say. The inner and unconscious ideal which guides their life is precisely what touches the child; their words, their remonstrances, their bursts of feeling even, are for him merely thunder and comedy; what they worship—this it is which his instinct divines and reflects.

The child sees what we are, behind what we wish to be. Hence his reputation as a physiognomist. He extends his power as far as he can with each of us; he is the most subtle of diplomatists. Unconsciously he passes under the influence of each person about him, and reflects it while transforming it after his own nature. He is a magnifying mirror. This is why the first principle of education is: train yourself; and the first rule to follow if you wish to possess yourself of a child's will is: master your own.

HENRI-FREDERIC AMIEL.
Entry for Jan. 6, 1853
in his "Journal Intime."
Translation by Mrs Humphrey
Ward.

70

TEN COMMANDMENTS FOR PARENTS

By Paul M. Pitman

(Used by Margaret Kendrick in her P. T. A. booklet)

I. Thou shalt love thy child with all thy heart, with all thy soul, with all thy strength, but wisely, with all thy mind.

II. Thou shalt think of thy child, not as something belonging to thee, but as a person.

III. Thou shalt regard his respect and love, not as something to be demanded, but something worth earning.

IV. Every time thou art out of patience with thy child's immaturity and blundering, thou shalt call to mind some of the childish adventures and mistakes which attended thine own coming of age.

V. Remember that it is thy child's privilege to make a hero out of thee, and take the thought to be a proper one.

VI. Remember also that thy example is more eloquent than thy fault-finding and moralizing.

VII. Thou shalt strive to be a signpost on the highway of life rather than a rut out of which the wheel cannot turn.

VIII. Thou shalt teach thy child to stand on his own feet and fight his own battles.

IX. Thou shalt help thy child to see beauty, to practice kindness, to love truth, and to live in friendship.

X. Thou shalt make of the place wherein thou dwellest a real home—a haven of happiness for thyself, for thy children, for thy friends, and for thy children's friends.

THIS MATTER OF DISCIPLINE

Several weeks ago I visited one of Dr. Whittlesey's rehearsals in Dallas, and tried to discover the reasons for his amazing discipline. It was an extra rehearsal of about 50 boys and girls of Junior High age. They came in, took their places, and waited quietly (without one poke or giggle) for the rehearsal to begin.

At the opening signal, a tone on the chime, everyone, without exception, straightened up and was at attention. Such discipline doesn't just happen. The ability to get it is either a gift or an achievement. With Dr. Whittlesey, I think it is a natural gift, but for most of the rest of us to attain such an orderly rehearsal would be an achievement. And so, for us less gifted directors I tried to probe the qualities that

71

made it possible. They might be summarized into the four P's: poise, prevention, purpose, and, for lack of a better word, politeness.

Dr. Whittlesey doesn't speak of his *kids;* the boys are addressed as *gentlemen.* Nor does he shout and rail at them. If he ever did, he would have to forfeit his most valuable quality—poise. Whenever we get angry enough to interrupt a rehearsal to reprimand a child, that child has taken charge.

I came in before starting time; some of the children were already in their places, and Dr. Whittlesey was standing quietly at the piano. Everything was in order; there was no last minute housekeeping to distract him from the immediate job of conducting a rehearsal in which every minute counted for something gained.

I am sure that Dr. Whittlesey works on the theory that prevention is better than cure. The children were to leave their coats in the hall, and pick up their bulletins and hymnals at the door. Those who forgot were reminded before they got to their seats. Every detail of the service was rehearsed: how to stand, where to put their hymnals, how to hold the head and hands, and there was no levity or deviation. The service was to be televised, and this rehearsal of minute details was to eliminate any chance for distraction.

Attention to detail can become picayune unless it fits into the pattern of an over-all purpose, and it is obvious that the purpose of this man is synonymous with dedication. As leaders in public worship, every member of every choir must be willing to give his very best—not occasionally, but habitually. And because he himself exemplifies that kind of dedication, the children have no choice but to follow.

If the children think of discipline as something forced upon them by the whim of the director, there will never be any discipline. But if discipline means behavior demanded by the importance and dignity of the office they fill, and exemplified by the director, then there's hope.

SOCIAL HABITS TO DEVELOP

1. Respect for authority.
2. Obedience.
3. Cleanliness.
4. Self-control.
5. Resourcefulness.

72

6. Self-respect.
7. Reliability.
8. Initiative.
9. Industry.
10. Respect for physical fitness.
11. Poise (ability to accept success or defeat gracefully).
12. Judgment (ability to face a difficult situation and select a good solution).
13. Independence (not a leaner).
14. Orderliness (a sense of system).
15. Sense of difference between right and wrong.
16. Courtesy (consideration of the feelings and rights of others).
17. Sincerity (not "putting on").
18. Honesty (with one's self and with others).
19. Appreciation (of kindness from others).
20. Friendliness (ability to make and keep friends).
21. Modesty (not blowing one's own horn).
22. Tolerance (Permitting others to have their own opinions).
23. Leadership (wise and unselfish).
24. Acceptance of leadership (from teacher, or majority vote).
25. Persistence.
26. Promptness.
27. Respect for property.
28. Courage.
29. Good teamwork.
30. Generosity.
31. Helpfulness.
32. Sympathy.
33. Patience.

Which of these social habits can be developed in Primary children? Which, at Junior age? What choir situations can help to develop them?

The Laws of Learning

Children learn most easily if:

They are given something to do which appeals to them as worth while and keeps them busily at work.

New learnings are built on old learnings.

They are in a frame of mind to learn.

The thing to be learned catches the interest.

The thing to be learned is presented slowly, patiently, and if drill on it is spread methodically over a considerable period of time.

Their individual abilities and needs are recognized.

SAMUEL SPIVENS

By Luby Pollack. Reprinted from *Better Homes and Gardens.* Copyright by the Meredith Publishing House, and used by permission.

Are you worried about discipline? Then meet Samuel Spivens. Samuel Spivens makes it easy for boys and girls to be good, because he keeps them so busy teaching him how to behave.

Samuel Spivens is just a doll, with a red velvet coat and white stocking hands, who fits over the fingers of Mrs. Dorothy Waldo Phillips. Together, they go to visit schools, as child guidance specialists. They never lecture the children on the art of being good—oh, no!—but Mrs. Phillips confesses shamefacedly some of the very naughty things Samuel Spivens has done and asks the children's advice in teaching him to behave properly. The children understand the situation perfectly, and are eager to tell Samuel, because maybe just the day before they had done the very same thing.

Mrs. Phillips calls this the "turnabout" approach of correcting a child without making him lose his self-respect. "No need to say, 'Boy, you did thus and such. You were wrong.' He told himself, in telling Samuel Spivens, so it was dignified and tactful, and if a fellow tells himself the rules, he jolly well remembers them. Now you have avoided the need of confronting him directly, so he will not have any need for putting up defenses."

Mrs. Phillips is loved by thousands of children because she is willing to come down off her adult pedestal, and because they know she loves them in turn.

"Samuel," queries Mrs. Phillips, "we can't teach character from four to five on Thursday afternoon, can we, Samuel? It's a full-time job, isn't it, Samuel, with papa and mama (and choir director) doing most of the studying, isn't it, Samuel?" And Samuel nods a thoughtful, "Yes."

KEEP VOICE LOW

From *Musical Learning: A Guide to Child Growth.* By Marion Flagg. Published by C. C. Birchard.

One of the most important teaching techniques is in the use of the voice. When the air gets tense, lower the voice, and ease its production. A low, resonant tone will cut under confusion, where a loud,

74

forced tone increases nerve strain and resulting noise. The teacher's voice should be calm, and directions given without emotion. Voices of children and teachers, if pleasant, have much to do with the feeling tone of the room and the school.

The feeling tone of the room can also be heightened by a positive good humor in the teacher's attitude, and give the impression that she really likes boys and girls, and has a good time teaching. There can be a healthy give and take between teacher and children as a group, without sacrifice of mutual respect. The schoolroom, and especially the music room, should be a joyful place, with children and teacher happily at work in experiences which must be pleasurable, if they are to reach first base as education.

ONE COIN

Dr. Whittlesey had one boy in his choir who was troublesome. How did he meet the situation? Nagging? No, he drew the boy into conversation, found that he was keenly interested in coins. At the next rehearsal, Dr. W. presented him with one from his own collection. At the next encounter the boy said, "Guess what! I was offered $5.00 for that coin you gave me. But I didn't sell it. No sir!" The next step will be a visit to a famous collector in a nearby city. There is no longer a behavior problem.

MARGARET KENDRICK ON DISCIPLINE

The Question: "What are the characteristics of each age group, and how can one fill their needs and interests so that discipline isn't a problem?"

The Answer: "This *is* a real sixty-four-dollar question. We will assume that our questioner has at least three groups, probably four, i.e., Beginners (ages 4, 5), Primary (ages 6, 7, 8), Juniors (ages 9, 10, 11), Intermediates (ages 12, 13, 14, 15, 16).

It is to be hoped that none of the groups meet together, since it would be almost impossible to interest even two of the groups at the same time. You could find an excellent chart of the characteristics and needs of these groups opposite page 68 in the 1947 Yearbook of the Association for Supervision and Curriculum Development of the N. E. A., 1201 Sixteenth Street, N. W., Washington 6, D. C. This would be a very helpful book on certain phases of child study.

Another splendid book is *Understanding Children* by Lewis J. Sherrill, Abingdon, Cokesbury Press. The first book gives the viewpoint of the public school, while the second stresses religious education.

We must remember that all children are different, yet the group can be interested by the same thing. Plan carefully, trying to understand the needs of the whole group. Plan more than you need. A *busy* child rarely gives trouble, and an idle one gives little else.

Be sure that you are at the choir session before the children. Remember that the first ones there usually "set the pace."

Do not choose to learn something too hard, for then they will become discouraged and give up easily; and do not insult their mentality by the choice of too easy material.

Do not issue any orders you cannot enforce without a scene.

Expect their respect and good order, and you will usually get it. Never let them feel that you are uneasy in their presence, or that you are uncertain about being able to do a good job with them.

Finally, really be *interested* in them, in their hobbies, their studies, their home life, and their friends. They *know* whether your interest is pretended or real, and will co-operate with you accordingly.

I don't think very highly of *discipline*. If you and your choirs learn to live and work happily together, you will not need to use the big word.

Question: What would you do with a boy of thirteen who is musical, but just will not pay attention?

Answer: A boy of thirteen is emotionally unstable. He is often an adult in size, but lacks the experiences, the knowledge, and the calm judgment of the grownup. At this age, he often thinks he "knows it all" and is very restive at any kind of restraint. He has a strong desire to be like someone he knows, and above all, he will do nothing that he thinks is "sissy."

He is coming to the choir, I expect, because his parents *make* him come, and they are failing to see that they are doing him harm, and possibly building up a resentment toward music which will rob him of much enjoyment later on. It is too bad they cannot be the choir director for a time to see what such enforced attendance does to the director, to the other members of the choir, and to the boy himself.

What to do? I would have a friendly talk with the boy, trying to make him see that you are "on his side." Ask him to tell you why he comes to choir, since he does not get much from it because of lack of attention. If he really dislikes coming, I would go to his home, if possible, and explain that you feel that his time and yours are being wasted by his continued attendance, and ask his parents to let him drop choir for a year at least, or until *he* wishes to return with a real desire to participate in its program.

I think it is usually a good thing to have the boy present at this discussion, and to let him express himself, too. Of course, you may have talked it over with the mother before you discussed it with him present.

Whatever the cause, lack of interest, fear of being called sissy, lack of self-confidence, a wish to assert his own desires instead of obeying his mother, or just plain laziness, it is not going to help him any to continue as a member of the group. I would try to make his mother feel that it is for his own good, that she should allow him to stop coming. If she wants him to continue, ask her to come for a visit, so that she may see and understand just what you are up against.

Miss Kendrick put the question to one of her seventh grades, and shares some of the answers with us. And quite revealing they are.

Boy of 14: "When a boy is thirteen, his voice starts to change. The boy doesn't like to sing because his voice goes up and down. When the boy gets out where no one can hear him, he sings to himself. When a boy is in front of a crowd, he is afraid to sing. He might have the voice of a man. That's why I think he pays no attention."

Boy of 13: "I think the teacher should try to find out why he is not paying attention. Maybe the teacher could change her way of teaching, or something of the kind."

Girl of 12: "If the boy doesn't pay attention maybe its because he is growing up, and doesn't like music any more. Maybe he has something to play with, and that is why he doesn't pay attention. The choir director can't do anything about his growing up, or not liking music. She can do something about his playing, though."

Boy of 13: "I think the teacher should have a talk with him."

Girl of 13: "I think he doesn't pay attention because he thinks he knows all there is to know about music. His teacher should not let him come to music until he can pay attention."

Girl of 12: "If he doesn't pay attention, he must not be very interested in music. The teacher should ask him if he wants to sing. If he doesn't, there is no sense in wasting time on him."

Girl of 13: "I think the reason he doesn't pay attention is that he wants someone always paying attention to him. Also he is the kind that does not like to sit in one place long."

Boy of 12: "He probably is musical, but isn't interested in the kind of music they are doing, so he doesn't pay attention to it. There is nothing much the choir leader can do except *make* him behave until they do what he likes."

Boy of 12: "Because he thinks it is cute. I think he does it to annoy the teacher. The teacher should punish him by sending him to detention hall, and if that doesn't work, take him out of the choir."

And finally—this from a boy who *knows:* "A thirteen-year-old knows music, but is too lazy to sing, and pays no attention. No matter how many times he is gotten after, he keeps this up until he is out of the choir—and wishes he was back in."

DO YOU TALK TOO MUCH?

The magazine *Coronet* tells the story of a young mother who, in order to avoid a very delicate operation, had to maintain absolute silence for six weeks.

"I made my first discovery within two days: mothers talk too much. We besiege our children with an unremitting barrage of words, mostly ineffective."

How about us directors? At the next rehearsal check to see how much of what you say is really indispensable.

"Wear your hat and rubbers," I used to tell my son when I saw rain. He balked, and I insisted. This whole battle is bypassed now, when I silently deposit his hat and rubbers next to his books."

It might be good practice for all of us to think twice before we speak—and then maybe not speak.

CROSS OF MERIT

I recently organized an Intermediate Choir for girls. It is much better to have the Junior High separated from grade school ages, and discipline is much easier. I have purchased ten Jerusalem sterling crosses as awards of merit, to be earned each month from one performance to the next. Their record has to have the three checks (different colors) on each rehearsal: one for attendance; one for conduct; and one for effort and co-operation. The change is *astounding!* They are worn only at the service, and no one knows the selected ones until they are vested.

KATHRYN RAWLS, St. Luke's Methodist Church, Washington, D. C.

78

CONFLICT

The High School choir rehearsal had been a total loss. Two of the boys had talked and interrupted constantly, and balked every effort at actual rehearsal. Finally, about twenty minutes before closing time, I said, "This is a waste of time, yours, and mine, too. The choir is dismissed. (Silence) I hope to see you Sunday morning ready to make use of the precious little time we have." Rather startled, they left.

I was glad to have a week for serious thought before meeting them again. In my irritation, my first reaction was to give them back to the organist who had given them up as hopeless. During a night of fitful sleep, I tried to concoct a plausible reason for deserting them; but I knew that they would recognize any scheme for what it really was: giving up.

Calmed somewhat by the unconscious decision not to be a quitter, I began to look for help, and found it providentially in an article "Why We All Have Ups and Downs" (*Getting the Most Out of Life*—a compilation of Readers' Digest Selections). It was encouraging to know that we all have regular emotional cycles, times when everything seems hopeless, and times when we can tackle any problem with courage. I decided to wait for the emotional upswing to help plan a course of action. In the meantime, there was time to give my own attitude somewhat honest scrutiny. If my real purpose was to help these boys and girls, how could I possibly act out of resentment and hurt pride? If I expected them to display evidences of maturity, I had better do so, too. There was therapeutic value in forcing me to admit the real problem to myself.

With my mind set on the children now, instead of on myself, and the emotional cycle on the upswing, I was ready to act with calm and purpose. The miserable rehearsal had been Sunday night; on Thursday I sent each of them a copy of "Choir Attitudes" and added a personal note to each one. To the obnoxious one it was, "The motto that Rosalind Russell's father gave her—'A winner is never a quitter, and a quitter is never a winner'— is a pretty good one. I'll see you Sunday morning."

I did see him, too, and saw him privately. He was immediately on the defensive against the expected tirade. Instead, I suggested that he had so many qualities of leadership that there was no telling what he might be able to do, if he would permit his positive self to take charge instead of his negative. (No need to mention that I had had to learn the same lesson.)

Sunday morning everyone was present, and everyone worked. Sunday night there were two new members. Every week since there have been new members; and now the chancel is beginning to be too small for the choir.

Rehearsals are by no means models of decorum, but now the choir is as interested as the director in making better use of our time. And the director, having once removed the cloud of his own ego from the situation, sees the children in the bright light of understanding. When that light dims, he will look first within himself for the source of the shadow. "He that ruleth his own spirit . . . ."

Mae Nightingale's Observations on the Teen-Agers

They need someone outside the home in whom to confide.

They love gangs, but are very resentful of interference from older people.

You must be smart enough to make them think "it was their idea first."

You have to take a real interest in sports and things that interest them.

They like to change their names—be sure to respect them.

Find jobs for them.

Have an organization; every officer works; no figureheads.

Test them in a range where they will not be embarrassed by having their voice break.

Select music that provides somewhat of a challenge in music or thought.

Provide for boys with changing voices, who may have a range of only three notes.

The changing voice has the same quality as the junior, but with more pressure.

Practical range of the teen-age choir:

SOPRANO   ALTO   ALTO TENOR   BARI-TONE

HELPFUL QUOTES

"Children need models more than they need critics."

"The great teachers are those who *expect* the best from their pupils, but do not *demand* it."

"Start a daily prayer period. Take one problem child in your thought. Go over your analysis of him carefully, look at yourself critically in relationship to him. Read some words of assurance from the Bible. Pray."

A woman, whose daughter had just been sentenced to the reformatory, cried out, "But Judge, I always thought that if you sent your child to Sunday School and church, this wouldn't happen."

The Judge replied, "Did you say, 'send'? As a parent you ought to know that children won't go to any institution you don't believe in enough to attend yourself. You can't *send* children. You take them to church with you."

CHOIR PROCEDURES

To clarify procedures for its members, and to give new members a greater sense of security, the officers of the First Methodist Church Choir, Santa Barbara, California, assembled a mimeographed booklet of choir procedures. Its general outline may be helpful to other choirs.

Choir practice starts at 7:30 Thursday night; and we shall all be vested and ready to practice at 10:30 Sunday morning.

Vestments are expensive and must be treated with care. Hang them up carefully, and keep them off the stairs when going up or down.

You will notice that your vestment and hymnal have the same number.

No jewelry, earrings, necklaces, bright hair combs, or ornaments are worn. Wear dark shoes; men wear black ties.

Responses and hymns on the blackboard Sunday morning.

Get lined up in choir room, go down in order, and remain so in the narthex.

Silence in the narthex before and after the service.

Do not start singing in the processional until you are out from under the balcony.

In processing and recessing, hold the Hymnal in outside hand with other hand on top.

In processing and recessing, keep only the distance of two pews between couples.

Couples keep together and in step.

If there is an uneven number of men or women, always have a couple at the end, with the single person next to the last.

The processional and recessional are sung in unison, and the middle hymn in parts. Doxology is in unison, and the Amens are in parts.

Hold Hymnal at side when you stand, and face the altar for singing the Doxology. Keep open at next hymn, with finger in page.

Have a spirit of reverence during the service. Don't look for hymn page during prayer.

Stay at attention after finishing anthem or hymn, and do not close music until you sit down.

Dues are 15c a month, and are used for cards, flowers, etc.

Courtesy demands that quiet prevail among choir members while director is talking, or working with one section.

If chorister is able to be at only part of the rehearsal, it is best to come late, and stay through to the end.

If anyone misses a Thursday night rehearsal, he must be at the 10:30 practice Sunday morning to sing that day. If anyone misses two Thursday rehearsals in a row, he cannot sing the following Sunday.

Either the director or president must be called when you are going to be absent, or it will be counted as an unexcused absence. Three unexcused absences will drop you automatically from the choir. Absences should be reported as far in advance as possible.

ODE TO POSTURE

Good posture is an asset
Which very few possess;
Sad to relate, the favored ones
Seem to be growing less.

We see the folks around us
All slumped down in a heap;
And the way that people navigate
Is enough to make you weep.

Some elevate their shoulders;
Some hollow in their backs;
Some stiffen up their muscles,
And some just plain relax.

The one who walks with grace and poise
Is a spectacle so rare,
That even down on gay Broadway
The people turn and stare.

If you would cut a figure
In business, sport, or school,
Just mind the Posture Precepts,
Obey the Posture Rule.

Don't thrust your head out turtlewise;
Don't hunch your shoulders so;
Don't sag and drag yourself around;
No style to that, you know.

Get Uplift in your bearing,
And strength and spring and vim.
No matter what your worries—
To slouch won't alter them.

Just square your shoulders to the world,
You're not the sort to quit.
"It isn't the load that breaks us down,
It's the way we carry it."

From "The Central Chorister"
Central Presbyterian Church.
Atlanta, Georgia.
Hubert V. Taylor, director.

83

Choir Diary

It is one thing to have a theory of education; it is quite another matter to make that theory function. In order to keep in touch with realities, I have adopted a choir, and in the diary of our experiences, you may find the reflection of some of your own situations.

Our choir is made up of children from a small and rather disorganized Junior Department. There is no supervised music in the public schools, and comparatively few of the children study privately. About a third of them have difficulty carrying a tune, and there seems to be no outstanding talent to set the pace.

The sanctuary of the church is a "barnlike" auditorium; the congregation is social rather than worshipful; there is no choir room for rehearsals. That is the picture.

There were about twenty at the first rehearsal—far too few. I showed them my Choristers' pin, and told them they would find out next Saturday how they could earn one. Next week, everyone was to bring a notebook cover. I gave them each a sheet of paper to show proper size.

Saturday, October 11. Gave them first three pages for their notebooks. Used colored paper. First page: space for name and address, and for picture of the church; second page: outline of credit system, with space for a record of credits earned. (Pointed out the credits for bringing a new member. Built up some enthusiasm for making this the best choir in the city, and for having as many boys as girls.) Third page: meaning of the design on the antependium or pulpit hanging, explanation of vestments, cassocks, cottas, how to act when wearing them. Made statements regarding them with blanks for the children to fill in.

Had the music on their chairs before rehearsal began. It was a disturbance rather than a help, because the children don't read music at all, and words only haltingly. Will pass out music only as it is used next time; must be careful that it doesn't become a chance for general talking.

Have to go slowly on rhythm work. They can tap whole notes, half and quarter, but are all off on eighth notes. Next week, I'll concoct a tune to the three words: running, walking, strolling, and see if they can keep time with those movements. But, first, we will review quarter, half, and eighth notes on the board.

Running running .. .. Walking walking .. .. Strolling .. ..

Saturday, October 18. Five new members: three boys and two girls. None of the boys can carry a tune. Both girls have clear voices and good range, but they are only 8 years old, and their voices are small. Got some of the boys around the piano before rehearsal; had them match tones with each other. Didn't get much tone, but established the will to try, which is more important. Tomorrow is Founder's Day, and the choir is to sing. Important that they should begin to develop good church behavior. Told them that some people don't like to have the Junior Choir sing because they can't sit still. I don't agree with them, because you can do most anything, no matter how hard, if you know that you must. Just like an Indian baby. Did you know that an Indian baby never cries? Long ago, the tiniest sound from a baby might give away their hiding-place, and the whole village might be killed because of it. So, when a newborn baby begins to cry, the mother quietly puts her hand over its nose and mouth. If it begins to cry when she gives it a chance to breathe, she does it again, and again, until the baby learns that it must not cry. If a tiny baby can learn never to cry, I think you can learn not to talk or wiggle for an hour, don't you?

Sunday, October 19. Most of the children were pretty good Indians, but as usual George and Mickie did more talking and squirming than all the others put together. But here is the payoff. After service, George presented me with a list of all the children he had seen talking.

Saturday, October 25. Before rehearsal got George and Mickie off in a room by themselves to discuss between themselves how they could manage to sit beside each other, and not talk, or whether it would be better to give them separate seats.

Several absences again today. Must map out a program of parent education on that matter. Am reading one story from *Bird Life in Wington* each week. One of the boys (who won't join the choir) made a model church for us. We call it the Wington church, and set it up for the story hour. Wish they were as interested in the whole rehearsal as they are in the story hour.

For note work we used the scale, drew a picture of a flight of 8 steps, and sang:

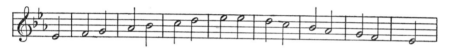

The scale is such a sim-ple thing. It walks right up and down a-gain. Step, step, step, step, step, step, step, *up*. Step, step, step, step, step, step, step, *down*.

Four children won a piece of candy by singing it correctly alone. Wonder how long it will be before they can all sing the scale correctly?

Saturday, November 1. "The scale is such a simple thing" was a good idea. We tried it again today, and this time practically everyone could sing the scale correctly. Last week, only four.

Caught George and Mickie before rehearsal to get their decision on the matter of talking. Their decision: "We've decided to keep on sitting together, and just not talk."

Jerry taught me today that high and low are poor terms to use in relation to pitch distinction. When I asked him which of two notes I played was the higher, he asked which end of the piano was high, and which low. I'm quite sure that high and low are arbitrary terms in music, and no help to the children at all. In fact, the very thought of singing high can be the cause of some of the usual tightness on those tones. I'm going to be very careful of my use of high and low, and gradually substitute fast and slow (if we must have terms) for that is what pitches actually are: faster or slower vibrations.

Sunday, November 2. Children in the service again. Good chance to test the boys' decision. It worked; neither George nor Mickie said a word. They were the best behaved in the whole choir. Afterwards George explained the phenomenon: Mickie had a funny book. On the Benediction, the children were all set to dash for the door. They looked more like an athletic field than a church. More education necessary.

Saturday, November 8. Three new notebook pages today, much to their joy. They would like to have them every week. Two pages were words of Christmas songs they are to learn. The two solid pages were lightened and made more palatable with Christmas designs. The third page, however, was a result of last Sunday's benedictional scramble. "Our Worship Service" is a copy of the page (see page 96). I hope the parents will read it; maybe some of them will discover, as well as the children, that there are purposes other than sociability in the worship service. Asked Mrs. Brett, one of the mothers, to hear the children's words for credit before and after rehearsal. She will be responsible for starring their songs and memory work.

Purely by happenstance, we have started a club—the Hoo-Hoo Club—that meets around the piano before rehearsal for some voice training. Hoo-Hoo Owl is one of the favorite Wington characters, and one time when the children were singing a rather flat oo vowel, I told them to sing it like Hoo-Hoo Owl. The tone improved, and our pre-rehearsal session had a name.

Started on the Christmas music. Have found it wise, since many of the children read very slowly, to read the words together, and discuss some of the texts, before introducing the music.

Sunday, November 9. George sat with me in church today. After the offertory, he leaned over and whispered, "That's in 4/4 time, isn't it?" Sure enough, it was. The music training is beginning to *take*.

Saturday, November 15. My husband's birthday. Considerable commotion before rehearsal. All explained when Gay Brett came down the aisle to him at the piano, with an enormous birthday cake. Everybody on his birthday gets a little bluebird tag that makes him an honorary member of the Wington church. The children insisted that Leslie get one, too. The chairman of the Music Committee, a wonderful old man, appeared with a present, too. We made him our guest of honor, and sang one of our Christmas songs for him. A good chance to put them on their toes musically.

Saturday, November 22. Leslie took the rehearsal alone, since I was in Tulsa for the festival there.

Attendance just does not hold up. In spite of the prospect of choir pins, and the interest in their notebook material, only a nucleus

ჿı the choir is dependably regular. This is proof to me that the co-operation of the parents is absolutely essential; and it can be done, even in a choir with as mixed a background as this one.

The enthusiasm over rhythm work is amazing. The progress and increased assurance are noticeable at each rehearsal. Must be partly because we have added only one thing at a time, and kept repeating (with variations) the things they could do fairly well. Besides, it gives them a chance to do something alone.

Saturday we introduced dotted notes. Around the room we went with running and limping steps. Rhythm travels best from the feet to the head, rather than the other way around.

We're developing some notion of tone. Played a recording of two English boys singing "Brother James Air." They listened attentively, and the first question was, "Was that just two boys, or a whole choir?" This was the chance to work on tone projection. With their minds on the job, they got quite a clear, ringing tone. They liked the sound of it—their expressions said so. Then we tried to put that same tone quality in a song. It wasn't nearly as good as the arpeggios had been, but a good deal better than it had ever been before.

We've finished all the useful stories in "Wington," and I've learned something about children's stories since. 1. They must be short. 2. Within the experience or imagination of the children. 3. And in their phraseology. "Peter, the Adventures of a Boy Chorister," left them fidgeting. Palestrina from *The Boyhood of Great Musicians* was no better until fate played into our hands, and brought a model of St. Peter's in Rome to the city. We're going down to see it after rehearsal next week. And instead of reading the stories about the great musicians, we're playing Musical Sherlock Holmes. I tell them the story, and then ask them questions to see if they are good detectives. You should hear them snap back at me that Palestrina got his name from his home town; that he was born in 1524; that he was a composer and a choirmaster; the kind of music he wrote is called polyphony; polyphony is several different melodies going on at the same time. We experimented with a little polyphony of our own—namely, "Three Blind Mice." We had some trouble with it, and wondered how people could manage some of Palestrina's music that has 8 or 10 melodies all going at the same time. Next week we shall play some polyphonic music. Everybody is excited about going to see the model of St. Peter's, and we've invited the other Juniors to go along. You would think we were actually going to Rome.

Discipline just doesn't stay put. Sent Mickie out of the room today because he persisted in talking. It doesn't pay to get irritated to that extent. Publicly disciplining a child doesn't improve his attitude, nor your own, and it disturbs the rehearsal more than the whispering. We will have to come to an understanding of what each one has a right to expect of the other. "I have to try as hard as I can to interest you, and you have to try as hard as you can to be interested." Fact of the matter is—I hadn't prepared that rehearsal as carefully as I should have.

Well, we went to Rome today, and had a wonderful trip. And we know about three phony kinds of music: monophony, polyphony, and homophony. Mickie is a traffic patrol at his school, so he was put in charge of the procession down to the exhibit. He was most efficient and businesslike about it, and used good judgment at the street corners. I made it a point to compliment him.

The millennium is not yet here. Sunday behavior is not perfect by any means, and some of the children are still not convinced that Saturday means Saturday, not Sunday. Two girls could not sing Sunday because they were not able to repeat the words of their song Saturday—in spite of due warning. And they reacted differently. Donna came back the next Saturday with her words memorized for two weeks hence. Shirley did not appear at all.

Life is never dull in a children's choir. Rather than scold Mickie and Rusty publicly for misbehaving in the service, I called a special meeting of all the boys after rehearsal. I hadn't counted on the curiosity of the girls. The boys played up, of course, and implied that a very special club (for boys only) was in the make. That was too much, so the next Saturday morning before rehearsal, Mr. Jacobs was called into a very special conference with half a dozen of the girls —object, top secret. The net result of the boys' conference was that Mickie, the only real offender, came up with a plan for improving behavior. "Why not have an army plan, like the Scouts have? Whoever is good for five Sundays gets to be a Sergeant, and so on up." I am tempted to try Mickie's plan, mainly because it came from Mickie, and give him the job of making the chart and keeping the records.

There are three sets of twins in the choir, and two of the sets look exactly alike. We took a picture of them in their vestments, and the Press-Scimitar used it along with a story about the confusion caused by not knowing who's who.

Now that we are singing so frequently, we've neglected our note and rhythm work. But we did try an experiment Saturday. Our processional hymn for Palm Sunday is "Hosanna, Loud Hosanna," and we introduced it by using it as a rhythm exercise. The staff confused the children, but when I wrote the same rhythm on the board, it was easy.

They were quite pleased with themselves when they discovered that three of the four phrases were exactly alike. The rhythmic patterns learned, Mr. Jacobs played the hymn while we clapped it. (Tympani section of the orchestra). Next we read the first stanza. I've found with this group that it is always best to get the words before we attempt to sing any song, because their reading is slow. Then we sang and clapped it at the same time; gave ourselves two minutes to learn the first stanza; sang it again without our books; and by that time it was pretty well learned.

The Saturday before Easter we are going to surprise the children with an Easter Egg Hunt after rehearsal.

P.S. After Easter, I think I'll write the rhythmic pattern of all the songs the children have learned on the board, and see how many they will recognize.

The new season brought us about a dozen eight-year-olds. Since the first rehearsal had been planned on the ten-year level, we had to shift gears. Must be more careful to make the children familiar with the words before they try to sing them, otherwise they are completely lost. Must also lay aside some of the more ambitious anthems and start with simpler ones. It takes very little to have these youngsters break out into gales of laughter; the slightest deviation from familiar routine is cause for amusement. They have to be kept doing things. We're doing considerable marching; our goal—in three weeks to have everyone in step through three stanzas of a hymn. Some of them make terribly hard work of marching; we won't be satisfied until they can keep in step without watching their feet.

Put some simple rhythm patterns on the board; everybody loves them. They practice them before rehearsal and want to be the first to do them right.

Must be careful about building up tone—both in quantity and range. Their top is B flat. Last year it was high C. The little ones will have to learn how to use their voices before we can try for range or projection. It will come in time.

The prospect of earning a pin is already showing its influence. Billie who was off again, on again last year, and full of excuses, has been present and on time every week because he wants a pin. And because of the pin, the memorizing is going along at a great rate; we run out of stars.

Will have to begin checking on orderliness. After rehearsal last week, the floor was littered with papers and hymn books. From here on out, the last job *before* dismissal will be housekeeping check up.

I'm wondering what Mike will do the first time the choir sings. He sits with me in church, and it seems that he just *cannot* sit still. We'll see.

Last Sunday was Communion, and it is the custom here for the smallest children to go forward with their parents for Communion. Mike said to me, "I tasted that stuff, and it's good." I think our next notebook project should be on the meaning of Communion. Don't you?

Every year we have to start all over again to convince the children that we really mean it when we say that they must have memorized their music to be permitted to sing with the choir. Always there is the day of reckoning, with some of the children making extravagant excuses, and others learning their lesson. And the parents. Some of them say, "I'll see that she knows her words next time." Others act as if their children had been subjected to inhuman atrocities. And some just don't bother one way or another. The children sang "St. Francis' Hymn" by Olds, (Hall and McCreary) with the adult choir, and did it well. On Monday, a letter went out to all the parents reminding them that the children were required to say their words before they could sing, and announcing when and what they would sing next.

The Simmons twins got a special prize Saturday for having learned all their words two weeks before the deadline. The choir has certainly had an influence on them. Leslie says that every time he goes down the aisle in the procession, he sees out of the corner of his eye that they both are holding their hymnals just *so* and singing lustily, even if they can't read the words. And when the processional hymn is one they know, they add a few decibels to the congregational tone.

Mike sat amazingly still during the service. Maybe because his mother was sitting in the balcony opposite, but maybe because he knew it was expected of him. But in rehearsal he is not as restrained. When something amuses him, he lets out a particularly Mike-ish snort that irritates the rest of the choir. The president thinks they should really do something about Mike, and I advise a unified program of patience and kindness. She prefers something more dramatic.

The eight-year-olds are coming along well. They settled down to real work in the second rehearsal, and their tone is improving rapidly. They are ready now for some of the numbers that had to be postponed earlier.

With some of the money they earned last season, we hope to get electric candles for their Christmas processional. The Church School is going to give "A Christmas Carol Pageant," by Diller and Page (G. Schirmer), and the choir will sing most of the carols. With their lighted candles, they will form the background for the action of the pageant.

Irene, our president, wants to know who is to sing the solos. She aspires! Thus starts *self*-consciousness. But her need for being something special is being filled to some extent by helping the Primary Choir, and she is a real help.

There are 12 carols to learn for the pageant, and two pages of words look rather formidable; but we sang them all through, and they found them all easy, and everybody got a star for knowing "Silent Night"— which left only 11 to learn.

The Sunday after Thanksgiving was Rally Day, and after checking attendance, the entire Church School assembled in the sanctuary. To hold the attention of this wide age range and to present the total program of the Church School as forcefully as possible, the committee planned a pseudo-radio program with the master of ceremonies interviewing representatives of all the different activities. The children took the place of the Senior Choir. Some of them asked afterwards—all popeyed—"Were we really on radio?"

By the time the Christmas season is over, the choir will have memorized 19 songs since September. They are much more prompt with their memorizing now, and are beginning to vie with each other to be the first one done. Several of the mothers are on hand before and after rehearsal to hear words. Some of the children get by with a rather sketchy performance. But if we can make them realize that they must know the words to be able to sing, the next step will be fairly easy—that they must know them *well*. The parents are beginning to take choir requirements more seriously, too, and help the children with their memory work. It is a good way to get in a little adult education; they learn the songs themselves by teaching them to the children.

I wonder if we realize how profound the influence of the choir can be on the child, the home, the church. I wonder how many of us are able or willing to open up these avenues of influence. Certainly not if we lack the strength of character to hold ourselves and our church to the highest standards of which they are capable. Being expert in making excuses, or lax in accepting them, is not a quality of leadership.

In a recent copy of *Christian Herald* there was a story about Gordon Crosby, a minister who believes that a church, to be vital, must make demands on its members. "Becoming a member of his church is difficult; candidates must take at least a year of group study and pass four courses: Christian Doctrine, Christian Ethics, Christian Growth, and Bible Study. He feels that we need to honor God by loving Him with our intelligence, and to deserve Him by working to improve our lives."

Do we want the children's choir experience to represent growth: self-discipline, group-discipline, discipline of mind and heart? There is no easy way to acquire those qualities. And it can't be done at all unless the leader exemplifies them.

George's attention is like a flea. He has a good voice, but doesn't use it consistently enough to be of any benefit to the choir. George is also an officer (vice-president) but without specific functions. As of today, however, he is a man of some importance; he is responsible for the gummed reinforcements on the new notebook pages for the choir. Besides giving George official status, it should help to keep the notebooks in better condition, too. We'll see what happens!

For the past three Saturdays I have been gone, and Mr. J. has had the rehearsals alone. He is more lenient with the children than I, so they had to adjust themselves to a sterner discipline again.

I put the rhythmic pattern of a new song on the board, and most everyone could clap it without much difficulty. But when we reversed the procedure, clapping a measure, they had a lot of trouble trying to write it correctly. Will have to use an intermediate step: write a series of measures on the board, let them clap them; then clap them at random, and let the children recognize which one it is; then finally erase them, clap one and ask for volunteers to write it on the board. That will be our procedure next week, and we will use the rhythmic patterns in one of the songs we are learning.

Mike and his mother attended a recital a few weeks ago, and Mike, as usual, sat next to me. His mother said she had gotten an interesting book from the library, *Great Musicians as Children,* and Mike promptly told me about Bach who copied by moonlight some music his brother would not let him have. I said I remembered the story, but thought it was Handel or Haydn. "No, it was Bach," said Mike. I asked him to find out for sure, and let me know if I was wrong. This was Mike's answer, done on his mother's typewriter:

DEAR MRS JACOBS

THE QUESTION YOU ASKED ME ABOUT WHO TOOK THE MUSIC WAS JOHANN SEBASTIAN BACH. HE TOOK THE MUSIC BOOK AND HE HAD A NOTEBOOK THAT HE WROTE IN, EVERY NIGHT THAT THE MOONLIGHT WAS OUT LITTLE SEBASTIAN WOULD COPY OUT OF THE MUSIC BOOK UNTIL LITTLE SEBASTIAN COPIED THE WHOLE BOOK COPIED LITTLE SEBASTIAN COULD HARDLY WAIT TO PLAY THE BUETIFUL MUSIC EVERY NIGHT HE WOULD PLAY WHEN HIS BROTHER WAS GONE TO A CHURCH SERVICE LITTLE SEBASTIAN WOULD PLAY THE BUETIFUL CHURCH MUSIC ONE NIGHT HIS BROTHER CAUGHT HIM PLAYING THE MUSIC HE SAID YOU STOLE THE MUSIC PLEASE GIVE IT BACK TO ME' BEAGED LITTLE SEBASTIAN HIS BROTHER SAID IT WILL DO YOU NO GOOD

THAT IS THE END OF MY STORY OF
JOHANN SEBASTIAN BACH
Sincerely, Mike

Not bad for an eight-year-old, is it? Who says a Children's Choir isn't fun?

OUR WORSHIP SERVICE

Organ Prelude. It reminds us that we are in God's house.

Collect. A prayer we all say together.

The Lessons. From the Old and the New Testament.

Apostles' Creed. What we Christians believe.

> * I believe in God the Father Almighty, Maker of heaven and earth;
>
> And in Jesus Christ His only Son, our Lord: Who was conceived by the Holy Spirit, born of the Virgin Mary; Suffered under Pontius Pilate, Was crucified, dead, and buried; He descended into hell; The third day He rose again from the dead; He ascended into heaven, And sitteth at the right hand of God the Father Almighty; From thence He shall come to judge the quick and the dead.
>
> I believe in the Holy Spirit; The Holy Christian (Catholic) Church, the Communion of Saints; The Forgiveness of sins; The Resurrection of the body; And the Life everlasting.

The Lord's Prayer. The prayer Jesus taught us.

> *Our Father, Who art in heaven: Hallowed be Thy Name; Thy kingdom come; Thy will be done on earth, as it is in heaven; Give us this day our daily bread; And forgive us our trespasses, as we forgive those who trespass against us; And lead us not into temptation; but deliver us from evil; For Thine is the kingdom, and the power, and the glory forever. Amen.

Offering. We gladly give back to God a part of all He has given us.

Doxology. A short hymn of praise.

> *Praise God, from whom all blessings flow,
> Praise Him, all creatures here below,
> Praise Him above, ye heavenly hosts,
> Praise Father, Son, and Holy Ghost.

Gloria Patri. Glory to the Father.

> Glory be to the Father, and to the Son, and to the Holy Ghost. As it was in the beginning, is now, and ever shall be, world without end. Amen.

Benediction. Asks God's blessing on us.

A GOOD CHOIR MEMBER

Goes to church regularly.
Treats the church as the house of God.
Sings the hymns.
Joins in the prayers and lessons.
Listens to the sermon,
And gives a tenth of what he earns.

* marks the place for a star when you have memorized that part of the service.

96

The Primary Choir

In the long-range view, the Primary Choir is the most important one in the whole choral organization of the church. It represents the child's first formal introduction to music. A large proportion of kindergarten and first grade children cannot carry a tune. This inability comes generally from the lack of any previous musical experience, and can almost without exception be corrected in the first choir season. Children learn more easily in the first grade than in the second to carry a tune. In the third grade it is still more difficult. What is simply a process of absorption in the first grade, may become a problem to overcome in the third grade. The earlier a child's musical training is begun, the more readily it is absorbed.

The Primary Choir is the place, above all others, to present a balanced musical experience. Not only should the children learn to recognize and produce accurate pitch, but rhythmic expression and outlet for the creative sense are equally as important. All three can become different facets of the same interesting experience. For the Primary Choir, it is far less important that the children learn an anthem for an occasional public performance than that they have abundant enjoyable experience in expressing themselves through music. The material will consist largely of short action songs, many rhythmic games, and opportunity for original expression.

The voice of the Primary child is very small, and dares not be pushed. It is comparatively high in range. If the director cannot model the songs in that range, he may teach them in a lower range, and when the children know them, gradually raise the pitch to the place where the voices find their natural clear light quality. But he must be forever on his guard against a chest tone.

No other group is as unaffectedly responsive as the Primary Choir. Their active uninhibited participation in musical activities is the finest foundation for a co-operative, enthusiastic Junior age choir.

Cherub ? Choir

From Edwin Karhu's Choir paper, and I agree! . . . "I am the mother of one of these 'Cherubs' but believe me, he fits Webster's definition of a cherub in only one particular—he is a 'child'— but by no stretch of the imagination is he an 'Angel.' In fact, if he and the rest of the children understood the connotation of the term, I'm sure they'd do their best to disprove the epithet. We dubbed the choir 'Cherub' to connote an age group. There must be some more fitting name for this gang. Won't someone relieve them of such a misnomer?" A Cherub? mother, First Methodist Church, Oklahoma City, Oklahoma.

The Beginning Choir

When the child is starting his formal school education, it is not too early for him to start choir education also. Many of the basic qualities that will make for an enriched life through music and the church can begin to be instilled in the child at five, six, and seven years of age. Some of these are: the elements of good singing by insisting on correct posture, breathing, ease of singing, and correct pronunciation; being on time; being dependable; teaching the beginnings of sight reading; respect for appointed authority as invested in the director; respect for the church and its music; reverence and some of the meanings of worship, etc,

Rehearsals should start on time with some definite signal—maybe the ringing of a bell, or a chord on the piano, or (what I use), the striking of a tuning bar. The starting signal means no more talking, and may aptly be followed with a prayer. The rehearsal should be begun with an admonition for, and illustration of, good posture and by tone matching and sustaining. I find the A tuning bar interests the children, and I have them tune their voices to it first. Then I take other tones for matching, also up and down a short "ladder" (three tones), a medium "ladder" (five tones), and the long "stepladder" (scales). In teaching children, it is best to make games; action songs or active vocalizations interest them.

In patterning for your children, it is important they hear the pitch clearly and accurately given, without vibrato, and that the pronunciation, inflection, and mood be correct. It may be, if the director is a woman, that the director can do it effectively. In lieu of that, a young lady should be found whose voice meets the requirements. She should sit in the choir regularly (at least in rehearsals, and it may be necessary at performances also) and sing exactly as the director wants the children to sing. A violin, played well in tune without vibrato, is a possible substitute for the above arrangement. A piano or organ for patterning is not too good. Remember, children are natural imitators and learn primarily by following an example, and by repetition.

The repertory should consist of a few simple hymns ("Away in a Manger," "Silent Night"), a few songs which might be used in services ("We Bring You Glad Tidings"— Bohemian Christmas Song; "Prayer of Norwegian Child"— Kountz refrain; "A Child's Prayer"— Taylor), and many interesting teaching songs. In this last category one book is indispensable for me; it is *Our First Music,* published by C. C. Birchard, Boston. This book has many numbers, both sacred and secular, through which the children will have fun and profit. Some have to be adapted, transposed lower, etc., but its 362 pages will provide a treasure house of workable music for the very young chorister.

DR. FEDERAL LEE WHITTLESEY

Teaching the Primary Choir

Mrs. Boyter's demonstrations at Green Lake were a revelation in Primary teaching technique. The whole rehearsal was a series of little games, but each game developed some phase of music technique. Children with such training will become valuable members of the Junior Choir; they will know note values, have a reliable sense of rhythm and pitch, good tone, creative freedom, and excellent choir habits and attitudes.

If you plan to organize a Primary Choir:

Keep the age range limited, preferably four and five, and six to eight.

Work closely with the mothers; have them attend rehearsals regularly.

Expect regularity and promptness.

Plan every detail of the rehearsal.

Use very short, simple songs.

Every minute of rehearsal should be enjoyable and profitable.

Include a little singing, rhythm, ear training, creative activity, religious education in every rehearsal.

Use a variety of equipment: rhythm instruments, blackboard, pictures, drum, etc.

Remember that the span of attention is very short.

Set definite goals to be accomplished in a certain time.

PRIMARY REHEARSAL PATTERNS

Based on Mrs. Boyter's demonstration rehearsals at the Lynchburg, Virginia, Summer School

Lesson I

1. The Telephone Song. Page 17, *Tone Matching Tunes*—Coit and Bampton—Flammer.

   Sing the song to each member of the class.

   The child sings the answer into a toy telephone.

2. Play simple rhythms on the drum.

   Call on individuals to repeat.

   Guide their hands, if they have trouble with the rhythm.

3. Sing a short phrase to each child.

   Child repeats.

   Vary both melody and rhythm to suit the ability of the child.

4. Sing a question.

   Child answers with an original phrase to complete the melody.

   Suggested questions:

   > Do you like to sing?
   > Do you love your mother?
   > Can you sing a little tune?
   > Do you have a sister?
   > What color is your dress?
   > Have you a happy face? Etc.

5. Play and sing short phrases.

   Children repeat together.

6. Play rhythms.

   Suggesting walking, running, skipping, sleeping, galloping.

   Children go around the room single file, imitating the movement.

   Use *An outline of Physical Education for First and Second Grades*. Published by A. S. Barnes

100

7. Sing several songs from *Song Wings, Book II*, Birchard, with and for the children.

"My Offering."

"God Make My Life a Little Light."

"Thanksgiving."

Lesson II

1. Vocal Exercises

1-2-3-4-5-4-3-2-1 on "La"

8-7-6-5-4-3-2-1 on "Loo"

1-3-5-3-1 on "Mee"

2. Repeat some of the songs started in previous lesson
3. Start a new song.
4. Sing "Twinkle, Twinkle, Little Star."

Let different children tap the rhythm on the drum, while children sing.

5. Pass around a bag of miniature toys (small enough to hide in the hands).

Each child takes one toy.

Teacher sings, "Who has the . . . . ?"

Child who has the toy mentioned, answers, "I have the . . . . ," repeating the same tune the teacher used, and returns his toy to the bag.

6. Show the children a tiny figurine of three puppies.

Say, "Three little puppies went out to play."

Whoever makes up a second line to rhyme gets a figurine (picture seals could be used instead).

7. Start learning another song.

Lesson III

1. Let two children bounce a large ball to each other in rhythm while the rest sing:

Bounce, bounce,   bounce,   ball bounce, bounce,   bounce,
 catch   catch   catch the   catch   catch   catch the ball.

2. Same song: use ball, drums and cymbals.
3. Telephone game.
4. Continue songs learned in Lessons I and II.

101

5. Let class respond to walking, running, galloping and skipping music.

6. Scarf game
    Have two children hold the corners of a large silk scarf, and let it balloon up and down in time to music with a smooth rhythm.

7. Show pictures of the instruments of the orchestra.
    Children learn to recognize the members of the string family.
    Instrument charts are available from J. W. Pepper & Son, 1423 Vine St., Philadelphia 2, Pennsylvania.

Lesson IV

1. Vocal Exercises
    1-2-3-4-5-4-3-2-1 on *Ma*
    1-3-5-3-1 on *Fa*

2. Songs
    Begin training in following a director.
    Signals for rising and sitting, soft, sustain.

3. New songs

4. Flash Cards (note values).
    Child raises his hand as soon as he recognizes the note. See who will have the most cards at the end of the game.

5. Review the string family of the symphony orchestra.

6. Play the music for walking, running, etc.
    Let the children pick out the picture that represents that music. Find quite large pictures of a child skipping, swinging, running, etc., and mount them on heavy colored paper. Put the pictures on the board before the rehearsal begins.

7. Difference between happy and sad chords (Major and minor).

8. Raindrops
    Draw a picture of a house on the board. Let the children take turns marking raindrops on the roof in response to the music played; slow, fast; heavy, light.

9. High and Low
    The doggie has chased the kitty up a tree. Whenever he barks (cluster of low notes) put a mark on the doggie. When kitty meows (cluster of high notes) put a mark on the kitty.

102

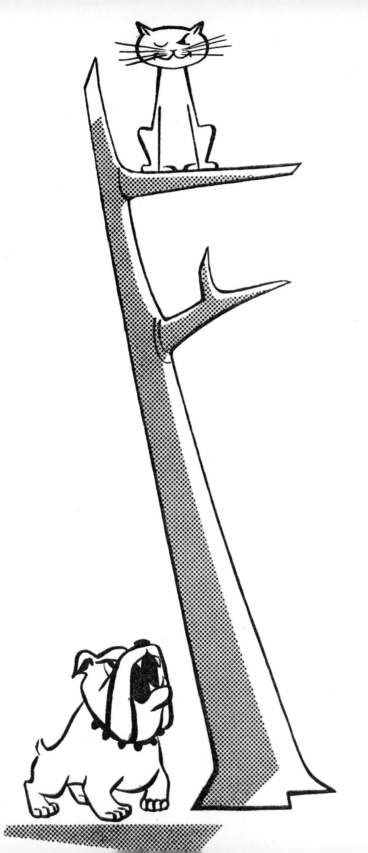

Lesson V

1. Recognizing pitch

   Two notes on the piano. Same or different? Same procedure with voice.

2. Five tones up and down on

   Ma; la; mo; ho; moo; loo; poo; too; soo; boo.

3. Songs

   Correct mistakes in pronunciation or pitch, etc.

4. Flash cards. Notes and rests

   Show them to the children and tell them what they are called. Write same values on the board, and show flash card to match.

5. Flash cards

   Treble clef, bass clef, measure, bar, double bar

   p. pp. ppp. mp. f. ff. fff. mf.

6 "The elephant's walk is steady and slow,

   His trunk like a pendulum swings just so,

   But when there are children and peanuts around,

   He swings it up, and swings it down"

   Have children in small groups imitate the elephant, while others recite the jingle in rhythm.

7. Speech rhythms

   "Pitter, patter, pitter, patter, hear the raindrops fall."

   "Pussy cat, pussy cat, where have you been?

   I've been to London to visit the Queen."

   Children mark the rhythm with chalk on the board, or with rhythm sticks.

8. Pass out little pictures of a doggie

   The children who make up a song about the doggie may keep the picture.

   Example:

   "This little doggie saw a cat.

   Guess what happened after that."

Lesson VI

1. Practice in following directions for rising and sitting.

2. Familiar songs

   Sing them at different speeds to keep them alert.

104

3. A "Listen Song" (The song used was "Listen to the Song-Birds Sing")
   Play and sing it for them.
   Have them sing the melody on *la.*
   Show picture of birds (preferably in color).
   Play a recording of the song; have children join in the chorus.
4. Song: "God, Our Loving Father" (a question and answer song)
   Play recording of the song; children sing answer.
   Have someone in the choir sing the questions.
5. Prayer Song
   Teach them to bow their heads and fold their hands when they sing it.
6. Review familiar songs.
7. Rhythm. Ear training.

Class sings:

Up the lad-der we must go, etc.   Down the lad-der we must go, etc.

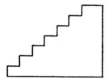 Children take turns tapping the steps in rhythm while others sing.

8. Picture Charts
   Tuba, trumpet, trombone, French horn.
9. A box of blocks with a letter of the alphabet and a picture of something beginning with that letter.
   Children form a circle, each takes a block and makes up a song about the picture on his block.
   They have a tendency to repeat the same tune. Suggest new intervals.
10. Post Office
    Each child comes to the mailbox (skipping, running or walk-ing, as the music being played suggests). He draws a card out of the mailbox, and does whatever it tells him to do—play the ladder game, find the trumpet, find the French horn, choose a partner and mark pitter-patter on the board, choose a partner and keep time with the scarf, find the cello, play

105

the telephone game, find the harp, find the trombone, tell if this tune goes up or down, find the tuba, point to the picture the music plays (sleeping, swinging, etc.), find the violin, etc., until you have covered all the work to date, and each child has drawn a card.

11. Children file out to music.

Lesson VII

1. Five tones up and down on *ma; moo.*
    Arpeggios on *ha; ho.*
2. Sing the songs that they have learned so far.
3. Introduce a new song by Bach.
4. Learn meaning of word "composer"— one who writes music.
    Introducing the three B's.
    Repeat Bach, Beethoven, Brahms, in unison and in rhythm.
5. Flash cards.
    Divide the class into two contesting sides.
    Instruments of the orchestra.
    Instruments of the orchestra: name instrument and family to which it belongs.
6. Picture of a little boy with three kittens.
    What shall we name the little boy?
    They make up a little poem about the kittens.
    They make up a tune to go with the poem.
7. Another picture: same procedure.
8. Clapping note values: always demonstrate first.

Now that we have come to the end Mrs. Boyter's demonstration classes, you are on your own. By this time, let us hope that you have established a system of your own, but to keep you from feeling stranded in a cold and cruel world, we recommend two books to use as guides in planning the first stages of group music education.

Discovering Music. By Wadley and Allison. Boston Music Co.
The Child's Unfoldment Through Music. By Knapp. Willis Music Co.

An Experienced Primary Choir Teacher

"Some children just sing naturally, but most of them have to learn. The Primary Choir is so very important, because that is their first real experience with music. That is why their songs have to be very short and very simple, because the main thing is that they enjoy singing. It must not be work for them. The whole rehearsal must be a happy experience.

We use a lot of games. One that they love is "Train." I am the engineer, and I give each of them a different toot. If they can answer back with the same toot, they may get on my train. Some of them have just a one-note toot, and those that are better get a harder toot—maybe four or five notes. Then all those that could answer the engineer's toot get on the train (they put their arms around each other's waists, and form a line) and we go chugging around the room.

But their favorite game is baseball. I throw them a ball (a simple phrase), and if they can throw it back correctly, they make first base. Second base is a little harder phrase, and third and home plate still harder. Later in the year, when they are more sure of themselves, we have teams and play that way.

I tell them a story at every rehearsal. I never read it, but work hard to learn to tell it well. We are working on our Christmas music now, and last week I found a beautiful little story in *The World's Great Madonnas*. It was called, "The Little Donkey That Carried a King." For Christmas we are going to do "Christmas Around the World," with still pictures, and I want the songs and the places they come from, and the people they come from to be very real to the children.

We're having a party tomorrow afternoon. We always have four parties a year—Halloween, Christmas, an Easter Egg hunt, and a picnic.

Primaries love immediate rewards, and individual ones. More than the older children they love to have their birthday recognized. We always have a candle for them, and sing "Happy Birthday," and I always send them a birthday card. When they have sung especially well, I have a little reward for them, maybe a tiny lollypop, and I give it to them right after the service. It means so much more then than it would a week later.

I correlate choir and worship very closely. Since I'm in charge of both I can do that very easily. They learn to be quiet and attentive in church, and to take part in their little service. The choir leads the worship service, so they have to learn their songs very well. I want the service to become both a habit and an experience with them.

Of course people should understand that you don't have the same kind of discipline for Primaries. Everything is much freer, and they sit in a circle instead of in rows. When they begin to get restless, we play one of our games. I keep them for an hour, but we have lots of variety, and lots of play. You just can't expect them to sit still.

MRS. JOHN IMBACH

Primary Choir Activities

I haven't had too much experience with Primary choirs, but here are a few things that worked, in case you need some for your next issue.

One of the children takes attendance by singing, "Where is Susan?" (or whatever name I tell him from my attendance book) in a simple tune, and the child answers back in the same tune, "Here is Susan." The first week we all wear big eighth notes made of construction paper so we can learn names. Each child gets one as he comes in.

Then we have our singing exercises, standing up.

a. The Siren exercise. Simply to go low and high.
b. The Bird exercise. From my voluminous picture collection I bring a picture of a different bird every week or so, which we imitate: chickadee, whippoorwill, sparrow, etc.
c. The Detective exercise. Four phrases on the blackboard. I sing, "Where am I?" and someone comes up, points to the right one and sings, "You are here."

Last year we made songbooks. I mimeographed their songs, and we put one in their songbook each week and took it home. Mothers kept asking for copies so they could practice at home, and even though some of the children couldn't read, they loved their songbooks. Early comers can make pictures for them, notes and time values can be discussed. Third graders get used to holding music in rehearsal, before going into the Boys' and Girls' choirs.

The story, *Millions of Cats* by Wanda Gag, Coward-McCann publishers, is a favorite. It has a little poem that keeps recurring, which we all (or individually) sing up the scale every time it comes: (c) hundreds of (d) cats, (e) thousands of (f) cats, (g) millions and (a) billions and (b) trillions of (c) cats.

The Episcopal Hymnal has two songs they especially like: "Remember All the People," and "Twinkling Stars."

RUTH RUDEBOCK, Baldwin, New York

Primary Songs Index

Do you need song material for your Primaries? Are you wondering how to improve the singing in the whole department? Phyllis Munyan of Montavilla Methodist Church of Portland, Oregon, has the answer for everyone who works in a Methodist church. She indexed all the songs in the Closely Graded Primary series, and collected them in a loose-leaf binder. The children learn the songs in choir, and you have no idea what it does to the department singing. Whatever your denomination, find out what the board of education provides—*and use it.*

PLAN FOR DEVELOPING MUSICIANSHIP

By LOIS OLIVER for the Choristers' Guild *Letters*

First Month

Suggested materials:

1. A miniature set of steps made of strips of wood ½-inch thick and 3 inches wide. Length of each step given in diagram:

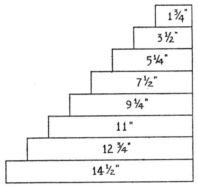

2. A metronome (borrow one if necessary), preferably the wind-up kind.

The most vital part of Theory teaching is Ear-training. Its importance cannot be overemphasized; nor can it be started too early! Learning to recognize and sing scale degrees and intervals can begin at age four. In every phase of the work—whether tone-matching, rhythm, acquiring a sense of direction, or developing music appreciation—there must be both *listening* and *participation.*

A Suggested *Tone Matching Approach*

"Can you sound like the wind on a blustery day?" (a siren may be used instead.) Call for demonstrations.

How did you learn to do that? By listening to the wind (or siren) many times! That is how we learn to sing—by listening until we can sound like what we hear. I wonder if you can hear something *just once* and imitate it? You need awfully good ears to do that, but let's try." Proceed with tone matching—single tones at first, of course, but sing each tone twice, slowly, on "loo" or imitate a horn with "toot-

toot." Avoid long-drawn-out tone matching exercises which involve one child at the time while those waiting are bored. Hearing small groups is better (in competition, if desired), and you will be able to spot the uncertain singers. Two or three children may be singled out each week, of course. Surely every director uses *Tone Matching Tunes* by Coit and Bampton (Flammer).

The Meaning of *Tone*

Teach the meaning of the word "tone" immediately, and use it often.

Have children listen with eyes closed to various sounds—non-musical and musical, and tell you what they heard. "Is this a pretty sound?" (pencil tapped on desk) "Can you sing it?" Repeat question with piano tone sounded. "Why couldn't you sing the first sound? Because it wasn't a musical sound." Older children can be taught that the ordinary sound has no highness or lowness (pitch), and therefore cannot be sung. "A musical sound has a special name: *Tone*. You have been singing tones."

Teaching *Up* and *Down*

Tones can go up and down, the way you go up and down the stairway. Sing to the children:

"This is how the music sounds when tones go up the stairs.
         1   2   3   4   5 5   5   5   1   2   3   4   5
This is how the music sounds when tones go down the stairs."
         1   2   3   4   5 5   5   5   1   2   3   4   5

Use the story and picture of "The Little Mouse" in Croninshield's *Stories That Sing* (Boston Music Company) to create interest in listening for up and down in music.

Show the miniature set of steps, or draw one on blackboard until you can build your set. Five steps will be sufficient at first (your set can be assembled in two sections, 5 and 3) with the top three added as needed.

"Let's call this our musical stairway, since it is going to help us sing tones up and down. Can you count the steps as I point? Which step is this ......? and this ......? Listen while the piano sings the number for us. Now see if you can sing the numbers up and down as I point."

The children who cannot sing up and down might be used to point the steps as the group sings. This would afford them a better opportunity to listen. As a reward for being able to sing all five tones up and down correctly, occasionally allow a child to walk a tiny doll or other toy up and down the steps while the group sings.

If you are fortunate enough to have access to a set of Ludwig Tuned Resonator Bells (many of the public schools use them), place one on each step to form the scale. Then you really have a musical stairway!

Teaching Music Symbols

Teaching music symbols (call them music signs or pictures) can be more fun than you ever dreamed, if you will secure the outstanding new book, *How to Help Children Learn Music* by Madeleine Carabo-Cone and Beatrice Royt (Harper). In the meantime, make a display of symbols on a large poster or bulletin board and place in the rehearsal room. Make no mention of them to the children for a few weeks. More later on the subject.

Teaching Rhythm

Along with the usual rhythmic activities, such as marching, skipping, running, etc., as the music dictates, have you tried using a windup metronome, so the children can watch the motion of the pendulum as they hear the steady beat? They will enjoy swinging uplifted arms back and forth in imitation as they watch. Playing rhythm sticks along with the metronome might follow at next rehearsal. Incidentally, may I suggest the best "skipping" music I have found? It is *Streabogg's Study*, Opus 63, No. 11.

Music Appreciation

For the most delightful musical stories with sound effects to be played on the piano, get *Musical Story Book* by Zepp and Montague (Pro-Art Publications). The entire Zepp-Montague Kindergarten Course is an excellent source of material and ideas.

Second Month
Tone Matching Suggestions
Musical Ball Game

"If I pitch a ball to you, can you pitch it back to me?

If I pitch a tone to you, can you pitch it back to me?

Let's try!"

      (One child might pitch the tone to another child in turn, after a little practice.)

Train Game

"I'm the engineer and if you want to be a car on my train, just echo my toot-toot!"

(As each child matches the tone, he gets in line to form a train—hand on the shoulders of the child ahead of him. Call attention to the *Engine* and the *Caboose*. Anticipation of the game and the accompanying activity will serve to keep the waiting ones from becoming bored (I am trying not to contradict what I said last month)! The action part of the game will provide a useful rhythmic activity for many rehearsals, as it is a favorite with children. The train moves around the room as the children shuffle their feet along in short steps to appropriate music written in eighth-note patterns, M.M. ♪= 100.

Woodpecker Song. Page 11 in *Tone Matching Tunes* by Coit and Bampton. First show picture of Woodpeckers and discuss briefly.

Telephone Song. Page 17, *Tone Matching Tunes*. Use two toy telephones that can be dialed. The children love it.

Listening Activities

Ear training can hardly be treated as a separate topic, since it is a part of all the things we are doing! May I suggest that as you have the children listen for the usual tone relationships (high or low, same or different, side by side, or far apart) *and* the direction of the tones, you also show them these relationships on your miniature stairway or blackboard drawing, and have them point to the steps as they sing up and down. Sing the step numbers alternately with "Now we're going up, now we're going down," or any similar wording.

After much drill of this sort, try this plan for developing a vocabulary of oft used intervals:

"Now that we know how the music sounds when tones go up and down the stairs, I wonder how it would sound if we took a jump from the top step down to the bottom one (5-1)? Listen! Why, that sounds like part of a song you know!"

Director: Children:

For our home and   dai-ly food, Thank Thee, Heav' nly Father, etc.

From: *Father, Hear Thy Children Sing.* Hall and McCreary.

112

What are the numbers of the steps on our musical stairway that sound like "Thank Thee"? Yes, 5-1. Could you come and play it on our stairway, Betty, as we sing the song? Now, if all of you can remember till next week which steps sound like "Thank Thee," someone else will get to play it (or point) as we sing!"

The other intervals to look for in the songs you are teaching are:

3-1 "Cuckoo"

1-3 —"How Strong and Sweet My Father's Care. *(Hymns for Primary Worship)*

3-5—"Brahms' Lullaby (actually 3-3-5)

1-5 —"Twinkle, Twinkle, Little Star"

5-3-1 —"Come, Thou Almighty King" (Your preschool children will not be singing this, but will probably recognize it as a familiar tune).

1-3-5 —"Trot, Trot, Trot   Trot, My   Pony,   Trot"

Diatonic Successions, such as 1-2-3, or 3-2-1 should follow these intervals of the tonic chord. The older children who are singing the entire scale will, of course, have still more intervals within the chord than those listed above.

For the younger children, one interval each month, thoroughly learned, is probably enough. I have given you enough for the entire year already!

Teaching Music Symbols

First week: Pass a box or basket of large cutout symbols or symbol flash cards, and ask each child to take one. Use Staff, Treble Clef, Bass Clef, Quarter note, Quarter rest, etc., having several of each kind. Ask the children to study the bulletin board a moment, and to raise their hands when they discover a picture to match theirs. Line up for a tiptoe march (it's about time for a little activity now) to the bulletin board to match pictures. Then go back to seats, and collect pictures for use another time.

Second week: Pin on each child a large treble clef (about 6 inches high), which he may take home to paste in a scrap book, if you have a scrap book project. Teach its name and show its place on the grand staff.

113

Third week: Bass Clef.

Fourth week: Have a large grand staff on bulletin board minus clefs. Ask one child to place a Treble Clef in proper position so that you may fasten it with thumb tacks. Another child places Bass Clef, and still another might point to the clef that sings high or low.

Rhythm

It is highly advisable to continue for a long time to develop the pendulum concept of rhythm, in order to establish a feeling for rhythmic ebb and flow, rather than a mechanical progression from stress to stress, as implied by emphasis on beats. Other ways in which it might be developed in addition to the metronome idea given last month are:

Watching and imitating a pendulum type clock.

Making pendulums of tape measures that unwind and spring back into round metal containers. These are useful because differences in tempo can be demonstrated by shortening or lengthening the tape.

Swinging an apple from a string. This suggestion by Mrs. Jacobs is an excellent pendulum idea.

Imitating the motion of an elephant's trunk as he walks slowly along.

Ringing church bell. This helps to develop a feeling for pulsation. Use slow, heavy music, or this little song which is also good for tone matching, and for teaching the interval 3-1.

CHURCH BELLS
From *Guide to Music Readiness Program*
by Sister M. Xaveria (Seraphic Press)

Ding, dong, Ding, dong, What do church bells say?

Ding, dong, Ding, dong, Come to church and pray.

Music Appreciation

Distinguish between music describing a mouse running and music that sounds like an elephant walking; or sleep music and march music.

114

Determine whether the day is sunny or cloudy by listening to major and minor chords of music.

Teach two musical instruments that are very different such as a drum and a violin, showing pictures and, if possible, playing a bit of a record illustrating the difference in their "voices."

Hymn appreciation: Each month acquaint the children with one of the great hymn tunes by playing it as they leave the rehearsal room, asking them to see if they can hear it all the way down the hall, which means they must go out quietly! Do not reveal the song title for several weeks. Secrecy sometimes adds interest to a thing you want learned, and someone might discover the title between rehearsals!

Volumes I, II, III of *O, Say Can You Hear?* by L. Margueritte House (Mills Music Co.) will provide you with stories of well-known classics you may want to introduce to the children.

Third Month
Tone Matching Suggestions
1. Echo Game

    Have an assistant "planted" in an adjoining room, or behind a screen to serve as your echo. Ask children to listen. Sing "Yoo hoo" on scale degrees 5-3. Echo answers. Find out if the children know what an echo is. Ask two or three children to sing and listen for the echo. Then, as a variation, ask several children if they would like to take turns being the echo. With a game of this kind, you sometimes get response from a timid child who has not produced a sound so far.

2. Quack-quack

    By this time you probably have more tone-matching songs than you can use, but I must mention one priceless little gem in the excellent book, *Discovering Music* by Wadley and Allison (Boston Music Co.). It is the "'Duck Song," in which the director sings questions about a little yellow duck, the children answering with "quack-quack" on scale degrees 5-1.

Rhythm
1. Mystery Rhythm

    Remember the radio program, "Mystery Melodies"? Can you think of a song that moves like this?" Clap one phrase of a song the children know well. If they fail to guess its identi-

115

ty, try another. It may prove difficult at first for the younger children. If they identify a song, however, ask: "How could you tell without hearing the song?" Yes, by the way it moved. Well, we are now ready to learn a new music word: *Rhythm.* Rhythm is the way music moves. Let us all clap the rhythm to .... while the pianist plays it. A little of this type of drill each week is worth while.

2. The next step might be reproducing a short rhythmic pattern after *one* hearing, using drum or rhythm sticks, if preferred.

3. Clap-touch Rhythm Drills
   Sometimes we hear music that seems to say, "*loud*-soft, *loud*-soft"; and some music seems to say, "*loud*-soft-soft, *loud*-soft-soft." Listen, and tell me what this music is saying (play 2/4 or 3/4 rhythm)? Can you clap when it says loud, and just touch your hands together when it says soft?

4. Making Rhythm Pictures
   We have noticed how some of our musical sounds last longer than others. Today we are going to draw pictures on the blackboard of the long and short tones in some of our songs. Example: "Hot Cross Buns."
   This same procedure is good to use in picturing the up and down in their songs.

Developing Reading Readiness

If your Primary children have had a year or two of choir training, here is a valuable project to prepare them for note reading and sight singing. After they have learned a song well, prepare a large song chart with only the melody in India ink on white cardboard. Each week ask one or two children to take turns pointing out the notes as the group sings and observes the melodic and rhythmic design. Do not have the words on the chart—*notes only.* Try to present one new song each month. Urge the children to point and watch the notes as they sing familiar songs at home. A mothers' committee can make the charts.

Ear Training

Since you will find it necessary to continue the same listening activities week after week, I wish to emphasize just one thing this time. As you have the children listen to determine if tones sound close together or far apart, ask them to show you *how far apart,* on your miniature set of steps, or blackboard picture. Remember to use only five

116

steps with preschool children and with Primary children who have had no previous training.

Teaching Music Symbols

1. Prepare a 5x7 flash card (staff lines ½ inch apart) as follows:
On one side: On other side:

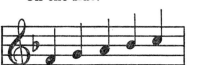 

Review briefly, pointing to a large note, staff, and treble clef on your bulletin board: "You have learned that *this* is a note, *this* is a staff, and *this* a treble clef. Today you are going to get together in a picture to show us when to sing up the steps and when to sing down." Show flash card and sing:

"This is how the music looks when notes go up the staff."
1 2 3 4 5 5 5   5 1 2 3 4 5

Turn card and sing in reverse.

2. Another week, each child might be given a copy of the flash card to take home with the suggestion that he sing it, pointing to the notes as he does.

Since preschool children will be taught only a few symbols (staff, treble and bass clefs, whole notes, half notes, quarter and eighth notes, and quarter rest) you may review these many times in various ways, such as:

1. Using flash card drills.
2. Providing colored pipe cleaners out of which to fashion different symbols (only one each week). This is preferably done as home work, the finished product to be brought back for display at the next rehearsal.
3. Providing a large symbol lightly sketched in pencil, to be taken home and traced over with a colored pencil.

Do not explain difference between   𝅝 𝅗𝅥 𝅘𝅥   at this stage.

Music Appreciation

No added suggestions this month. Continue along the lines suggested last month, as your time schedule permits. Since it is impossible to crowd into a rehearsal all of the things you would like to present, I feel that the most important thing is to cultivate an appreciation for the *best* in church music.

Fourth Month

Rhythmic Activities

These are activities you have most likely used before, but I mention them in case you may have forgotten about one of them.

1. Ask the girls to bring their dolls on a certain rehearsal day, and rock them to the rhythm of a lullaby.
2. The boys might bring a rubber ball to bounce on beat "one" of 3/4 music, saying: "Bounce, catch, hold."
3. Have the children push an imaginary friend in a swing, forward on beat "one," stepping back on "two."
4. Imitate the motion of a seesaw, with outstretched arms. Explain that since a seesaw is made of board, we must keep our arms stiff.

Ear Training

Melodic

You have learned how to listen for the up and down in music. Tell me, does this melody go up or down?" (Play the same tone three times.) "Ah, I tricked you! It doesn't go up *or* down! It moves on a level."

"Now, sing "Mary Had a Little Lamb," and show with your hand whether the melody moves up or down or on a level. Sing it again as I draw a picture of the way it moves."

```
                                              tle lamb
  Ma-          lit  tle lamb                lit
     ry    a                 lit  tle lamb
        had
```

Teach difference between a scale and a chord. Have children listen to both major and minor scales and chords, and tell if they heard a happy scale or a sad chord, etc. When they can differentiate fairly well, teach them to use the terms major and minor.

"Sing 1-2-3-4-5. Now, listen, as I play it. One tone is going to drop out. See if you can tell which one." (Play various ways.)

Rhythmic

"I'm going to play 'Twinkle, Twinkle, Little Star' while you listen and decide how it should be clapped (loud-soft). That's right. Clap it this time and watch what I draw on the blackboard."

Have two children at a time come to board and draw rhythmically as group claps and pianist plays. Any other song may be used, of course. At another rehearsal, use 3/4 time, playing quarter notes as children draw:

| | | | | | | | | | | | |

Explain that writing what you hear is called "taking dictation."

Staff Study

Number the lines of a treble staff, and drill the children on finding quickly line 3, or 5, as called. Then show a series of flash cards, each having a staff with lines drawn in black except for one line which should be red, or any color you choose. Have children tell which line was colored. This is an important drill, as you will discover later.

Keyboard Study

Show a large picture of a piano keyboard, asking what it is. Someone will surely say, "a piano." Shake your head. "No, it is not a piano! It is just one part of a piano—the keyboard, and these are keys. You thought a key was something to unlock a door! Well, it is. These keys unlock the door to some wonderful sounds.

"Since the piano is going to be our helper for a long time, we are going to learn something about it, and even play on it a little. Would you like to learn how to make it sound like going upstairs and down? Then, here is a little map that will help you. Take it home and stand it behind the black keys anywhere on your piano (or your neighbor's), and play just the keys that have a number over them— up to 5 and back to 1. Sing the numbers as you play." (If the children do not read numbers, they can soon learn them up to 5.)

1	2	3	4	5

Music Appreciation

Show pictures and explain orchestra, conductor, baton.

Many of you have been using Mrs. Boyter's grand idea of displaying pictures of people or animals in action (walking, running, etc.) and asking the children to point to the picture suggested by the music being played. You might vary this by asking the children to

119

find and bring to rehearsal pictures to fit some of the music you have been using. These pictures would, of course, be displayed.

Review Suggestions. It is about time to check up on just how much has been learned up to now.

Flash Card: "Does this note tell us to sing high or low?"

Flash Card: "Do these notes tell us to sing up the steps or down?"

"Can you sing this "step-tune" (interval)?" (Point to any two steps of your stairway.)

"Which song has this 'step-tune' in it?" (Play an interval.)

"Which song moves like this?" (Clap a rhythm pattern.)

"Does this music say 'loud-soft-soft' or just 'loud-soft'?"

"Can you point to these steps on the musical stairway?" (Play an interval that has been taught.)

"Can you find a treble clef on the bulletin board?" (Have a display of symbols and musical instruments that have been presented.)

Discovery: Gamble Hinged Music Company has heavy Manila cards with 5 line staff printed boldly on both sides, for use in preparing your flash cards and song charts. Two sizes are available: 7x11 inches and 7x22 inches.

Fifth Month

Tone Matching Suggestions

Live Stairway. Line up stairsteps of children; each sings his note of the scale when he is touched on the head.

The entire group might first be drilled in singing up the scale: "I can sing right up to the top," or "Climbing, climbing up the stairway," or "Singing, singing up the C scale," (any scale). On descending scales, sing, "Coming, coming down the stairway," or "Singing, singing down the C scale."

The choir boy chart can be used as a substitute for the live stairway, children taking turns pointing to each choir boy as they sing.

Use opening phrase of "Joy to the World" to demonstrate how the descending scale is used to begin a song.

Preparation for Sight Singing

Continue to develop visual awareness of the melodic line by having the children draw melody pictures of songs they sing. Rhythmic values can be indicated in the same procedure, after a short discussion such as this:

"Which would you rather have, a whole dollar, a half dollar, or a quarter? Why? Yes, it is worth more—and I imagine it would last longer than a half dollar or a quarter, if you wanted to buy an ice cream cone every day. Twice as long, or four times as long. Well, in music we have whole notes, half notes, and quarter notes. Which do you suppose lasts the longest? Why of course, the whole note." (Here, if you wish, you may present each of these notes and merely teach the name.)

"We have been drawing short lines and long lines to show how long our tones last. And we have drawn pictures of the up and down in our songs. Do you suppose we could put them together in one picture? Like this?"

(Sing "Lightly Row," or any other song, as you draw the lines)

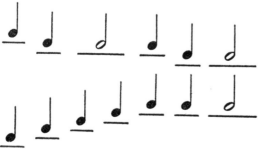

Light-
ly   row
the
o'er
glass-
y
light-
ly   row
waves we
go   etc.

After much drill of this sort, say: "Our short marks mean we sang quarter notes, and our long marks mean half notes, since they lasted twice as long. We won't use whole notes yet. Watch me place the right kind of note on each little line."

"Now as I point, will you clap the notes and sing: 'Quarter, quarter, half note,' etc."

Another procedure I find helpful in developing eye memory or image retention is based on the same principle as the plan used by the Air Force for increasing the span of vision, in which objects are flashed on a screen for 1/100th of a second, and the men in training are asked to identify the object.

My plan begins with non-musical flash cards, on which are drawn or pasted pictures of two unrelated objects. Each card is shown for just a second, then the child is asked to tell what he saw. Later, the pictures are replaced with lines, or circles placed at different angles; then finally, a music staff is shown with one note on it. The child is supposed to tell which line the note was on, etc.

Keyboard Study

Purpose at the moment: To acquaint the child with the piano as an aid to singing.

As soon as the children can play up and down the five note scale with the aid of the little "map" given on page 119, teach them to sing a simple song in numbers as you point to those steps on the miniature stairway or blackboard picture of steps. Then show them how they may play the song on the piano (with one finger, if easier) just by following the numbers on the "map."

Call attention to the black keys and the white keys, with a comment about the blacks getting together in groups as children do when playing games. Mention that keys have names, as you and I do, but their names are A, B, C, or D. Teach them only one at a time, beginning with D, with the rhyme: "Hi, dum, diddle, D's in the middle."

After teaching the name of a new key, have several children line up at the piano for a game of "Leap Frog," locating D's or C's up and down the keyboard.

Tone Matching and Rhythmic Activities

Just a few suggestions in the way of songs you may not know about:

"High-low Song" Page 13 in *Follow the Music*. (Coit and Bampton).

"Clap Your Hands" Page 2 in the same book.

"Scarf Game" Page 15 in the same book.

"Come Out to Play" Page 11 in *All Through the Year*. (Hall and McCreary).

"The Rhythm Band Song" in *Rhyme, Rhythm and Song.* (Hall and McCreary).

Extra: Idea for Checking Attendance

Some of your adult choirs already use pegboards with name or number tags, which the members themselves move from the "absent" to the "present" side as they arrive. Your children will love marking their own attendance if you secure a small snapshot of each of them, cut out the face in a circle and glue it to a name tag. This idea is for the preschool children, since they cannot usually read their names. Collecting the snapshots, mounting them, and preparing the pegboard will be another job for your mothers.

Sixth Month
SONGS FOR PRESCHOOL CHILDREN
Content

Preschool children like songs that tell a story. Consider how many nursery rhymes are little dramas. "Jack and Jill," "Little Miss Muffet," "Little Jack Horner," "Pat-a-cake, Pat-a-cake, Baker's Man," "Polly, Put the Kettle On," "Jack, be Nimble," and so on ad infinitum. For the first introduction to music, there is no better resource than an illustrated volume of nursery rhymes.

They enjoy songs that give opportunity for natural expression. When they act out "Three Little Kittens Who Lost Their Mittens," they really become the three little kittens, unless some stupid adult tries to formalize the little drama.

They need songs that deal with familiar experiences: bed-time and wake-up songs, helping songs, friends, animals, the seasons. Rev. Grime's little Christmas song "Gid-di-ap, dear little donkey" (Carl Fischer) is an ideal experience for the small child, especially if he is acquainted with one of the tiny Mexican burros that have become such popular pets. The very simple music fits the very simple words:

"Gid-di-ap, gid-di-ap, dear little donkey,
Bend your friendly head up and down,
Gid-di-ap, gid-di-ap, dear little donkey,
Carry Baby Jesus to Nazareth town."

Songs that suggest attitudes can help to establish behavior patterns. Try singing this little song on a gloomy morning, and see if it doesn't raise your spirits. Even to think of it performs a mild kind of mental prophylaxis. It does the same for children.

123

"I wake in the morning early,
And always the very first thing,
I raise up my head, and I jump out of bed,
And I sing and I sing and I sing."

Texts for preschool songs must be simple, but of the kind of simplicity that remains charming to the adult. One can sing "I wake in the morning early" with enjoyable amusement over the many sour mornings one has experienced, but such a song as "Climb up, Sunshine Mountain" only calls attention to infantile motions that he has long since outgrown.

Melodic Qualities

Small range: simple intervals; repetition; one note to a syllable; and the music should fit the words both in rhythm and mood. A good example of all these qualities is "Twinkle, Twinkle, Little Star."

"Twinkle, twinkle, little star,
How I wonder what you are,
Up above the world so high,
Like a diamond in the sky."

There is a repetition not only of the phrase, but of the individual notes. The range is only six steps, and the rhythmic pattern puts some twinkle in twinkle.

Presentation

Do not try to *teach* a song to a four- or five-year-old. Just sing it to him. But sing it lightly and clearly, in the spirit of the words. Accompaniment is not necessary; it can easily become an intrusion. Sing the song through without interruption or explanation. Permit the

124

children to make their own response to the music; some will sing, some will not, some will respond with action, some will not.

Relate the song to their own experiences and observations. Each repetition should be an enjoyable experience.

Seventh Month

Suggested Materials

Flannel boards. At least one, preferably two, with large grand staff drawn with a black crayon. Size: approximately 17½x23 inches. Available at book stores.

Ada Richter's My First Note Book, Part I, (Presser). Contains large staff and note cutouts to use on the flannel board staff, with ideas for teaching note reading with staff games.

Large grand staff for each child, drawn on heavy paper or cardboard, and at least 10 notes cut from black construction paper. A better plan is to have each child own one of the Richter books. He will be able to use it profitably for at least two years.

Cardboard Keyboards. One for each child. Large ones may be cut into octave lengths, or sketches may be given the children, with the black keys to be colored in.

Large Cutout Letters, A through G; seven of each. Anagrams are fine.

Flash cards, each bearing the notation of a different major scale. C, D, E, F, and G scales are sufficient.

Flash Cards, each showing an interval or musical figure taken from a song the children have learned.

Song Charts, each bearing the melody of an entire song the children have learned. Use songs from which you have chosen intervals and figures for your flash cards.

Presenting the Musical Alphabet (preschool age)

"You have learned already that the keys on the piano have A B C names. Notes have the same names, because they are pictures of the sounds you hear when you play a piano key. There are only seven of them to learn. That will be easy, because you have more friends than that, and you know all of their names, don't you? Let's line up these letters on the blackboard and read their names. 'A' is not always number 1 in music. Sometimes 'B' leads the parade, or 'C' or any other letter."

"Suppose we wanted five of them to march up our stairway. We could number them and sing their numbers or their names, couldn't we?" (Arrange three groups of letters on the blackboard as follows:)

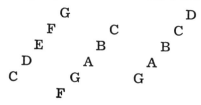

"Here is a song to help us learn to read the letters." (Point to each letter as the children sing.) Later the song can be sung from the notes on a song chart, as a beginning experience in note reading. Only the notes should be on the chart.

slowly

SING: 1 2 3 4 5 C D E F G 1 2 3 4 5 F G A B C

1 2 3 4 5 G A B C D Each one has his turn——.

Eighth Month
Developing Sight Singing (Primary ages)

Major Scales:

Each week, thumbtack the notation of a different scale on the bulletin board above the picture of the choristers on stairway covering the original D Scale. Compare to a procession or parade in which Johnny is leader sometimes, Mary sometimes, etc. In other words a different person can be number *one* each time. So it is in scales. Always have the group sing the scale by numbers with one child pointing out the notes. Letter names may be sung later, when you feel that the children are ready. When they do sing letters, have the words "sharp" or "flat" sung after the letter name affected (explaining, of course). For easy recognition, these notes may be marked with an x, or circled.

Greater interest in singing scales will be sustained if each child is given a complete scale "map" to use in finding all of the major scales on a piano. Simply extend the pattern given under "Keyboard Study" on page 119.

Song Patterns (musical figures)

Discussion: "Did you ever watch your mother cut out a dress or a shirt by a pattern? Was the pattern all in one piece, or in several parts? Yes, and some parts were just alike, for instance, the two sleeves. Songs are made from patterns, too, and some of them are alike." (Call attention to similar phrases or even intervals in one of the familiar songs.)

"Remember this pattern (sing 5-1 on "la")? How many of our songs is it in? You will hear it in many songs, so you need to know

126

its step numbers, and also what it looks like in music. Here is a picture of it taken from the song, "Thank Thee, Heavenly Father" (show pattern on flash card).

Now show the entire song (melody only) on a song chart, and ask a child to find the pattern just studied. Ask how many times it appears. Have entire group sing the song, watching the notes, as one of them points. Treat other songs and patterns the same way.

Chord Tunes:

Write the C scale on blackboard, then ask children to watch closely as you remove all except the most important tones. Erase all notes not contained in the tonic chord (1-3-5-8). Ask which numbers remain, then which letter names. Then ask them to sing wherever you point. Fragments of familiar melodies beginning on chord tones can be pointed out for the children to try to recognize, such as the first phrase of "Star Spangled Banner" and the "Marines' Hymn." Continue this sort of drill week after week, eventually adding the notes between the chord tones, and adding five tones beyond the scale (to G above treble clef). Other tonic chords should be used when the children are ready.

Ninth Month
Keyboard Study

At the Piano:

Line up seven children to the left of the piano. Give each child a large cutout letter C to place on a corresponding key. Another group of children can place another letter up and down the keyboard.

At the Table:

Provide each child with a one-octave keyboard picture, and drill in locating the keys called for. Markers can be used, or the child may simply point to the key. Make it a speed drill as soon as possible.

Staff Study

Using a flannel board or blackboard staff, teach the line and space numbers, treble first, of course. Line up a group of children in front of the staff, and have them take turns pointing to the line or space called for. Number the bass lines and spaces downward rather than upward as you were probably taught. Then call for first line "upstairs" or first line "downstairs," etc. Use this also as a table game, if each child has a staff.

Place notes at random on the staff, and spend much time having the children tell whether each note is a line note or a space note. Be sure to make it clear that a line note always has a line through his middle. Saying *on* a line usually confuses children. *Around* or *across* a line is less confusing.

The next step is to have the children take turns placing notes on certain lines and spaces as called. Use line notes only for a long time. This drill can be lots of fun if you use two flannel board staves, divide the children into two competing teams for a relay—the first child placing his note correctly winning a point for his team.

Explain that line notes cannot live next to each other, nor can space notes. Next to each line lives a space, and vice versa. Point to each line and space *in succession,* having the children say with you: Line 1, space 1, line 2, space 2, etc.

Rhythm

On flash cards or blackboard, show these four patterns, one each week:

Ask the children to begin clapping steadily and to watch your pointer as it moves from note to note. Ask how many claps you waited on the long notes. Then have them say: quarter, quarter, half note, half note dot, whole note counts four, two-eighths, as the case may be, while you point again.

Dictation:

The Primary children can begin actually to draw notes of different value rhythmically, as you play eight measures of 2/4 or 3/4 music. Call it "marching the chalk," if you like. Explain that the quarter notes we are going to draw will have to be little skinny ones since we must draw them with one quick stroke. Here are the steps in the procedure:

Count "1 2 1 2 1 2 1 2" or say "Quarter-ter, quarter" to each stroke.

Draw / / / / / / / /

Next, add stems. Count 1 2 1 2 1 2 1 2.

Half notes (a series of four) Count "1 2," or say "half note."

Write (∪) forming 0

Add stems on count 1.

Dotted half notes are made in three strokes, of course. Do not attempt to teach any other kind of note. Instead, combine quarter and half notes in simple patterns.

Projects and Special Activities

Community Training School

One of the rarest virtues is unselfishness, even among musicians. We will work with others, if we are given a position of importance. But to work hard for a cause that brings us no personal credit— that is a sure sign of Christian character, the very object of our Children's Choir work. In every community represented by the Guild members, there is need of such unselfish promoters, willing to put their shoulders to a community-wide training school, using as teachers local people who have been particularly successful in some field. A successful businessman could teach organization and administration. Many a school principal could give us musicians new light on dealing with children. Most public school music teachers are abreast of new methods of music teaching, and would be willing to share their knowledge. There will be a preacher who knows how to make Bible study interesting. It is not necessary to import a leader; there is much good in Nazareth, if we are willing to recognize it. Why not attempt such a Children's Choir training school this spring? Church school teachers of all denominations have done it with marked success; certainly musicians are as broad-minded, and as willing to learn.

If there are only one or two other children's choirs in your area, informal club meetings of the directors could serve the same purpose.

One of the largest church music organizations in the country started in just that way.

Church Gardens an Interesting Project

In Carmel, California, a church has enjoyed the project of creating a Biblical garden, planting one of each plant mentioned in the Bible. In areas where the climate is similar to that of Palestine, this could become a fascinating study for the Children's Choir.

At Garrett Biblical Institute, in Chicago, in a corner of the grounds, there is a little garden. A sign at the gate, beautifully carved in wood, is an invitation to quiet reflection. Inside are secluded benches and shrines where man and God can commune, alone and uninterrupted.

I think there are many churches and choirs in this wide land that would reap a rich harvest from the planning and care of a "worship garden."

Church Arts Class

Edward Johe, First Congregational Church, 444 E. Broad St., Columbus, Ohio: The opening session of our Church Arts Class will be Saturday, November 1. This year's course will be "Our Heritage of Great Music." It is designed to acquaint the children with great choral and instrumental literature, and to introduce them to the personalities and nationalities of the composers. This class follows the rehearsal period. The class is optional this year, and the registration shows 88% of the choir electing the course.

Mothers' Class

Mrs. Haskell Boyter, Atlanta, Georgia, as one would expect, has come up with a splendid new idea. In connection with her Children's Music School she is holding three series of four classes for the mothers. In November the classes will be on "What we hear in music." In January there will be four lectures by a fine psychologist on "Family Relations," and March will bring another series on "What We Hear in Music." There is so much interest that double sessions have had to be arranged for each series.

Story of the Bible

An event celebrated by all Protestant churches in 1952 was the publication of the new Standard Revised Version of the Bible. There could have been no more appropriate time to choose as the study project for the choir "The Story of the Bible." There are many facts

130

about the writing and the assembling of the books of the Bible that would make both fascinating and informative stories for the choir. Such a study is, furthermore, in order at any time.

For Christmas

Ernestine Peebles, Delaware, Ohio, at a Christmas breakfast for her class, used white paper tablecloths, each with a crayoned border of a carol tune. Each table had to recognize and sing its particular tune.

She also encouraged 39 families to give their children a church Hymnal with their name in gold lettering on the cover. The children were very proud of "my very own Hymnal" and a number of regular Hymnals found their way back into the church. The parents were grateful for the suggestion.

Baby Sitters

"A front page article, with a picture, features Ernestine Peeble's choir baby sitters. "So That Others May Sing" is the caption, and the very human story is about a group of women who take care of children every week, so that the parents can attend rehearsals regularly. They, too, are contributing to an effective music ministry. There is more than one way to serve.

Publicity

Hubert Taylor, of Central Presbyterian Church, Atlanta, Georgia, is to be commended on his promotional booklet, *Sing Ye*, the story of the choir program in excellent pictures. He plans to use it to recruit new members, and to arouse interest in the general community. It is placed in magazine racks, in doctors' offices, in business offices, colleges, schools, etc. The back cover of the booklet is a picture of the capitol tower, and the church spire across from each other, with the caption "The church in the heart of the city has a place in its heart for you."

Beggar's Night

In Delaware, Ohio, on Halloween Night, the children, instead of "trick-or-treat," go begging for material to "mend-or-make" clothing for the poor in Europe. The P. T. A., radio, newspapers, schools, churches, all support the project.

Annual Sunday School Parade

Council Bluffs, Iowa, in which 800 Sunday School children, representing 21 churches participated. The theme of the parade was "Sing Unto the Lord." Thirty-two colorful floats illustrated as many favorite hymns. Three high school bands played marching hymns. A robed choir of 80 voices formed a living cross. Invitations were sent to all churches within a 50-mile radius. Churches sent in requests for the hymns they wished to illustrate. Local merchants gave window space, and churches wishing to sponsor a window drew lots for location and subject. One window, sponsored by all the churches, featured a collection of old hymnals. The publicity committee used newspaper and radio releases, auto stickers, handbills, sound trucks, advertising tie-ins, public announcements, letters, and a poster contest among the Sunday School children. The General budget amounted to about $50, and was shared by all the churches. The average cost of the floats was $15. Prizes were not awarded to any of the floats, nor was anyone named the best. The parade, a mile and a half long, was witnessed by an estimated 10,000 people. There was no loud talking, or applause. Instead, the response was one of close and thoughtful attention. A brief service of prayer and community singing, held in the park, terminated the parade.

Lending Library

George Litch Knight, West Side Presbyterian Church, Ridgewood, New Jersey, has inaugurated a lending library, and church families are encouraged directly and indirectly to make use of it. It is located in an alcove that members are bound to pass whenever they enter the church, and there is always some interesting display to attract attention.

Whole Church Learns Hymns

In Trinity Presbyterian Church, Atlanta, Georgia, a hymn of the month folder was issued every month. Each folder contained the words of the hymn, and some interesting notes on the hymn and the tune. A statement in the church bulletin read, "Do accept this personal invitation to become a part of our plans for a Festival of the Singing Church. We are joining with churches from coast to coast to revive the fine art of congregational singing. Do put this folder in a prominent place in your home. Have a contest to see who in your family can memorize the hymn first. The tune will be used by our organist during the month. Watch for it! Make a notebook of your Hymn-of-the-Month folders."

132

Hymnal Markers

Alberta Westby, Toledo, Ohio, stitches three narrow ribbons to the upper binding of the choir hymnals to mark the three hymns of the service. The children mark the hymns at rehearsal, thus avoiding distraction during the service.

Annual Seminar

The Choristers' Guild chapter of Appleton, Wisconsin, makes it a practice to sponsor an annual one-day seminar on some practical phase of church music.

South-American Seminar

Ruth Parkhurst, Caracas, Venezuela: "I am to hold a three-day music conference in the interior of Venezuela, where the small churches are even more separated from materials and know-how than we are. The repertoire lists from the Guild *Letters* will be the most valuable thing I can give them."

Vacation Singing School

Foster Hotchkiss, First Baptist Church, Milledgeville, Georgia, held a one-week singing school during the summer vacation. The school met every morning from 9 to 11:30, and included a worship period in the chapel, vocal instruction, rhythm drill, note reading and writing, hymn singing, and a story period. On Friday night there was a talent show. The parents were invited to this and to the final hymn sing. Membership was not restricted to choir members.

Musical Valentines

Margaret Sigafoose, Wheeling, West Virginia, had her choir children bring a homemade Valentine that had something musical about it, to their Valentine party.

Young Couples Make Music Education Toys

Mrs. John Imbach, wife of the minister of the Presbyterian Church of Carpinteria, California, had the Mariners Club (younger married couples) of the church provide equipment for the children's choirs. Her letter is self-explanatory: I was so inspired by the help I received at Choir school this summer that when I came home and began to dream of the things that could happen here I was really amazed. I suggested to the Mariners that perhaps they could have as one of their cargoes, equipment for the four youth choirs of the church. Right away many were interested. Many of their children

133

are members of the choirs and, as in the case of all good parents, if they can help their children they are always standing ready.

We met as an executive group where I explained what I wanted for the children:

A ladder with steps on two sides to help the children sense differences in pitch. One of the men, who is a carpenter, said he would lay it out and bring it to our workshop. He did. Some of the other men helped put it together, and some of the women painted each step a different color to please the eyes of the little folks. It has a hinge on top, so that I can store it easily.

I wanted some tone pipes. One of the men, a welder, said he would find some castoff pipe and bring it to the meeting. He did. He also brought along a saw that is used for metal, for we found that we had to saw off some of the pipes, inch by speck-of-inch, in order to tune them.

The tone bottles were produced by the women saving up "Vermont Maid" syrup pitchers (the 59 cent size). We found, however, that the higher tones take the 31 cent size. Three people spent their time that work-evening adding drops of water to tune the bottles, while two others painted the stands for both bottles and pipes.

One of the men, who is part owner of a lumberyard, brought a beautiful nail keg painted a nice blue. One of the other men, who has a friend at a music store, stretched a used drumhead over it to make us a lovely sounding drum.

Short pieces of doweling, and sandpaper tacked to wooden blocks, helped to supplement the rhythm instruments.

The confusion and fun of the evening were unmatchable. Every now and then someone asks me, "How do the children like their instruments?"

The children all signed their names to a large sheet of butcher paper with the heading, "Thank You," to tell the Mariners what fun they were having with the instruments.

Festival of the Singing Church

Barbara Tuttle, Elizabeth, New Jersey, sent this clipping from the *Elizabeth Daily Journal*. "First Presbyterian Church has joined a nation-wide campaign, Festival of the Singing Church, the purpose of which is to improve congregational singing. Motto of the drive is 'The Church That Sings Together, Clings Together.' The church has sent a letter to all members of the congregation encouraging the singing of hymns at home. Children of the Bible School and members of

134

the choir will memorize at least twelve well-known hymns during the year. Words of the hymn, 'When Morning Gilds the Skies' will be distributed to children of the Church School tomorrow morning. It will be sung at both the school session and the 11 a.m. service, and will be the organ prelude at the latter rite. It also will be sung at meetings of church organizations during the week." Barbara adds a note: "Do you know Chester Kingsbury's organ arrangement of 'When Morning Gilds the Skies,' 'Fantasia on the Hymn Laudes Domini'?" H. W. Gray, publishers.

Choir Day

Madeline Ingram, Lynchburg, Virginia: I must tell you about our Choir Day. We had the dedication service, and then at 5:30 we had a Choir Family Night. Each member of every choir was to bring every member of his family and one dish to serve 8 people. The choir mothers had done a lot of telephoning, so that some brought salads, some hot casseroles, some desserts, etc. That afternoon the High School choir girls set and decorated the tables. At the door, each choir member was given a distinguishing music note to wear. Each choir had its color. They ate together in families, and then we had group singing which amazed me. I thought I would have to pry the oldsters loose, but they caught the enthusiasm from their children, and we made the rafters ring. I did all kinds of stunts with the songs for variety.

The boys sang the solo part in "Lord, I Want to Be a Christian." I had all sorts of stunts mixed in, too. Then we had three films: one on the Christian home especially for the oldsters, an Abbott and Costello short for the juniors, and a "Woody Woodpecker" for the little ones. I had the most glowing sense of satisfaction over the whole day, and felt it was definitely worth all the trouble. Everyone is asking when we will have another Choir Family Night.

Sing It Again

Willa Crawford, Lawton, Oklahoma. Her church sponsored an all request program of favorite hymns and gospel songs. They called it a "Sing It Again" Song Service. The Korean boys who are training at a nearby air field were the special guests. The welcome song for the Koreans was "In Christ There Is No East Nor West." The Korean officers also sang a Christian hymn. Although some of the music was not what a good musician would recommend, Mrs. Crawford felt that the pleasure of the old timers was worth the concession. Her reaction was, "Never in all my experience in the Presbyterian Church have we had such singing."

New Year's Eve

Dr. Newman at First Methodist Church in Memphis, Tennessee, is building up the custom of having the young people celebrate New Year's Eve at the church. The program begins at 7:30 with an excellent dinner which is without cost to the guests. This is followed by a well-planned program of nonsense. (This year it was a truth and consequence program with lots of good laughs for all, and plenty of audience participation). At 10:30 there is a special feature, either a speaker or a film, and at 11 o'clock they go to the sanctuary to participate in the communion service. Last year the young people were rather hesitant about celebrating New Year's Eve at church. Now they begin to prefer it to anything else.

Thanksgiving Service

An Order of Dedication of the Seed, the Soil, and the Sowers. (Simple, dignified and meaningful.) Copies available through Rural Church Department, Southeastern Jurisdictional Council, 404-408 Wesley Memorial Building, Atlanta 3, Georgia.

Pilgrim Thanksgiving Service

As used in Pilgrim Congregational Church, Des Moines, Iowa, the order of the service is as usual, but the setting is different. A drummer boy, outside the church, calls the people to worship; the choir, men, women, and children, come in as a group, father leading with his musket over his shoulder; the minister times his sermon with an hourglass; huge wooden boxes are used for the offering; the ushers are in colonial costumes; the men and boys are seated on one side of the church, the women and girls on the other.

Horn of Plenty

Edwin Irey, minister of music, Second Baptist Church, Little Rock, Arkansas, uses for the Thanksgiving service, two huge golden Horns of Plenty which are filled with gifts of food, and distributed afterwards to the needy.

Handout or Helpout

In *The Parish School,* a United Lutheran publication, Ruth Steininger tells how the combined churches of her community counteracted the secularism and vandalism of Halloween "Tricks or Treats," by

136

gathering a contribution for the United Nations International Children's Emergency Fund. The project was given wide publicity by church announcements and bulletins, as well as by press and radio. The children wore identifying armbands, carried special slotted containers, and worked in pairs. Between 5 and 7 o'clock they collected more than $500.00. The children knew that they were foregoing their customary Halloween fun, but they took pride in interpreting the meaning of UNICEF to their elders, as they also did in sending such a substantial contribution to the cause for which they had developed a real concern.

Thanksgiving Did Not Originate with the Pilgrims

Thanksgiving did not originate with the Pilgrims. In Old Testament times, the Hebrews had a festival of thanksgiving in the fall when their fruits and grains were harvested and stored. It was called the Feast of Booths or Tabernacles. Jews still celebrate this Festival. Before the festive meal is served the mother lights the sacramental candles, covers her face with her hands and repeats, "Blessed art Thou, O Lord, our God, King of the universe, who hast sanctified us by Thy commandments, and commanded us to light the festival lights." The whole family says, "Blessed art Thou, O Lord our God, King of the universe, who hast brought forth bread from the earth." And the final blessing after the meal is, "Blessed art Thou, O Lord our God, who hast given us life and hast preserved us, and enabled us to reach this season."

Easter Projects

Make small crosses from palm fronds, and let several of the children give them to the congregation as they enter the church on Palm Sunday.

Get a bulb and an individual pot for each child to water and tend. Plant in time for Easter blooming. Use the flowers in the Easter service, and let the children give the flowers either to their mothers, or to some hospital or old people's home.

Have an Easter egg coloring party.

Let the children sing at the sunrise service, and hold an Easter breakfast for them afterwards.

Make a sand-table model of Jerusalem and the Mount of Olives.

Study the events of Holy Week. Guide the children in preparing a booklet, with the events, a Scripture reading, and a prayer for each day of Holy Week.

Learn appropriate Holy Week hymns:
Palm Sunday
"All Glory, Laud and Honor." Teschner
"Hosanna, Loud Hosanna." *Hartig's Vollständige Sammlung*
Gethsemane
"Into the Woods My Master Went." Lutkin
Last Supper
"Bread of the World in Mercy Broken." Hodges or Franz
Crucifixion
"O Sacred Head Now Wounded." Hassler-Bach
"I Bind My Heart This Tide." Conant
Easter
"Christ the Lord Is Risen Today." Lyra Davidica
"The Strife Is O'er." Palestrina

BASIC INFORMATION ON CHRISTIAN SYMBOLISM

The Church Year

ADVENT: The word means Coming. The Advent Season speaks to us of the three-fold coming of Christ: His coming in great humility to the world, His coming in great glory to judge the world, and His coming into our hearts.

CHRISTMAS: The birth of Jesus, our Savior.

EPIPHANY: The word means Showing Forth. It is the period during which we celebrate the visit of the Magi.

LENT: Forty days of fasting and penitence before Easter. The word means the lengthening of the days of springtime, the prevailing of light as Jesus prevails as the Light of the World.

PALM SUNDAY: This day begins Holy Week, the week that commemorates the Lord's suffering and death.

EASTER: Commemorates the resurrection of our Lord.

PENTECOST: The word means fifty. It was a feast of the Jews fifty days after the Passover. It is the day on which the Holy Spirit came upon the Early Church.

TRINITY: The season beginning with the first Sunday after Pentecost and continuing until the first Sunday in Advent. It emphasizes the growth of the church through the power of Father, Son, and Holy Spirit, concluding with the Last Judgment.

The Church Colors

White is the color of happiness and rejoicing. It is used at Christmas, Easter, Ascensiontide. It is the proper color for baptisms, weddings, and confirmations.

Green is the universal color, the color of nature, and is used in the season of Epiphany, because it teaches that Christ came for *all* mankind, not only for the Hebrews. It is also the color for the long Trinity Season, during which the whole general course of Christian doctrine is presented.

Violet or purple is the penitential color, and is used for Advent and Lent.

Red is for Whitsuntide, as a reminder of the tongues of fire on the first Day of Pentecost. It is also used in All Saints' Day, Reformation Days, and special festivals.

Black is the color of mourning, and is reserved for Good Friday, and for burials.

The main value of the Christian Year is that during every period of twelve months the principal events and teachings of our Lord are brought to the attention of the worshipers, thereby preventing undue emphasis on certain features of the gospel to the neglect of others. The change in color is a visible sign that all parts of the gospel are important. Such changes are often made in the hangings about the altar, the antependia on the lectern and on the pulpit, and in the vestments.

Although in many of our churches there is no altar, and both the Church Year and the meaningful use of color are disregarded, nevertheless these are all symbols and traditions that are the rightful heritage of all followers of Christ, and an integral part of the knowledge of the church musician.

The Cross

The chief symbol of the church is the cross. It was first used publicly during the reign of Constantine the Great (324-337), but Christians no doubt used it secretly before that. It represents Christ, His death on the cross for us, and reminds us of our dedication, as Christians, to Him. There are about 400 forms of the cross. Some of the most commonly used ones are:

139

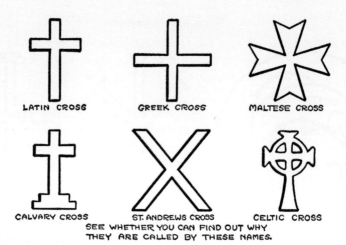

SEE WHETHER YOU CAN FIND OUT WHY
THEY ARE CALLED BY THESE NAMES.

The Latin Cross. The proper proportion is 7 squares long, and 5 across.

The Greek Cross. With arms of equal length. Five small Greek crosses are generally carved in the top of the altar: one in each corner, and a slightly larger one in the middle. The five crosses symbolize the five wounds of Christ.

The Maltese Cross. The cross has also been adopted by many orders of knighthood. Perhaps the best known of these is the cross of the knights of Malta. It is a white cross of eight points on a black ground and is the proper Maltese cross, a name which is often wrongly applied to the cross patée.

The Calvary, or Graded Cross. The usual type of altar cross. The steps, beginning with the upper one, represent Faith, Hope and Charity.

St. Andrew's Cross. Tradition says that St. Andrew preached the gospel at Cythia and Achaia, where he is reported to have been crucified on a peculiarly shaped cross, which hence is known as St. Andrew's Cross.

The Celtic, Ionic, or Irish Cross. The circle is an emblem of eternity. This is one of the most ancient forms of the cross. A number of them are to be seen in England and Ireland, where they were erected in ancient times as wayside and cemetery crosses.

140

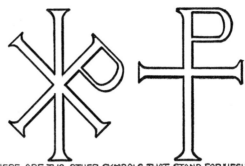

HERE ARE THE INITIAL LETTERS
OF THE GREEK WORDS WHICH MEAN
"JESUS CHRIST, SON OF GOD, SAVIOUR"
IT IS PRONOUNCED "ICHTHOS".

HERE ARE TWO OTHER SYMBOLS THAT STAND FOR "JESUS".
THEY ARE MONOGRAMS, FOUND IN THE CATACOMBS.
YOU WILL NOT SEE THESE AS OFTEN AS THE *IHS*, BUT
KEEP ON LOOKING AND YOU WILL FIND THEM SOMEWHERE.
IT MAY BE RIGHT IN YOUR OWN CHURCH, PERHAPS IN ONE
OF THE WINDOWS. OR YOU MAY NEED TO VISIT SOME OTHER
CHURCH IN ORDER TO FIND THEM.

~ THE SHIELD OF DAVID ~
IS A SYMBOL FOR GOD, THE CREATOR.
EACH OF THE SIX POINTS HAS MEANING:
1. POWER, 2. MAJESTY, 3. WISDOM,
4. LOVE, 5. MERCY, 6. JUSTICE.
ALTHOUGH IT IS SOMETIMES USED IN CHRISTIAN
CHURCHES, IT BELONGS PARTICULARLY TO
THE JEWS. LOOK FOR IT IF YOU SHOULD
GO TO VISIT A JEWISH SYNAGOGUE. OR, IT
MAY BE THAT YOU CAN FIND IT SOMEWHERE
IN THE OUTSIDE OF A SYNAGOGUE.

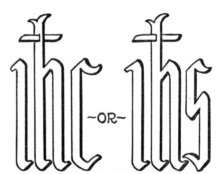

~OR~

THIS IS MORE ACCURATE.   THIS IS MORE FAMILIAR.
IF YOU ARE PLANNING TO USE THE SYMBOL ON
A TABLE COVER, BOOKMARK, OR SOME OTHER OBJECT,
IT MAY BE WISE TO CHOOSE THE MORE FAMILIAR FORM.
ALWAYS REMEMBER THAT IT HAS ONLY ONE
MEANING. IT MEANS *JESUS*, AND NOTHING ELSE.
WHEN YOU SEE THIS SYMBOL IN A STRANGE CHURCH
PERHAPS IT WILL DO FOR YOU WHAT IT DID FOR
EVIN —— MAKE YOU FEEL AT HOME.

141

The Five-pointed Star

"And lo, a star appeared in the East, and shone o'er Bethlehem."

"Behold wise men from the East came to Jerusalem, saying, 'Where is he who has been born king of the Jews? For we have seen his star in the East, and are come to worship him.'"

In the representations of the Nativity and the coming of the Magi, the star is an almost unfailing accompaniment of the scene.

The Rose

"Lo how a rose, e'er blooming,
From Jesse's stem hath sprung."

The rose has been used only since the thirteenth century as a Christian symbol, and is used usually in conventional form. It is often seen in Gothic architecture, and is known as the Gothic Rose. Among its many meanings are: Messianic Promise

The Nativity (Christmas Rose)
The Virgin (White Rose)
Death of Christ (Rose on a cross)

The Nimbus or Halo

a. The halo with the three arms of the Greek cross is used only for the Deity.

b. The double halo is frequently used for the Virgin Mother.

c. The plain nimbus appears on representations of angels and saints.

We kneel for prayer, we stand for praise, we sit for instruction.

THE PRINCE OF PEACE

There lives at this time in Judea a man of singular virtue whose name is Jesus Christ, whom the barbarians esteem as a prophet, but his followers love and adore him as the offspring of the immortal God. He calls back the dead from the grave and heals all sorts of diseases with a word or touch. He is a tall man, well shaped, of an amiable, and reverend aspect, and his hair of a color that can hardly be matched, falling in graceful curls, waving about and very agreeably touching upon his shoulders, parted on the crown of his head, running as a stream to the front fashioned after the Nazarites. His forehead high, large, and imposing; his cheeks without spot or wrinkle and beautiful with a lovely red; his nose and mouth formed with exquisite symmetry; his beard of a color suitable to his hair, reaching below his chin and parted in the middle like a fork; his eyes bright blue, clear and serene, look innocent and dignified, manly and mature. In proportion of body, most perfect and captivating, his arms and hands are most delectable to behold. He rebukes with majesty, counsels with mildness, and his whole address, whether in word or deed, being eloquent and grave. No man has seen him laugh . . . yet his manners are exceedingly pleasant, but he has frequently wept in the presence of men. He is temperate, modest and wise; a man for his extraordinary beauty and divine perfection . . . surpassing the children of men in every sense.

This description of Jesus Christ was written by Publius Lentulus, president of Judea in the reign of Tiberius Caesar, to that monarch in Rome and was first seen in the writings of Saint Anselm of Canterbury in the eleventh century.

AFTER EASTER PROJECTS

Because a number of letters recently have asked about ways to keep the choir interested and active after Easter, I sent out a questionnaire to a cross section of our members, asking them about their methods of sustaining interest through the spring and summer.

We are grateful for their prompt reply, and pass on their ideas to others who may be able to adapt them to the needs of their own choirs.

Welcome Party

Mrs. Fredrickson, Tuscola Street Methodist Church, Saginaw, Michigan. "The girls in the choir learn numbers to sing for the Mother-Daughter Banquet.

"The choir plans for Mother's Day, and also for Children's Day in the Church School. We will have several parties in June, to welcome those who are eight into the Junior Choir, and those who are twelve into the Youth Choir."

Scholarship For Junior Camp

Summer project: "Our Methodist Church has a fine Junior camp which we encourage the children to attend. They also have Vacation Church School. If a child has regular attendance in Church School and choir, $10.00 of his fee to Junior camp is paid by the church."

Pictures and Recordings

Mrs. Vivian Johnson, Elim Evangelical Lutheran, Duluth, Minnesota. "I usually take pictures of the Junior Choirs after Easter. They love to be along for that. Last year we gave a pageant-cantata, based on the life of Christ. I have also recorded each voice individually for some years."

Children Take Service

Mrs. Cecil Stewart, First Methodist, Alliance, Ohio. "We work toward Children's Day, when the children take the morning service all by themselves, singing all responses, etc."

Music in Vacation School

Dr. Austin Lovelace, First Methodist Church, Evanston, Illinois. "In the summer we have a Vacation Bible School at which music is given a prominent part, including time for fun songs, rounds, as well as study of hymns."

Through the Year Program

Dr. Federal Lee Whittlesey, Highland Park Methodist Church, Dallas, Texas. "Refresh the choirs on numbers used through the year, then present a program, 'Through the Year with the Youth Choirs,' for another church. Broadcasts. Surprise trip, with a picnic and a program at some philanthropic institution."

144

Guest Choir and Special Interest Class

Mr. Edward Johe, First Congregational Church, Columbus, Ohio. "Have invited the Junior Choir of the First Presbyterian Church of Delaware, Ohio, (Ernestine Peebles) to be our guests for: 1. Rehearsal. 2. Luncheon. 3. Period of recreation or program demonstration of recorders.

"Arrange a period in which to meet choir members with special interests, abilities or needs, and prospective members, in a Summer Choir School! This is a fine time to help and encourage members The time and program can be more leisurely. Briefly, it is a special-interest class which allows the director time to discover and aid individual needs."

Vacation Vocal Camp

Marvin Reecher, Boston Avenue Methodist Church, Tulsa, Oklahoma. "Vacation Vocal Camp—Mondays, Wednesdays and Fridays for the month of June."

Children's Choir Festival

Mary Louise Shore, George Washington Lee Memorial Presbyterian Church, Winston-Salem, North Carolina. "This year we are concentrating on music for the Children's Choir Festival, planned for the final Sunday of Music Week, and sponsored by the local AGO chapter."

Hymn Festival

Mr. John Gabbert, Redford Avenue Presbyterian Church, Detroit, Michigan. "Hymn Festival—combined choirs—using some of the material the choir has used throughout the year."

Operetta

Mr. Lyman Bunnell, Immanuel Congregational Church, Hartford, Connecticut. "Usually sing in Junior Choir Festival in May. Always give an operetta in May or June. Have used Birchard's simplified 'Pinafore, Pirates of Penzance, Mikado,' also 'King Puddinhead.' In June, the music for Children's Day is a special project. We always have a choir picnic when school is out. The Junior Boys' Choir has an overnight camp trip."

Hymn Service

Mrs. Harlan S. Kirk, Methodist Church, Appleton, Wisconsin. "Hymn worship service in May, in which we use the hymns, Scriptures and anthems learned during the year. I use some as solos, and some as duets. A grand time to present the choir awards."

Litany Service

Mr. Donald Kettring, East Liberty Presbyterian Church, Pittsburgh, Pennsylvania. "The most successful project we have tried is a Litany service at the end of the choir year. This is a festival service with all the choirs of the church participating, and closing with a Litany in which each choir in succession sings a response. Then, at the end, all the choirs join in something like the Sibelius' 'Onward, Ye Peoples'!"

Church Music Festival

Mr. Alwyn Howell, Southside Baptist Church, Jacksonville, Florida. "We have a church music festival for our five choirs in May. This takes a great deal of our time, and the members look forward to it. Awards and certificates are presented to those making a good record during the year."

Special Interest Studies

Ruth Rudebock, First Presbyterian Church, Baldwin, Long Island, New York. "Last year we had a 7-week's study of the organ, using the first 10 or 15 minutes of each rehearsal. Introduction (with movie, 'The Singing Pipes' from the Canadian Film Service, New York. A little old for them; might be better as a conclusion, but it worked fine). 2. Pipes. 3. Manuals. 4. Pedals. 5. Stops. 6. Registration. 7. Chimes and Carillons. We made a huge chart to which we added pictures and information as we went along. After week 4, each choir member was entitled to a half-hour organ lesson, if he wanted it. Most of them did, and enjoyed it tremendously (I have 100 kids!). I had planned this year to do a similar project on the Hymnal, studying its parts, and making a miniature hymnal. I haven't worked it out yet, though, and so many have asked about organ lessons that I may repeat the organ one."

THE
BOYS AND GIRLS
in your
CHOIRS
Have 8 to 12 Weeks of Vacation Time
Why Not Co-operate with Other Directors to Plan a Program
of
WHOLESOME ACTIVITIES
USE THE RESOURCES
Of Your Community to Develop Christian Character for Your
Community

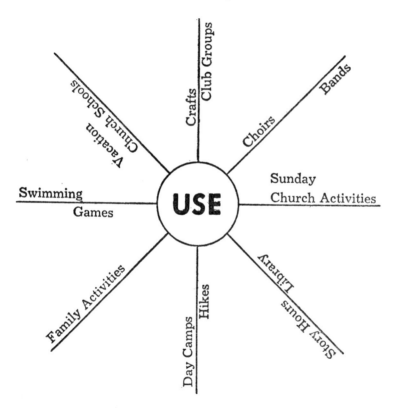

FOR A
COMMUNITY SUMMER PROGRAM
(design copied)

OF COURSE
>To Carry Out Such a Program Would
>>Take much of your own vacation time,
>>And your gray matter,
>>And perhaps—some of your money.
>You would have to learn to work with others,
>>But that is good exercise for anybody.
>And it could be *fun* to unearth the hidden treasures
>in your community—such as hobby supervisors,
>and craft materials, and free passes, etc.

OTHERS HAVE DONE IT . . . CAN'T Y O U ?
>"The saddest folks of those who live . . .
>Are those who never learn to give."
>And nobody is so poor but that he can give *himself*.

A YEAR'S CALENDAR FOR A CHRISTIAN HOME

Prepared by the Department of Home Life, Board of Education of the American Baptist Convention. Used by permission of the American Baptist Department of Adult Work and Family Life.

January

1. Use "Secret Place" for daily family worship.
2. Conduct an inventory session, to determine how the family has grown in its love for each other, its appreciation of the church, its sensitiveness to the needs of others, and its stewardship of time and money.
3. Hold "open house" for neighbors and friends.

February

1. Ask God's blessing at every meal.
2. Make the acquaintance of a family of some other nationality or race. Invite them into your home.
3. Send birthday cards to missionaries.

March

1. Attend church service regularly as a family.
2. Make plans for a self-denial Easter offering for some cause needing Christian support.
3. Collect good used magazines and books for a Christian center, or for some community agency.

148

April

1. Plan a Family-at-Home night for family fun, fellowship, and worship.
2. Make friends with newcomers in the church.
3. Plant a flower garden, dedicating the flowers for church use and for distributing to shut-ins.

May

1. Organize a family council to discuss family problems and plans.
2. Celebrate Mother's Day as an anniversary in the home.
3. Conduct a home dedication service.

June

1. Celebrate Father's Day as an anniversary in the home.
2. Invite some family without a car to accompany you on a pleasure trip.
3. Deliver bouquets to the sick, or to shut-ins.

July

1. Arrange a family picnic.
2. Make visits to places of special interest, such as historic churches.
3. Co-operate with your church in the Vacation Church School by attending and giving leadership.

August

1. As a family, spend your vacation together. Attend a family camp in which there is opportunity to live, play, work, and worship together.

September

1. Visit new neighbors, inviting them to church and Church School.
2. Take neighbors to Church School.
3. Invite the children's Church School teachers to dinner in your home.

October

1. Attend Family-Night-at-the-Church.
2. Assemble a box of winter clothing for personal distribution, or for distribution by a community agency.
3. Help organize a garden club to beautify the church property, preparing flower beds, and planting bulbs.

November

1. Assemble a basket of provisions for some needy family at Thanksgiving.
2. Invite some lonely person into your home for Thanksgiving Day.
3. Attend Thanksgiving service as a family.

December

1. Invite your pastor and his family to your home for dinner.
2. Co-operate as a family in decorating your home for Christmas, delegating responsibility for the tree, greens, candles, lights, and a manger scene.
3. Conduct a home worship service on Christmas Eve or Christmas Day.

FOR THE BOY WHOSE VOICE IS CHANGING

The Order of St. Andrew

The Order of St. Andrew was founded at West Side Presbyterian Church, Ridgewood, New Jersey, in the fall of 1952. Its immediate ancestor was the order of St. Paul, of the Brick Presbyterian Church, New York City. Its purpose: to provide a service organization for seventh and eighth grade boys who were no longer interested in or able to share in the choir work.

Two factors determined the name: St. Andrew is the patron saint of Scottish Presbyterianism, and it is recorded that "Andrew brought his own brother to Jesus."

St. Andrew's Day is usually the last Sunday of November, providing an opportunity for recognition in the morning service. Preceding this there is an initiation (written by the author) in which there is a candlelighting ceremony using an X cross, traditionally the cross upon which Andrew was crucified. The hymn, "Jesus Calls Us O'er the Tumult," has a stanza which originally commenced, "As of old, St. Andrew heard it."

The Order of St. Andrew meets weekly on Sunday at 4 p.m. for a session of meditation (about 10 minutes) followed by work including service projects about the church, such as, picking up bulletins from the pews after the morning service, straightening hymnals, setting up chairs and removing them for various youth groups, operating the lighting rheostats, folding programs, stapling, and a host of other tasks always needed in a busy church. Sorting choir music, mending hymnals, and cleaning piano and organ keys are favorite tasks of ex-choristers. Sometimes there is an extended work session on Saturdays. Candlelighting, carrying flags in the choir procession, assisting with the offering at special services, and handing out palm branches to worshipers also provide welcome activities.

Boys in the Order of St. Andrew receive pins, silver with the blue cross of St. Andrew, at the end of the eighth grade. These pins are worn in the lapel of a suit coat on Sundays. Dues of 15c per meeting are collected, and will ultimately go toward a "shield" in one of the new church windows. The Order of St. Andrew always goes along with the singing choirs on field trips to other churches or to New York City.

GEORGE LITCH KNIGHT, Ridgewood, New Jersey

MAKE YOUR OWN
Rhythm Band Instruments

The Community Workshop of the Oklahoma City libraries, in cooperation with the Art Department of the public schools, sponsored a creative craft project on making rhythm band instruments. I am sure they would not object to having Guild members share the information.

People everywhere seem to have a feeling for rhythm. Savages, highly educated people, children and adults, all respond to rhythm in sound. It is fun to make rhythm instruments from materials you have around the house.

The instruments that make musical sounds which are somewhat alike may be grouped together something like this:

1. *Tinkling*
   jingle bells
   dinner bell
   sleigh bells
   bells on straps or
     sticks
   bottle cap bells

2. *Ringing*
   triangles
   metal rods
   cymbals
   knives
   forks
   spoons
   nails

3. *Tapping*
   castanets
   rhythm sticks
   wood blocks
   sand blocks
   wooden boxes
   wooden forks
     and spoons

4. *Rattling*
   tin can shakers
   cardboard shakers
   tambourines (with buttons)

5. *Booming*
   barrel drums
   kettle drums
   tambourines

1. Tinkling Sounds—
   A. JINGLE HOOP
      Materials
         One 6-inch dowel or other small stick
         3 jingle bells
         2 tacks
         3-inch leather strap
         4 pieces of thin wire
      Procedure
         Punch holes in the strap and fasten the bells to the strap
         with the wire. Tack the strap to the dowel. Use small
         tacks to avoid splitting the wood, or a hole may be drilled
         through the wood, and the strap anchored securely with
         the wire.

   B. JINGLE STICK
      Material
         2 bells
         wire
         tongue depressor
      Procedure
         Drill holes in the depressor and wire bells to the wood
         securely.

   C. BOTTLE CAP BELLS
      Material
         One 6-inch dowel, or other stick
         2 very thin nails (about 1 inch long)
         4 pop bottle caps
      Procedure
         Remove the cork from the bottle top. Make a hole in
         each cap with a nail that is slightly larger than the one
         to be used, in order that the cap may hang loosely on the
         nail. Tack to the dowel.

   D. JINGLE RING
      Material
         6 or 7 jingle bells
         ribbon
         ring cut from the top of a gallon can
      Procedure
         To make the ring, cut the heavy rim from the top of a

gallon can. Wrap this with ribbon or a strip of bright colored material to protect the child's hand from the tin. Thread the ribbon through the bell and tie to the hoop.

2. Ringing Sounds

A. Cymbals may be made from the lids of cans. Make a hole in the lids with a nail or ice pick and fasten to a spool or piece of wood for the handle.

B. Knives, forks, and spoons make a good ringing sound when tapped against scrap metal. The metal should be suspended by a string because it loses its ringing sound when held in the hand.

C. A large spike, or a horseshoe, when suspended and struck by a large nail makes a ringing sound.

3. Tapping Sounds

A. Castanets

Material

Wood scraps—3 ply or other thin wood

Thin wire

Coping Saw

Drill and small bit

Sandpaper

Paint

Procedure

Draw desired shape on the board and cut with a coping saw. Sandpaper each piece. Drill holes in places indicated, and paint. Small pieces should be wired loosely to larger piece.

B. Sand Blocks

Material

4 blocks of wood

4 nails or screws

Sandpaper

Lepage's glue

Procedure

Cut two pieces of inch thick wood about 2x3¾ inches. Cut two pieces slightly smaller, about 1¼x2½ inches. Center the smaller block on the larger one. Nail or screw securely. Cut two pieces of sandpaper, and glue them to the bottom of the larger blocks.

4. Rattling
   A. Shakers
      Material
         Ice cream carton
         ¾ inch dowel
         Thin piece of wood or tin
         1 screw
         Beans or gravel
         Glue
      Procedure
         Decorate the carton with crayon or show card paint.
         Fasten the handle to the lid of the carton, placing a small
         piece of wood or tin on the inside to prevent the head of
         the screw from pulling through the cardboard lid. Place
         beans or gravel in the carton, and replace the lid, which
         has been generously coated with glue on the inside rim.
         Metal spice boxes or baking powder cans may be used.

   B. Tambourines
      Material
         2 paper plates
         16 pop bottle tops
         thin wire
         ice pick
      Procedure
         Punch two holes in each pop bottle top with an ice pick.
         Place the bottom of the plates together. Punch 16 holes
         in each plate. Space the holes evenly to correspond to
         the holes in the bottle caps. Wire the plates together,
         placing the bottle caps between the rim of the plates.
         Decorate the plates with crayons or paint.

5. Booming Sounds
   A. Barrel Drum
      Material
         gallon can
         2 pieces of inner tube (not synthetic rubber, or one that
         is heavy)
         3 to 5 yards of heavy cord.
         lacquer or quick drying enamel
         brush for lacquer
         leather punch or ice pick

   154

Procedure

> Remove the ends of the gallon can and smooth the edges. Paint the can with lacquer or quick drying enamel. Cut two pieces of inner tube, about 4 inches larger in diameter than the can. Punch the same number of holes in each piece at least one inch from the edge. Place the two pieces of rubber over the ends of the can and lace together. Tie a cord securely around the ends of the drum and adjust the lacing until it is very tight.

B. Kettle Drum

> Stretch leather or rubber over a hollow receptacle, crock, or stew pan. Tie securely.

C. Tambourine

> Stretch rubber, wet leather, or wet chamois, over metal or wooden embroidery hoops.

RHYTHM BAND MUSIC

Eighteen Folk Tunes. Churchill. Boston Music Co.
Folk Tune Book. Diller and Page. Boston Music Co.
Rote Pieces for Rhythm Band. Diller and Page. Boston Music Co.
North American Tunes for Rhythm Bands. Gest. Boston Music Co.
Toy Orchestra Tunes. Jobson. Boston Music Co.

A "Must"

How to Teach the Rhythm Band. Diller and Page. G. Schirmer.

ENGLISH HAND BELLS

The use of English hand bells in the musical ministry of the church is a relatively new development in point of time. Present interest in and enthusiasm for bell ringing stems from famed Brick Presbyterian Church, New York City, where Dr. Dickinson continues to direct a vital and superior musical program.

Hand bells were really popularized in America through the efforts of Mrs. A. A. Schurchliffe of Boston, but primarily as a social or recreational project. It was with the organizational genius of Mrs. Doris Watson, youth choir and handbell director at Brick Church, that bell ringing became a part of the church program.

There are many possible uses for hand bells as an adjunct to the musical ministry. (1) They may be used for the familiar "Westminster Chimes" before the morning service in the absence of a church

155

bell. (2) They are helpful in combination with voices and organ in anthems and carols. (3) They may be used singly, or in parts, to play hymns or carols in connection with a service of worship, or for special occasions. However used, the bells provide an excellent vehicle for musical training as well as participation in worship.

The following churches (to this writer's knowledge) have sets of handbells: Brick Church; College Hill Presbyterian Church, Easton, Pennsylvania; The Reformed Church, Bronxville, New York; Westminster Church, Buffalo, New York; West Side Presbyterian Church, Ridgewood, New Jersey; there is, of course, the set owned by the Beacon Hill Bell Ringers in Boston and a fine set at Princeton University.

Hand bells are manufactured in historic Whitechapel Bell Foundry, London, and may be purchased in various numbers. The simplest set would be 13 bells tuned to a diatonic scale, and perhaps the most useful would be two chromatic octaves, commencing with the G above middle C, and progressing upwards. The low G is helpful as a "bourdon bell." Such a set, with duty, costs about $300.00. Delivery is about two years after orders are received at the foundry. (They may be purchased as memorials.)

Unfortunately there are no books of instructions available. Mrs. Watson has made many arrangements, in regular notation, of hymns, carols, changes, etc., and many persons from distant parts of the country have come to New York to interview her and to obtain information about arrangements. Mr. Scott Parry, director of the Bell Choir at Princeton University, uses a notation with letters, and has been successful in this method.

A natural for use of the bells is Dr. Dickinson's "List to the Lark," which can be used without adaptation. There are a number of other anthems which have good parts for bells.

It is well to suggest that churches with bells might pioneer in arrangements. The local situation will, in large measure, dictate the possible uses of the bells. Arrangers must bear in mind that each bell, when rung, gives off a number of overtones and this complicates harmonization considerably. Minor chords have a beauty which is almost unexpected.

Lest bells be a "novelty" in the church music line, it seems wise to suggest that they be used primarily as a part of the total musical program, preferably in divine worship, rather than as "program material." Bell ringing does provide a wholesome opportunity for young people to work as a group—without soloists—where the chief requirement is proficiency that comes with concentration and practice rather than superior natural endowments.

GEORGE LITCH KNIGHT. West Side Presbyterian Church, Ridgewood, New Jersey.

THE HISTORY OF BELLS

With the increasing number of hand bell choirs in our churches, some knowledge of the historic background of bells would seem to be timely. The use of bells was not original with Christian usage; archeological discoveries indicate that it goes back almost before historical record.

In the earliest civilizations—China, Assyria, Egypt—a variety of bells was used both for household and religious purposes. One of the early Old Testament traditions was that the priests should wear small bells attached to the hem of their garments, so that the worshipers might know when they were entering the sanctuary.

The prize given the winning contestant in the Grecian contests was a silver bell. Then it became customary to turn the bell upside down and drink a toast from it. Out of this custom, came the loving cup of our day.

Chinese parents attach small bells to the clothing of their babies, not to entertain the child, but to placate an evil spirit. Many hundred years ago it was prophesied that if a certain great bell were struck it would bring disaster. When the prophesy was disregarded, 1,000 children died suddenly. Ever since that disaster, babies wear small bells to placate the evil spirit living in the "Tabooed Bell."

It is understandable that bells should not play a prominent part in the customs of the early Christian Church. A group of people under the constant threat of persecution would not care to draw attention to themselves by any unnecessary sound.

However, when Christianity became sanctioned by the State, it was not long before bells began to add their particular beauty to religious customs. By the Middle Ages the church was the power that determined the daily life of the people, and the bell was the means of communication. The Gabriel bell awakened the people in the morning. The sermon bell announced that the sermon was about to begin. The pardon bell, immediately before and after the service, called to prayers of repentance. There was a small, clear-toned bell to announce a christening. A big, solemn-voiced bell sounded the death knell when someone was about to die, and then announced the death and the age of the departed one. The church bell was rung in a special way to

157

warn of a fire. It called attention to an approaching storm. The bell gave the signal for the closing of the city gates, after which no one could enter.

A number of our words in common usage have their origin in these mediaeval bell traditions. It was Alfred the Great who decreed that at a certain hour in the evening all the fires should be banked and people go to bed. In French, the word for covering the fire is "couvre-feu," and this became eventually the English curfew, with similar meaning.

The word, "noon," comes from the second of the three Angelus bells that was rung the ninth hour, "none," after sunrise.

The first big bell to be hung in a tower instead of an open scaffold was by the bishop of Campana, in Italy. So the big bell became known as the Campana, and the tower that housed it as the Campanile. That is why universities, such as California and Michigan State, call their bell tower the Campanile.

With bells playing such a vital part in daily life, it is not surprising that the people should believe them to have personality and miraculous power. Benvenuto Cellini, the great artist, designed a bell for Pope Clement VII in the sixteenth century. Its surface was an intricate interlacing of grasshoppers, snakes, flies, and all manner of insects, and the bells were rung to place a curse on the insects represented whenever they increased to plague proportions.

So much a part of the religious life of the people were the bells that a new bell was christened in an elaborate service before it was hung. After its baptism, it was thought to have power over evil. Stories of the miracles credited to certain bells were common knowledge. A man swearing "on the bell" was careful to tell the truth for fear that the bell would reveal him a liar. Bell superstitions have found their way into music as well, in such compositions as Debussy's "Sunken Cathedral." There are many stories of bells long submerged in lake or ocean that can still be heard ringing on certain days.

In many countries of Europe church bells still are an intrinsic part of the pattern of the day. In Switzerland, the ringing of bells in the clear mountain air adds much to the charm of the country. On a Sunday morning in village and city, the air is alive with bell tone. I remember well one Sunday in Lauterbrunnen when I went into the church as the bell began to ring, only to find myself alone there. The bell continued to ring for about fifteen minutes; at the end of that time there was a fair congregation and the service commenced.

Another memorable experience was on a clear moonlit night overlooking the roofs of Florence, when the bells of the city began to strike the midnight hour. Some near and booming, others small, clear and distant, no two of them striking together and no two of them having the same tone. But they swelled into an unforgettable tonal symphony.

It is regrettable that in our American cities, sirens and claxons and electrical devices should have supplanted bells so universally. There is a mystical, quieting, spiritual quality about bells that would be a welcome counterbalance to the stridency of American life. Almost the only remnant of the dinner bell, the sleigh bell, the fire bell, the school bell, the church bell, that some of you may still remember, is the Salvation Army lassie with her Christmas bell.

But there are welcome signs of a renaissance. Carillons are increasing in number in our country, and the manufacturers of hand bells find it impossible to keep up with their American orders.

It is to be hoped that those churches with newly acquired sets of hand bells will consider them as instruments of worship rather than recreational equipment. We dedicate our vestments, and our organs, to the service of God. It would be well in the same manner to dedicate our bells. They can add considerable beauty to a church service, sometimes used for a prelude, or offertory, or to accompany an anthem, or played on festival occasions from the tower, as is done in many places on Easter Sunday. Treated as dedicated instruments, they can be as vital a factor in the character training of young people as the choir. Certainly, their playing takes as much self-control, cooperation, and attention as does the discipline of a good choir, if indeed it does not take even more.

There are records extant of the hallowing of mediaeval bells which was a solemn ritual. It would be well, if we would consecrate our hand bells before using them. Part of the ancient ceremony was the singing of Psalm 28, consecrating the bell in the name of the Father, Son, and Holy Spirit, a prayer of blessing, and the singing of Psalm 76. After the consecration service, the bells could well be rung for the first time.

Music for hand bells is still very limited. Most hand bell choir directors make their own arrangements. Bells sound better in open harmonies. Chorales, and simple classics like those of Corelli and Mozart, are splendid for bells.

Those interested in a better knowledge of the history and use of bells should read *Bells* by Satis Coleman, published by Rand McNally. It is most informative, simply written, and full of illustrations.

SIGNS OF THE TIMES
College Credit for Children's Choir Class

Virginia Cheesman, after attending the Santa Barbara summer school, started a class in children's choir methods at Westminster Choir College in Princeton, New Jersey. Over eighty students registered for the class, and the school authorities have decided to run the class through the second semester. When children between the ages of 9 and 11 were invited to audition for a demonstration choir for the class, 90 appeared on the scene.

Church Music Clinic

Following the city-wide Junior Choir Festival held in the spring of 1954 in Toledo, Ohio, several of the leading church musicians met to evaluate the benefits. Out of this meeting evolved a purposeful educational program for this city of 400,000. Six professionally trained church musicians agreed to give one evening a week for two nine-week periods twice a year to teach some phase of church music, in a church music clinic. The clinic was to be non-sectarian; it was to help church musicians acquire technique, repertoire, and assurance in the performance of their work; to inform laymen, including choir members and clergy, for a better understanding and appreciation of church music.

The Glenwood Lutheran Church offered its facilities for the program, and gave a generous donation as well, which made possible the printing of announcements and syllabus.

The next step was to create a citizens' committee on church music—prominent people interested in bettering church music. Of all the people invited—laymen, several clergymen, a few professional musicians, the music critic of the local newspaper—there was not one refusal.

Four courses were offered, and a collegiate system of registration was adopted.

Fundamentals of Music, a non-technical approach to scales, key signatures and time, note values, intervals, triads, chords. In the first class there were the president of a drug company, the director of a welfare agency (Ph.D.), a secretary, a bookkeeper, an art student, a minister, and a student organist who had never known that a scale had structure. After the first term, this group continued in an advanced course, and a new beginners' class was started.

Choral conducting started with thorough training in conducting patterns and hymn directing. Many in the class had no idea that there

160

was such a thing as a universally accepted conducting pattern. Those who were too fearful to conduct were permitted to audit the class. Ten anthems, chosen for their good texts and simple, good, and interesting music, were studied, and soon found their way into the choir library of the churches represented. The anthems selected were: "Lauda Anima"— Mark Andrews (unison); "By Early Morning Light"— Dickinson; "O Lord, Increase My Faith"— Orlando Gibbons; "Let Us Now Praise Famous Men"—Vaughan Williams; "O Savior of the World"— Goss; "Break Forth, O Beauteous Heavenly Light"— Bach; "Immortal, Invisible"— Thiman; "Hosanna"— Bitgood.

Service playing and conducting from the Organ was attended by a group of shy and reticent organists. The teacher showed them how to play easy preludes and postludes; wrote out simple modulations on the blackboard to help them tie the service together; demonstrated how to play hymns correctly; how to conduct anthems from the console; and gave them a wealth of usable repertoire.

In Hymnology the class began with the hymns of the Old Testament up through the Psalms and into the early Christian hymns of the New Testament, finding the place of their origin on a large wall map, learning why and how they became a part of the service in liturgical communions, and re-creating their historic background. By singing the chants and hymns of the Greek Church, the Easter hymns of the early centuries, the class came to a new appreciation of the riches of our common heritage in hymns.

This Church Music Clinic is an intelligent and systematic approach to good church music that other progressive communities could adopt. The address is: Dr. Helen Allinger, Dean, Church Music Clinic, Glenwood Lutheran Church, Art Museum Square, Toledo 2, Ohio. It is possible that copies of the syllabus are still available.

Degree in Church Music

One of our large universities with the establishing of a program for the training of ministers of music in mind, has called specialists from all parts of the country to a consultative conference to consider such questions as: The Needs of the Church in the Area of Music; The Role of Music in the Life of the Church; The Aims and Purposes of a Program for the Training of Ministers of Music; and The Desirable Curriculum for such a Program. Children's choirs are to be an intrinsic part of the consideration.

All three of these isolated incidents are indications of the change that is taking place. Children's choirs are beginning to be recognized as a legitimate phase of a legitimate profession.

Special Services

ORDER OF WORSHIP FOR CHOIR DEDICATION SUNDAY

Processional Hymn

Minister:

It is a good thing to give thanks unto the Lord;
and to sing praises unto Thy Name, O Most High;
to show forth Thy loving kindness in the morning,
and Thy faithfulness every night.

Choirs:

I will praise Thee, O Lord, with my whole heart.
I will show forth Thy marvelous works. I will
be glad and rejoice in Thee. I will sing praises
to Thy Name, O Thou Most High.

Anthem

Scripture Reading

Hymn

Presentation of Tithes and Offering

Choir Dedication

Minister: You children, the like of whom Jesus took into His arms and blessed, do you promise to learn well all that shall be taught you in the Cherub Choir? Do you so promise?

Cherub Choir: We do so promise.

Minister: You who with eager hearts are learning to worship God, do you promise to serve and sing for Him in the Junior Choir? Do you so promise?

Junior Choir: We do so promise.

Minister: You who are giving your young lives in the service of praise, do you promise to live for Jesus every day, and to be faithful to Him by doing your best in the Junior High Choir? Do you so promise?

Junior Hi Choir: We do so promise.

Minister: You, who are seeking to discover the will of God in your lives, and have committed yourselves through the choir to the ministry of your church, do you promise with the help of God, that you will keep your daily life in harmony with your music, and fulfill to the best of your ability your duties as choristers in this church? Do you so promise?

High School Choir: We do so promise.

Minister: You, who with true stewardship of time and talent, have committed yourself to the discipline of choir membership, do you promise by the help of God that you will keep your daily life in harmony with your music, and that you will endeavor to meet all the obligations of membership in the Sanctuary Choir? Do you so promise?

Sanctuary Choir: We do so promise.

Litany of Dedication:

Minister of Music: To a conduct of life worthy of those who stand before others in the public worship of God,

Choirs: We dedicate ourselves.

Minister of Music: To help in the fostering of reverence in the house of God, and to the creating of an atmosphere of worship,

Choirs: We dedicate ourselves.

Minister of Music: To lead the congregation in singing the praises of God, and giving the honor due His name,

Choirs: We dedicate ourselves.

Minister of Music: To fill the house of worship with song and praise and prayer, and to help as we can in the lifting of the burdens of life from all who enter here,

Choirs: We dedicate ourselves.

Minister of Music: To lead others by song into the Kingdom of God,

Choirs: We dedicate ourselves.

Minister of Music: To testify in glad and tuneful music our gratitude and love to Thee,

Choirs: We dedicate ourselves.

Minister: Let us pray.

Choirs:
  God of all lovely sounds, grant us a share
  In Thy great harmonies of earth and air;
  Make us Thy choristers, that we may be
  Worthy to offer music unto Thee. Amen.

Minister: Oh God, Creator of this universe of rhythm and sound
  and beauty, bless these Thy servants and inspire them as they
  lead this congregation in worship, that their voices may worthily
  praise Thee, their thoughts glorify Thee, and their lives honor
  Thee; through Jesus Christ our Lord. Amen.

Minister: Do you, the members of this congregation, recognizing the
  devotion and the service of these choirs, receive them as your
  choirs, and in so far as possible support them by your encouragement, and faithful attendance at the worship services of this
  church? Do you so promise?

Congregation: We do so promise.

Hymn of dedication.

Benediction.

CEREMONY OF CHOIR DEDICATION

Service of Preparation

Minister: It is a good thing to give thanks unto the Lord; and to sing
  praises unto Thy Name, O Most High; to show forth Thy loving
  kindness in the morning, and Thy faithfulness every night.

Choir: I will praise Thee, O Lord, with all my heart. I will show
  forth Thy marvelous works. I will be glad and rejoice in Thee. I
  will sing praise to Thy Name, O Most High.

Congregation: Doxology
  (Then shall the minister admonish the choir of the meaning of
  service, and offer a prayer of dedication.)

Service of Dedication:
  (The minister of music shall rise and stand before the minister.)

Minister: Whom do you present for membership in the ....
  Choir of this church?
  (Then shall the minister of music call the names of the choristers,
  who shall stand as their names are called.)

Minister: The Lord be with thee.

Choristers: And with thy spirit.

165

Minister: The ministry of music is not to be entered into lightly. To lead the people in sincere expressions of praise and prayer requires dedication of self. But the rewards of such service are a finer self-respect, and a deeper sense of the nearness of God. Do you dedicate yourself to the principles for which your choir and your church stand: faithfulness to duty, thoughtfulness of others and loyalty to Christ?

Choristers: I do so dedicate myself.

Minister: May the Lord Jesus Christ keep you steadfast in your purpose and faithful in your endeavor, now and always. May the consciousness of His presence be and abide with you forever. Amen.
(Then shall the choristers kneel.)

Minister: Ministering in the name of the Lord Jesus Christ and of this church in which you serve Him, I place upon you the responsibilities of the office of a chorister. O Lord, Author of all things true and beautiful, bless these Thy servants and lead them in their worshiping that their lips may praise Thee, their thoughts glorify Thee, and their lives honor Thee, through Jesus Christ our Lord. Amen.

SERVICE OF CONSECRATION AND RECOGNITION

Written by Dr. Shepherd Knapp for the presentation of awards at Central Congregational Church, Worcester, Massachusetts.

Charge to the Choirs, by the Minister:
You are called to your work in the worship of the Church of Christ, not only by your fellow Christians, but by the voice of God himself. He needs you to lift men's hearts to Him in prayer and praise, to give to truth the strong wings of feeling, to stir our human consciences to new energy, to send men forth to live in hope and faith and Christlike love. Above all else, and as the indispensable foundation of all your service, do you take Jesus Christ as the Savior, Leader, and Inspirer of your lives, and pledge to God, your Father, your ardent devotion to the building of His kingdom and the doing of His will?

The Answer of the Choirs:
I pledge to God my devotion.
Then the choirs sing the first stanza of "I bind my heart this tide."

166

The Minister:

Today our choirs bring to a happy close another year of service, and already they are looking forward to the year ahead. I call upon them now, as presently I call upon you all, to consecrate themselves anew to Christ's service.

Choirs of .... Church, once more I set your own ideals before you, the ideals given you from the beginning by your leader, and by you loyally adopted and striven for: *Steady musical improvement,* including readiness to do anything that will advance your musical standards, constant fidelity to the meaning of all the music studied; and dissatisfaction with any but the highest attainable results; *the establishment of true fraternity among all the members of the group; a deepening love of all beauty; fuller understanding and wider sympathy,* as the true basis of song; and the acceptance of this fourfold personal responsibility: *responsibility to the work,* in regularity, honest effort, sincerity, co-operation; *responsibility to the choir,* in consideration for all others in the group; *responsibility to yourselves,* in holding yourself firmly to your best; *responsibility to the church,* in seeking for yourselves the experience of reverence, of worship, of devotion, which you would inspire in others. I call upon you now to renew your pledge of loyalty to this ideal. Taking it as your guide, will you give yourself and all your powers to the service of God both in His House, and for your Fellow Man?

The Answer of the Choirs:

I pledge myself to the service of God both in His House, and for my Fellow man.

Then the choirs sing the first stanza of "Now I resolve with all my heart."

Presentation of Awards:

The minister of music takes his place beside the minister in the chancel. As the minister of music reads the names of the choir members, they come forward to receive the award from the hands of the minister, who says, "In the name of this church which you have served with distinguished faithfulness, I give you this award." The choir members remain at the chancel steps until all awards have been made, whereupon the minister offers a prayer of dedication.

167

Minister:

In the worship of the church, the spirit and purpose of the worshipers in the pews is no less important than the spirit and purpose of the choirs in the chancel. When Sunday after Sunday, the people of the church come, truly seeking God, truly opening their hearts to Him, truly giving themselves to be moved by His spirit, eager not only to enter into vital fellowship with Him, but to share that experience with all who have come with them into the House of God, then does the worship of that church become indeed a reality, a vital moving force. Therefore in our final pledge of loyalty and devotion let all join who call .... Church their church. To the challenge which I shall voice, let us reply in the words of the hymn, "I bind my heart this tide."

All rise

Worshipers of .... Church, by your faithful and reverent participation in the worship of this church will you help to make it a true house of prayer? Taking Jesus Christ as the Leader of your lives, and making His ideal of faith and love the guide of your spirits, will you seek to draw all who enter here into oneness with God?

Congregational hymn, "I bind my heart this tide."

Prayer and Benediction

SERVICE OF RECOGNITION
For the Presentation of the Choristers' Pins

(The Choir shall stand as a body)

Minister: O come, let us sing unto the Lord; let us make a joyful noise to the rock of our salvation. Let us come before His presence with thanksgiving, and make a joyful noise unto Him with psalms. For the Lord is a great God, and a great King above all gods. In His hands are the deep places of the earth; the strength of the hills is His also. The sea is His and He made it; and His hands formed the dry land. O come, let us worship and bow down; let us kneel before the Lord our Maker, for He is our God; and we are the people of His pasture, and the sheep of His hand.

Choir: I will praise Thee, O Lord with my whole heart; I will show forth all Thy marvelous works. I will be glad and rejoice in Thee. I will sing praise to Thy name, O Thou Most High.

168

Then shall be sung the Gloria Patri.

Then shall the Choir be seated.

The minister of music shall rise and stand before the minister.

Minister: Whom do you present for public recognition of faithful and loyal service to Christ and this church in the ministry of music?

As the minister of music reads the names of those who merit recognition, the children shall rise and stand before the minister.

Minister: In the name of this church, I bestow on you this emblem of faithful and loyal service. May it be to you not a symbol of achievement, but of dedication of voice and will and life to Christ and His will for your life.

Then shall the minister of music give the Chorister's pins to the minister who shall in turn present them to the children.

Then shall all the members of the Choir stand.

Minister: Let us pray.

Almighty God, Fount of all love and wisdom, Source of all power, so guide and uphold the teachers of these children that by loving care, wise counsel, and holy example, they may lead them into that life of faith whose strength is righteousness, and whose fruit is everlasting joy and peace; through Jesus Christ, our Lord. Amen.

The Choir:

God of all lovely sound, grant us a share
In Thy great harmonies of earth and air;
Make us Thy choristers, that we may be
Worthy to offer music unto Thee. Amen.

Minister: The Lord bless you, and keep you, now and evermore. Amen.

FAIREST LORD JESUS

(A simple festival service, using hymn-tunes exclusively)

READER: During the reign of Tiberius Caesar, the governor of Judea sent this description of Jesus to the monarch in Rome: "There lives at this time in Judea a man of singular virtue whose name is Jesus Christ, whom the barbarians esteem as a prophet, but his followers love and adore him as the offspring of the immortal God. He calls back the dead from the grave, and heals all sorts of diseases with a word or a touch. He is a tall man, well-shaped, of an amiable and reverent aspect, and his hair of a color that can hardly be matched . . . . His forehead high, large and imposing

169

. . . . his eyes bright blue, clear and serene, look innocent and dignified, manly and mature . . . . He rebukes with majesty, counsels with mildness, and his whole address, whether in word or deed, being eloquent and grave. No man has seen him laugh . . . . yet his manners are exceedingly pleasant . . . . He is temperate, modest and wise; a man for his extraordinary beauty and divine perfection surpassing the children of men in every sense." It is He of whom we sing *Fairest Lord Jesus.*

CHOIR: "Fairest Lord Jesus"

READER: In those days a decree went out from Caesar Augustus that all the world should be enrolled. And all went to be enrolled, each to his own city. And Joseph also went up from Nazareth to Bethlehem to be enrolled with Mary, his betrothed, who was with child. And while they were there, the time came that she should be delivered; and she gave birth to her first-born son, and wrapped him in swaddling clothes, and laid him in a manger, for there was no room for them in the inn.

The first noel the angels did say was to certain poor shepherds in fields as they lay keeping their sheep on a cold winter night. They looked up, and saw a star shining in the east beyond them far. And to the earth it gave great light, and so it continued both day and night.

And by the light of that same star, three Wise Men came from countries far. To seek for a king was their intent, and to follow the star wherever it went. This star drew nigh to the northwest, o'er Bethlehem it took its rest, and there it did both stop and stay, right o'er the place where Jesus lay. Then entered in, these wise men three, full reverently, on bended knee, and offered there in His presence, their gold and myrrh and frankincense.

CHOIR: "As With Gladness" (organ starts playing the tune softly before reader finishes).

READER: And the child grew and became strong, filled with wisdom, and the favor of God was upon him. As he in the synagogue worshipped and praised God, let us too honor Him with voice and life. O come, let us sing unto the Lord, let us make a joyful noise unto the rock of our salvation. Let us come before His presence with thanksgiving, and make a joyful noise unto Him with psalms.

CHOIR: "The God of Abraham Praise"

READER: Jesus, when he began his ministry, was about thirty years of age. And he came to Nazareth, and he went to the synagogue,

170

as was his custom on the Sabbath day. And he stood up to read. He opened the book and found the place where it is written, "The spirit of the Lord is upon me, because he has anointed me to preach good news to the poor. He has sent me to proclaim release to the captives and recovering of sight to the blind, to set at liberty those who are oppressed, to proclaim the acceptable year of the Lord." . . . "Today this scripture has been fulfilled in your hearing."

CHOIR: "We Would See Jesus" (second stanza)

READER: And Jesus went about all Galilee, teaching in their synagogues, and preaching the gospel of the kingdom. . . . And there followed him great multitudes of people from Galilee, and from Decapolis, and from Jerusalem, and from Judea, and from beyond the Jordan. And seeing the multitudes, he went up into a mountain and taught them. And the people were astonished at his doctrines, for he taught them as one having authority, and not as the scribes.

CHOIR: "We Would See Jesus" (third stanza).

READER: In those days Jesus went out into the hills to pray; and all night he continued in prayer to God. And when it was day, he called his disciples, and chose from them twelve. And he came down with them, and stood on a level place with a great multitude of people from all Judea and Jerusalem, and the seacoast of Tyre and Sidon, who came to hear him, and to be healed of their diseases. And all the crowd sought to touch him, for power came from him, and healed them all.

CHOIR: "We Would See Jesus" (fourth stanza).

READER: O young and fearless Prophet of ancient Galilee: Thy life is still a summons to serve humanity; to make our thoughts and actions less prone to please the crowd, to stand with humble courage for truth with hearts uncowed. O young and fearless Prophet, we need Thy presence here, amid our pride and glory to see Thy face appear; once more to hear Thy challenge above our noisy day, to lead us triumphantly along God's holy way.

CHOIR: "We Would See Jesus" (fifth stanza).

READER: When Jesus on that last Sabbath entered Jerusalem, most of the crowd spread their clothes on the road, and others cut branches from the trees, and spread them on the road. And the crowds that went before him and that followed him shouted: "Hosanna in the highest. Blessed is he that cometh in the name of the Lord. Hosanna in the highest."

171

CHOIR: "All Glory, Laud and Honor."

READER: My Master was so very poor, a manger was His cradling place; so very rich my Master was, kings came from far to gain His grace. My Master was so very poor, they nailed Him naked to a cross; so very rich my Master was, He gave His all and knew no loss. . . . There was a knight of Bethlehem, whose wealth was tears and sorrow; His men-at-arms were little lambs, His trumpeters were sparrows; His castle was a wooden cross, whereon He hung so high; His helmet was a crown of thorns whose crest did touch the sky. . . . There was a knight of Bethlehem, whose wealth was tears and sorrows.

CHOIR: "There Is a Green Hill Far Away."

READER: In Joseph's lovely garden, the Lord Christ's tomb was laid, and there His broken body to rest was gently laid. A great rock strongly sealed it that death might have full sway, but God sent down an angel to roll the stone away. O Jesus, blessed blest Redeemer, all praise to Thee we bring. No power of death could hold Thee, our Savior, Lord, and King.

CHOIR: "Jesus Christ Is Risen Today" (tune—Llanfair)

READER: Though Christ a thousand times in Bethlehem be born, if He's not born in thee, thy soul is still forlorn. The cross on Golgotha will never save the soul, the cross in thine own heart alone can make thee whole. Hold thou! Where runnest thou? Know heaven is in thee; seekest for God elsewhere, his face thou'lt never see. O would thy heart but be a manger for his birth, God would once more become a child upon the earth.

CHOIR: "I Bind My Heart This Tide to the Galilean's Side."

THE LIFE OF CHRIST IN SCRIPTURE, ART, AND MUSIC

(This unusual and undoubtedly beautiful service was planned and presented by Mary Wigent, with the Primary, Junior, and Intermediate Choirs of the Garden City Community Church, Garden City, New York.)

ORDER OF WORSHIP

PRELUDE: Elegie .... *Flor Peeters*

Aria .... *Flor Peeters*

INTROIT: Glory to Thee My God This Night

PROCESSION HYMN 231 "Thou Didst Leave Thy Throne"

The Life of Christ in Scripture, Art and Music

172

THE ANNUNCIATION
"Annunciation of the Virgin" ....*L. van Leyden*
     Flemish—Renaissance ....(1493-1533)
Solo: "The Annunciation" ....*Eric Thiman*

THE NATIVITY
"Holy Night" ....*Correggio*
     Italian—Renaissance ....(1494-1534)
Anthem: "Snowy Flakes Are Falling" ....*Polish Carol*

PRESENTATION OF CHRIST IN THE TEMPLE
"Presentation of Christ" ....*Hans Holbein*
     German—Renaissance ....(1497-1543)
Anthem: "Presentation of Christ in the Temple"

FLIGHT INTO EGYPT
"Flight into Egypt" ....*J. J. Tissot*
     French—19th century ....(1836-1902)

THE DOCTORS
"Christ and the Doctors" ....*Johann Hoffmann*
     (1824-1895)

THE BAPTISM
"Behold the Lamb of God" ....*Dierick Bouts*
     Flemish—Early Renaissance ....(1410-1475)
"The Baptism of Christ" ....*Guido Reni*
     Italian—Renaissance ....(1575-1642)

THE TEMPTATION
"Temptation of Christ" ....*Pieter Brueghel*
     Flemish ....(1568-1625)
Anthem: "Forty days and Forty nights" ....*Martin Herbst*

JESUS THE FRIEND OF CHILDREN
"Jesus Blessing the Children" ....*Elsie Anna Wood*
     English—Contemporary
Anthem: "God My Father Loving Me" ....*J. H. Knecht*

QUIETING THE TEMPEST
"Christ and the Sea of Galilee" ....*Tintoretto*
     Italian—High Renaissance ....(1518-1594)
Organ: Lord Jesus Walking on the Sea ....*J. Weinberger*

PURIFICATION
"Christ and the Money Changers" ....*El Greco*
     Spanish—Renaissance ....(1541-1614)

CHRIST'S ENTRY INTO JERUSALEM
"Christ's Entry into Jerusalem" ....*B. Plockhorst*
German—Nineteenth Century .... (1825-1907)
Anthem: "Hosanna Be the Children's Song"
CONGREGATION AND CHOIRS sing
"All Glory Laud and Honor"

THE LAST SUPPER
"The Last Supper" ....*Leonardo da Vinci*
Italian—Renaissance .... (1452-1519)
Organ: The Last Supper ....*J. Weinberger*

SIMON OF CYRENE
"Christ and the Cross" ....*Caravaggio*
Italian—High Renaissance .... (1569-1608)

THE CRUCIFIXION
"The Crucifixion" ....*F. Cossa*
(1435-1480)

CONGREGATION AND CHOIRS sing
"O Sacred Head Now Wounded"

THE RESURRECTION
"The Resurrection" ....*Altdorfer*
German—Early Renaissance
Anthem: "Angels Roll the Rock Away" ....*Matthews*

HIS ABIDING PRESENCE
"Christ and the Pilgrims of Emmaus" ....*Velasquez*
Spanish .... (1599-1660)
Anthem: "Come Jesus Holy Child"

THE ASCENSION
"The Ascension" ....*Elsie Anna Wood*
English—Contemporary
Anthem: "The King Ascendeth into Heaven" ......*Healy Willan*

CHRIST IN GLORY
"Head of Christ" ....*Tintoretto*
Italian—High Renaissance .... (1518-1594)
Anthem: "Glory to the Father Give" ....*Healy Willan*

OFFERTORY
"All things come of Thee, O Lord,
And of thine own we have given Thee."

RECESSIONAL HYMN 454 "Once in Royal David's City"

174

BENEDICTION

CHORAL RESPONSE "Jesus Tender Shepherd Hear Us"

POSTLUDE

Listed below is the music that was sung in LIFE OF CHRIST service. We *rented* the slides from the Metropolitan. I believe it is fifty slides that are rented for two weeks for only $1.00.

The Annunciation. Eric Thiman from the Christmas Cantata, "The Flower of Bethlehem." Publisher, Curwen. Handled by G. Schirmer.

"Snowy Flakes Are Falling." Polish Carol. Setting by Healey Willan, as found in his book, *We Praise Thee*, published by Concordia.

"Forty Days and Forty Nights." Martin Herbst, as found in *Songs of Praise for Children*. Oxford University Press.

"God My Father Loving Me," found in *Songs of Praise for Little Children*, published by Oxford University Press. Also found in the Episcopal Hymnal, hymn number 239.

"Hosanna Be the Children's Song," as found in *Hymns for Primary Worship*, Westminster Press.

"Angels Roll the Rock Away." J. Sebastian Matthews. Printed in G. Schirmer's *Carol Collections Annual* No. 13. No. 6911.

"Come Jesus Holy Child." Setting by Healey Willan in his book *We Praise Thee*. P. 12.

"The King Ascendeth into Heaven." Setting by Healey Willan, same book, p. 41.

"Glory to the Father Give." Setting by Healey Willan, p. 48.

With this we had two ministers reading the Scripture divided between them.

THE LIFE OF CHRIST

In song and narration

(Planned and presented by William Giles, First Presbyterian Church, Middletown, Ohio.)

Narrator: Long before Jesus was born, wise men, called prophets, foretold His coming, and the people waited eagerly for the sign that would herald His birth.

Song: "How May I Fitly Greet Thee"
Chorale from Cantata 161. Bach (with flute). From *The 389 Chorales of Bach*. The Association of American Choruses, Princeton, New Jersey.

Narrator: It was the angel Gabriel who came to Mary and told her that the son she was to bear would be Jesus, the Son of the Most High, who would reign over the house of Jacob forever, of whose kingdom there should be no end.

Song: "A Great and Mighty Wonder"
Chorale by Praetorius. Stanzas 1 and 4, from *The Hymnal* 1940, The Protestant Episcopal Church.

Narrator: To fulfill what was written in the Scriptures, Mary and Joseph went to Bethlehem for the taxing, and while they were there, Mary's baby was born in a manger, because there was no room for them in the inn.

Song: "In That Poor Stable"
French Carol. Arranged by Gounod. Stanzas 1 and 3, from *The Oxford Book of Carols*. Oxford University Press.

Narrator: Shepherds on the hillside were the first to hear of the birth of Jesus. It was announced to them by choirs of angels, singing from above.

Song: "The Shepherds' Christmas Song"
French Carol. Arranged by Dickinson (with flute). From *The Coming of the Prince of Peace*. H. W. Gray.

Narrator: The Bible tells us very little about Jesus' life as a boy, but many legends have grown up about things He did when He was young.

Song: "Legend." Tschaikowsky. From *The Oxford Book of Carols*.

Narrator: We know that Jesus worked in the family carpenter shop when He was a young man, and we are sure that He did more than His share in every job, and that His customers were fairly

176

and honestly treated. Knowing the people Jesus chose to be His friends, we know that He thought highly of honest labor and skillful craftsmanship.

Song: "My Master Was a Worker." Hymn tune "Munich." Arranged by Mendelssohn. From *Singing Worship*. Thomas. Abingdon.

Narrator: It was not until Jesus was thirty that He left the carpenter shop and became a traveling preacher and teacher. All through His ministry, His favorite way of teaching was through parables, stories that pointed out what were the right and wrong ways to live with our fellow men.

Song: "The Good Samaritan." Lee Hastings Bristol. From *Songs from Luke*. Canyon Press.

Narrator: The part of Jesus' life we hear most about is the beautiful and terrible story of His last days on earth. On Thursday evening, He and His disciples gathered to celebrate the Passover, and when they had eaten, He went to the Garden of Gethsemane, to pray by himself.

Song: "Our Lord Jesus Knelt in the Garden." Swiss folk song. Arranged by Dickinson. H. W. Gray.

Narrator: Judas, one of Jesus' disciples, had betrayed Him to the authorities, and His prayer was interrupted by the mob that came to arrest Him. After a false trial before Pilate, the mob demanded that Jesus be crucified, and on Friday afternoon He was put to death on Golgotha, the place of a skull.

Song: "Were You There?" Spiritual. Arranged by David McK Williams. From *The Hymnal* 1940. Sung unaccompanied.

Narrator: For a while, the disciples and Jesus' followers thought that the end had really come, but on Easter Day they discovered that Jesus had risen from the tomb, as He had said, and their sorrow was turned to great rejoicing. Since that time, Christians have celebrated Sunday as the Lord's day, to thank God for His great mercies.

Song: "Alleluia, Alleluia." Bach (with flute). Chorale from Cantata 142 Cantata score. Galaxy.

UNUSUAL PRESENTATION OF "ELIJAH"

By Don Fischer

Mount Hollywood Congregational Church, Los Angeles, California

Here is an idea used in our church which anyone is welcome to use. The object was to sing excerpts from Mendelssohn's "Elijah" with a small choir of 24 (12 men). We also wanted to build a program with a wide appeal, that is, to Juniors as well as adults. So we wrote a script in simple storytelling style for our minister to read; we started the evening of music with a short hymn sing of favorites requested by the audience; and incorporated three hymns in the concert portion in the manner of chorales in the Bach oratorios. The script and music took about 45 minutes, and the incorporated hymns added 10 minutes more. The organ prelude and opening hymn sing added 20 more minutes for a total time of one and one-quarter hours. We started at 7 p.m.—early, so families could come together and be home early.

Continuity

Narrator: A long time ago—about 850 years before Christ—there lived a prophet named Elijah. It is at the time King Ahab and Queen Jezebel are ruling over Israel. Ahab has led many people away from their God into worshiping idols instead. He has even built a temple to Jezebel's God, Baal. Elijah is deeply concerned over this. He goes to the king and warns him of what will happen if he continues to worship idols.

Music: "As God the Lord liveth." *Elijah.* Page 3 (Schirmer edition).

Narrator: Soon the rivers begin to dry up. The people are hungry— even the children have not enough to eat. In desperation the people call on God:

Music: "Lord, bow Thine ear to our prayer." Chorus page 16.

Narrator: Now Obadiah, the governor of Ahab's house, was still a loyal servant of God. He also dared to hide one hundred prophets of the Lord when Jezebel had ordered, "Kill them all." Obadiah now asks the people, "Do you really want to find God? Then hear what God says we must do to find Him."

Music: "Ye People, Rend Your Hearts and not Your Garments." Page 20. "If with All Your Hearts." Page 21.

Narrator: Then the word of the Lord comes to Elijah saying, "Go to the east and hide yourself by the brook Cherith. There I will see

178

that the ravens bring you bread and meat." So Elijah does as God says. But after a while the brook dries up, and God sends him another message: "Go over to the city of Zarephath and stay at the house of a widow and her son. She will provide for you." Elijah obeys God again. But after a while the widow's son falls ill and she wonders, "Has this prophet brought a curse on my son? I must ask him."

Music: "What Have I to Do with Thee?" *The Widow and Elijah.* Page 41.

Narrator: Three years have gone by since Elijah first told King Ahab that no more rain would fall until God gave the word. The famine is merciless. Finally the word of the Lord comes to Elijah: "Go call on the king again I will soon send rain." Elijah goes to Ahab and says: "Let all the people of Israel be assembled on Mount Carmel along with the priests of Baal and of your other gods." When the people are gathered, Elijah asks them, "How long are you going to hold two opinions? If the Lord is God, follow him; but if Baal, then follow him. Therefore, let two altars be prepared with sacrifices. You call first on your gods; then I will call on the name of the Lord; and the God that answers by fire, let him be God." The priests of Baal prepare their altar and call on their god, but he does not answer. Then Elijah prepares to pray to his God.

Music: "Draw Near, All Ye People." Elijah. Page 75.
"Cast Thy Burden Upon the Lord." *Chorus.* Page 77.

Narrator: Elijah's prayer is answered. The fire of the Lord burns up the sacrifice. The people fall on their faces and say, "The Lord, He is God; the Lord, He is God."

Congregation and Choir: a suitable hymn.

Narrator: Then Elijah prays to God for rain. A little cloud begins to rise out of the sea, like a man's hand. Soon the sky is black with clouds and wind, and a great rain falls.

Congregation and Choir: "Praise to the Lord, the Almighty."

Music: "Hear ye, Israel." *Soprano.* Page 108.

Narrator: But Queen Jezebel still cannot believe in any other God but Baal; and even though the drought is over, she wants revenge on Elijah for causing it. Obadiah warns Elijah, "Jezebel's men will kill you on sight; go into the wilderness. You will be safe there. Hurry, and God go with you." But once hidden in the wilderness, Elijah begins to reflect on his failings, "It is enough; now, O Lord, take away my life, for I am not better than my fathers. Now let me die, for my days are but vanity. I have been very jealous for the Lord of Hosts: because the children of Israel have forsaken Thy covenant, thrown down Thine altars, and slain Thy prophets with the sword; and I—even I only am left, and they seek my life to take it away." Then he sleeps beneath a juniper tree while angels watch over him:

Music: "Lift Thine Eyes." Page 139.
"He Watching over Israel." *Chorus.* Page 141.

Narrator: But Elijah still feels he has failed because many people continue to harden their hearts against God; and again he wishes to die. An angel tries to comfort him:

Music: "O rest in the Lord." Page 149.

Narrator: Then the word of the Lord comes to Elijah: "Go, return upon thy way, for there are still 7,000 in Israel who have never bowed down to Baal." Elijah goes, saying, "I will suffer gladly for the sake of the Lord." Thus he continues to prophesy until the day God sends a whirlwind to carry him to heaven.

Music: "Then Shall the Righteous Shine Forth." Page 180.
"O Come Everyone that Thirsteth." *Chorus.* Page 188.
"Then Shall Your Light Break Forth." *Chorus.* Page 192.

Congregation and Choir: "Faith of Our Fathers."

Minister: Benediction.

Numbers which the children's choir could learn
"Cast Thy Burden upon the Lord."
"Lift Thine Eyes."
"O Rest in the Lord."

For a vivid account of the story of Elijah, read from page 223 "With Ahab the real troubles of Israel began" to page 241 "But when they spoke, it was too late" in Hendrik van Loon's *The Story of the Bible.* Perma Books. Available in most drug stores for 50 cents.

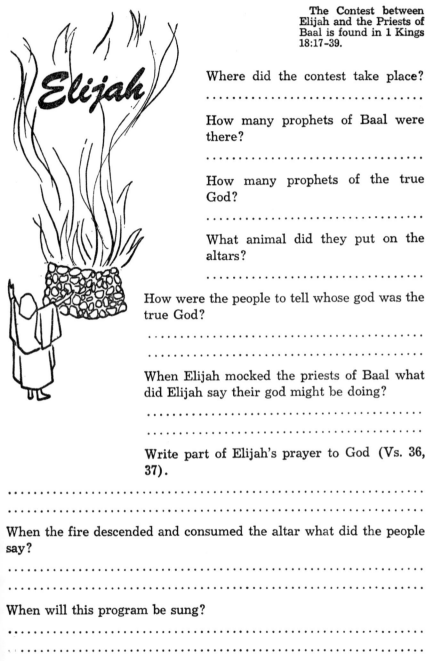

Elijah

The Contest between Elijah and the Priests of Baal is found in 1 Kings 18:17-39.

Where did the contest take place?

....

How many prophets of Baal were there?

....

How many prophets of the true God?

....

What animal did they put on the altars?

....

How were the people to tell whose god was the true God?

....

....

When Elijah mocked the priests of Baal what did Elijah say their god might be doing?

....

....

Write part of Elijah's prayer to God (Vs. 36, 37).

....

....

When the fire descended and consumed the altar what did the people say?

....

....

When will this program be sung?

....

....

Work-page designed by Dr. F. L. Whittlesey.

181

A DIFFERENT APPROACH TO MOTHER'S DAY

Wedding Day Service originated at Memorial Methodist Church, Lynchburg, Virginia. Madeline Ingram, Minister of Music.

Procession

Invocation

Hymn: "O Love Divine and Golden"

Our Christian Wedding Creed (to be said responsively)

M. We believe in God, our Heavenly Father, who has ordained that people should live together in families, finding joy and fellowship in mutual sharing.

C. We believe in the sanctity of marriage; that it is an honorable estate, instituted of God, and signifying unto us the mystical union which exists between Christ and His Church; which holy estate Christ adorned and beautified with His presence in Cana of Galilee. We believe that it is to be entered into advisedly, reverently, discreetly, and in the knowledge of God.

M. We believe that no other human ties are more tender, no other vows more sacred, than those assumed in Christian marriage, and that if these solemn vows be kept inviolate, and if we steadfastly endeavor to do the will of our Heavenly Father, our life will be full of joy, and the homes which we establish will abide in peace.

C. We believe in our children; they are a sacred trust as well as a joyous responsibility; they have a need for Christian teaching as a part of their total training for Christian citizenship.

M. We believe in the Church, as an institution established through the wisdom of Almighty God for the propagation of the Gospel of Jesus Christ, through personal work, teaching in church and home, and the ministry of the Word.

C. We believe in the importance of religion in our home for laying the foundations for courageous Christian living and for providing each member of the family with strength for daily living.

ALL: We believe that the spirit of Jesus Christ in the lives of individuals can transform home life to the extent that its members will find peace and happiness and power for radiant living. Amen.

182

ANTHEM

RESPONSIVE READING

> M. And these words which I command thee this day, shall be in thine heart. And thou shalt teach them diligently unto thy children, and shalt talk of them when thou sittest in thine house, and when thou walkest by the way, and when thou liest down, and when thou risest up.

> C. Thou shalt love the Lord thy God with all thine heart, and with all thy soul and with all thy might.

> M. Be ye, therefore, followers of God, as dear children; and walk in love, as Christ also hath loved us.

> C. Whatever ye would that men should do to you, do ye even so to them.

> M. Husbands, love your wives, as Christ also loved the church and gave himself for her. Fathers, provoke not your children to wrath; but bring them up in the nurture and admonition of the Lord.

> C. A new commandment give I unto you, That ye love one another; as I have loved you, that ye also love one another.

> M. and C. Entreat me not to leave thee, or to return from following after thee, for whither thou goest, I will go, and where thou lodgest, I will lodge; thy people shall be my people, and thy God my God; where thou diest will I die, and there will I be buried; the Lord do so to me and more also, if ought but death part thee and me.

GLORIA PATRI

ANTHEM

PRAYER

O God, who has set Thy children in families, and art the Head of all the families of the earth, we worship Thee in reverent love. The joy and brightness of life are from Thee, and in the dark places Thou art not far from any one of us. The strength of fathers and the tenderness of mothers are gifts of Thy love to us, and Thy goodness is revealed in the lives of children. We rejoice in the fellowship which our homes offer, and in the strength which we have in one another, and in Thee.

183

Help us to look on parenthood with reverence, and upon childhood with awe, and so live together that Thy kingdom may be carried forward in our homes. Help all parents who are worried or bowed down with heavy burdens to find strength in Thee. Give us repentance for the unconcern which allows fathers and mothers to suffer in needless ways, and to feel the stab of anguish because they cannot do for their own as love would prompt them. As we commend the mothers of the race to Thy protection, we pray that we also may sustain them in the travail of body and of soul with resources of skilled and loving care. And may there be life abundant for them and for their families.

Forgive us that we send mothers in grim necessity to toil outside their homes, while children are deprived of care. Forgive us that we use wealth recklessly, while families are hungry and in want. Save us from the folly of building institutions in such a way as to allow families to be oppressed. As we call Thee our Father, we pray that Thou wilt turn our feet into the ways of brotherhood, so that the Christ who moved amid the homes of long ago may dwell in our homes through love.

Grant that mothers and fathers may be satisfied by love returned, by lives lifted to Thee, and by Thy sway extended in the world. And when evening comes, may the light of the Eternal shine around them. Through Jesus Christ our Lord. Amen.

ANTHEM

OFFERING

HYMN: "O Perfect Love"

MESSAGE: "Qualities of Life Necessary for a Happy Home"

THE WEDDING VOW

To thee I renew my vow to take thee as my wedded mate, to have and to hold, from this day forward, for better, for worse; for richer, for poorer; in sickness and in health; to love and to cherish, till death do us part, according to God's holy will.

PRAYERS from the *Marriage Ritual*, followed by Our Lord's Prayer and the Benediction.

184

FESTIVAL OF THE CHRISTIAN HOME

The Mt. Hollywood Congregational Church in Los Angeles adds dignity to its Mother's Day celebration by making it *A Festival of the Christian Home*. The service includes a series of short talks on "What the Family Means to Me" by a father, a daughter, a son, and a mother. The minister speaks on "Religion in the Home," and all repeat the unison prayer:

> "Lord, make me an instrument of Thy peace.
> Where there is hatred, let me sow love;
> Where there is injury, pardon;
> Where there is doubt, faith;
> Where there is despair, hope;
> Where there is sadness, joy.
> O Divine Master, grant that I may not so much seek
> to be consoled, as to console; to be understood,
> as to understand; to be loved, as to love. For it
> is in giving that we receive; it is in pardoning
> that we are pardoned; and it is in dying that we
> are born to eternal life."

CHILDREN'S CHOIR FESTIVALS

Children's choir festivals are increasing in number. To a great extent, it is the amount of preliminary planning that determines the success of the festival. A fine festival is impossible without a great deal of preliminary work. Here are a few lessons learned from wide experience:

Limit the Age Range.
> Fourth grade through Junior High is the maximum; preferably fourth through sixth grade.

Contact every church in the area.

Set a participation fee; generally $10.00 for each church.

Set a date for a meeting of the directors.
> Ask them to bring copies of suitable music.

At this meeting:
> Select the music to be used.
>> Keep it simple.
>> Be ready with several positive suggestions.
> Set the time and place for the festival.
> Decide on the festival director, and any special feature.
> Set a date for the next meeting.

At Second Meeting (at the place where the festival is to be held):

Go through the music, with the festival director if possible.

Show directors where their choirs are to go for robing.

Pass out instruction sheets for the festival.

The order of the service.

Directions for the Choirs.

Date of massed rehearsal (preferably two of them).

Get exact number of children in each choir.

Appoint a publicity chairman.

Publicity Chairman Should:

Send out uniform publicity to all the churches.

Keep the papers supplied with material and names.

Before the festival, get a good group picture in the paper.

Keep a file of all publicity for future reference.

Shortly Before the Festival Date:

Send out a letter of final instructions.

Stress the necessity for promptness.

Tell choirs where to go upon arriving at the church.

First Final Rehearsal:

Rehearse the procession and seating.

Get balance of voices and organ.

Show choirs their robing rooms.

Go through the music; find numbers and spots that need extra work.

Final Rehearsal:

Choirs come directly to their appointed seats.

Put final polish on the music (allow an hour).

Send choirs to their robing rooms, and practice the order of entering and leaving, as it is to be at the festival.

Attendance at both final rehearsals should be required.

Consider the advisability of a reserved section for parents.

Hold a meeting of directors soon after the festival.

Evaluate the festival.

Suggest improvements.

Appoint chairman for next year.

Select music for following year.

For a Spring festival, the music should be in rehearsal in the fall.

LET US USE HYMNS

In *Child Guidance*, the teachers' manual for the Methodist Church, some months ago, there was an article suggesting the history of church music as a special Junior Department program. Starting with a Hebrew melody (most good hymnals have at least one or two) and proceeding with a Gregorian melody, a Bach chorale, a Scotch psalm tune, and a contemporary hymn, the whole program could be taken from the Hymnal. A commentary on each period by one of the choir children would add to the interest. Why not see how interesting a service you can create from the Hymnal?

Requests for festival material! Why not use the hymns we have been learning, and for once let the congregation become an active part of a festival?

Dick Helms, Kansas City, presented his choir in a special service as the final session of an interdenominational church music study. The call to worship, solo, anthems, the entire worship service came from the Hymnal. Few of us are conscious of the resources of the Hymnal.

A CHILDREN'S HYMN FESTIVAL SERVICE

(All Hymn numbers refer to the 1933 Presbyterian Hymnal)

Prepared by the Reverend George Litch Knight, assistant minister of the West Side Presbyterian Church, Ridgewood, New Jersey. Editor of *The Hymn*, Quarterly magazine published by The Hymn Society of America. National Chairman of the Members' Interests Committee of the A. G. O.

Organ Prelude: "Prelude on 'Jewels.'" *Bitgood.* (Based on a familiar Sunday school song of an earlier time.)

Processional Hymn 411. "O Beautiful for Spacious Skies"

Call to Worship. O come, let us worship and bow down. Surely the Lord is in this place. And Jesus grew in wisdom and in stature and in favor with God and man.

Collect and the Lord's Prayer

Explanation of the Service Theme

"O Sing a Song"
Based on Hymn Number 138 "O Sing a Song of Bethlehem."
Dr. Louis F. Benson

I. BETHLEHEM
(Here the Minister reads some appropriate Scripture)

187

Hymn 138. Stanza 1 (Sung by a small group of singers in a gallery, or separated from the rest of the choirs).

Hymn 454. "Once in Royal David's City" (Stanzas 1, 2)

Anthem: "O Saviour Sweet." Bach-Dickinson (first stanza only, with quartet or adults taking Chorale)

Hymn 448. "The Shepherds Had an Angel" (Optional)

II. NAZARETH

(Here the Minister reads some appropriate Scripture)

Hymn 138. Stanza 2 (Sung as before—*in unison*)

Anthem: "By Nazareth's Green Hills." J. Frederick Bridge (Novello). Can be arranged for children; also might have parts of it sung by adult group for contrast.)

Hymn 140. Stanza 2 *(Sing to the tune Materna)*

(Good for boys to sing alone; might preface it with first stanza if desired.)

Hymn 452. (Optional) "Saviour, Teach Me Day by Day."

III. GALILEE

(Here the Minister reads some appropriate Scripture.)

Hymn 138. Stanza 3 (Sung as before).

Hymn 444. "It Fell upon a Summer's Day" (Sing as a dialogue).

Hymn 442. (Optional) "I Think When I Read That Sweet Story."

IV. CALVARY AND EASTER

(Here the Minister reads some appropriate Scripture)

Hymn 138. Stanza 4 (Sung as before).

Hymn 154. "Behold the Lamb of God" (Stanza 1 by a mixed choir and stanza 3 by the children alone in unison).

Anthem (Optional) "While My Watch I Am Keeping." Adapt from the Gounod "Redemption." Very good for boy choir solo.

Hymn 157. "There Is a Green Hill," or Hymn 156, "O Jesus, We Adore Thee" (Latter good for adult participation also).

Hymn 168. "Come, Ye Faithful."

Closing Prayer

Recessional Hymn 431. "Hark, Hark My Soul" (My Junior Choirs' favorite hymn; they love "Angels of Jesus," etc.)

Benediction

Organ Postlude

188

The Story of Easter in Hymns

(Purpose is to have children see the Life of Jesus as a unit. So often they think of disjointed parts—Christmas, Easter, etc., and do not see the thread of continuity which runs through from Bethlehem to Calvary. These suggestions should not be followed literally, but should provide a basic skeleton for adaptation.)

Hymn: "Fairest Lord Jesus"
Narrator: Matthew 21:8-11
Hymn: "All Glory, Laud and Honor"
Prayer
Narrator: Mark 14:32-42
Prayer
Narrator: Mark 14:43-50, 53; John 19:1-22
Hymn: "There Is a Green Hill Far Away"
Narrator: John 20:1-16
Hymn: "I Say to All Men Far and Near"
Narrator: John 21:19-31
Hymn: "Christ the Lord Is Risen Today"
Narrator: Matthew 28:19-20
Hymn: "Take My Life, and Let It Be"

A Festival Service of Good Will

Processional Hymn: "Jesus Shall Reign" (Duke Street)
Call to Worship
Introit: to be sung by choirs and congregation. Tune: America.

> Father of every race, Giver of every grace, Hear us we pray.
> Let every land be free, may all men brothers be,
> All nations honor Thee, now and always. Amen.

Prayer of Invocation, followed by the Lord's Prayer.
Chorale: "Jesus, Joy of Man's Desiring." Bach.
The First Lesson: Isaiah 40:1-11
The Anticipation of Jesus' Coming
   "O Come, O Come Emmanuel" (Presbyterian Hymnal)
The Birth
   "Christmas Song." Holst ....G. Schirmer, unison
The Boyhood
   "O Savior Sweet." Bach ....H. W. Gray, unison
The Ministry
   "Jesus Walked This Lonesome Valley" ......"Singing America,"
      Birchard

189

The Second Lesson: Matthew 5:1-12

The Triumphal Entry into Jerusalem
"Hosanna." Bitgood ....H. W. Gray

The Crucifixion
"The Bird of Christ." Ross ....J. Fischer
(omitting solo)

The Resurrection
"Christ the Lord Is Risen Today" ....Tune: Easter Hymn

Litany of Brotherhood
Leader: How good and pleasant it is for brothers to dwell together
in unity. For God hath made of one blood all nations and
people to dwell on the earth.
People: We thank Thee, our Father, that all men are brothers
through our divine Brother, Jesus Christ.
Leader: There is no difference between Jew and Greek, bond
and free.
People: We thank Thee, our Father, that all men are brothers.
Leader: This is the message of the gospel, that we should love
one another, and that he who loveth God should love his
brother also.
People: We thank Thee, our Father, that all men are brothers.
Leader: We also have received the commandment that we should
do unto others as we would that they do unto us.
People: Help us Father, to keep this commandment.
Leader: "Inasmuch as ye have done it unto one of the least of
these, my brethren," said Jesus, "ye have done it unto me."
People: Help us, Father, to keep this commandment.
All: Teach us anew, our Father, that all peoples at home, and in
all the world, of every race, color, and creed, are our brothers,
and Thy children. Amen.

Anthem of Brotherhood
"Worship." Geoffrey Shaw ....H. W. Gray, unison

Prayer of Resolve
Response: "Lord, I Want to Be a Christian." *Fun and Folk Songs.*
Westminster Press

Benediction and Recessional Hymn

This program was the Twentieth Annual Youth Choir Service of
Good Will, held at the Madison Avenue Presbyterian Church, New
York, on February 17, 1952.

Hymn Festival Program

Prelude: Chorale Preludes on Gregorian Chant—Demessieux
From the Hebrew Service —"The God of Abraham Praise"
A mediaeval Latin Plainsong Hymn —"Of the Father's Love Begotten"
The Hymn-prelude: "A Mighty Fortress Is Our God"
Martin Luther's Great Reformation Hymn, "A Mighty Fortress," ar-
ranged by Mueller
A Psalm Tune from Calvin's Psalter —"All People That on Earth Do
Dwell" (as lined out by a precentor)
A Psalm Tune from the Scottish Psalter *Dundee:* "God Moves in a
Mysterious Way"
Finest Hymn of Isaac Watts, father of the English Hymn: "O God,
Our Help in Ages Past"
Offertory. Bach, the greatest master of church music: "Come, Blessed
Rest"
Charles Wesley's Most Famous Hymn: "Jesus, Lover of My Soul"
A Twentieth Century Hymn: "This Is My Father's World"
Postlude: Chorale Prelude on "Palisades." Sowerby
Lauretta Cotton, Milwaukee, Wisconsin

Twenty-third Psalm Theme for Morning Service

Hymns: "He Leadeth Me" and "Savior, Like a Shepherd Lead Us"
Anthems: "Brother James Air"
        "God Is My Shepherd." Dvorak
Scripture: Twenty-third Psalm Choric Speaking
Madeline Ingram, Lynchburg, Virginia

Festival Based on Twenty-third Psalm

The Twenty-third Psalm has inspired so much good music that it,
too, could well be the theme of a choral service. Appropriate to the
text are:

"Brother James' Air." Oxford University Press No. 1139. Unison.
"The Shepherd." Brook. Oxford University Press No. 149, two
part (or unison).
"The Lamb." Protheroe. FitzSimons No. 5002, two part (or
unison).
"A Song of Innocence." Davies. Novello (sheet music). Same
text as "The Lamb."
"Flocks in Pastures Green Abiding." Bach. Oxford University
Press SC 1631. Unison.

191

Thanksgiving Vesper Service—Glade Spring, Virginia, Boys' Choir

Mrs. B. M. Arington, Director

(Planned by the boys themselves)

Prelude

Call to worship: Psalm 100

Invocation and the Lord's Prayer

Hymn: "Come, Ye Thankful People, Come"

Psalm of Thanksgiving—1 Chronicles 16:1-15; 23-26. Read by Tommy
  McGlocklin

"We gather together to ask the Lord's blessing" ....Choir Boys

Poem: "Thankful" ....Floyd Ballou

"The Old Thanksgiving Basket" ....Milton Boyd

"Joyful, Joyful We Adore Thee" ....Choir Boys

Announcements and Offering

"The Boy of Today—The Man of Tomorrow" ....Dr. Valiant

Hymn: "O Beautiful for Spacious Skies"

Benediction and Postlude

Tulsa Festival Program

A Musical Meditation on John 3:16

Prelude—Air for G String. Bach

Call to Worship

Hymn: "O Worship the King"

Scripture Reading

For God So Loved the World

Praise—Rowley—Oxford University Press MA24 (used adult choir
  in antiphonal manner)

That He Gave His Only Begotten Son

Four Christmas Songs. Arranged by Lynn. *Jr. Choir Christmas Collection.* Ditson 332-40082

That Whosoever Believeth in Him

Hymn: "All Hail the Power of Jesus' Name." Tune: Miles Lane

"All in the April Evening." Robertson. G. Schirmer No. 8837

Offertory Prayer. Organ Offertory: "Prayer." Boellman

Short Talk to Parents

Should Not Perish

"Dona Nobis Pacem." Arranged by Wilson. *Rounds and Canons.*
  Hall & McCreary

But Have Everlasting Life

"All Hail to Christ, Our King." Rawls. J. Fischer 8533

192

Second Annual Youth Choir Festival of the Columbus, Ohio, Presbytery

Anthems:

"Praise to the Lord, the Almighty." Davis. E. C. Schirmer 1572

"If with All Your Hearts." Mendelssohn.

"O Lord Most Merciful." Franck. E. C. Schirmer 1571

(All three numbers in *Green Hill Jr. Choir and Duet Book)*
E. C. Schirmer

"Forward! Be Our Watchword." Kettring. *Anthems for Jr. Choir.* Westminster Press

Hymns:

"With Happy Voices Singing"

"All People That on Earth Do Dwell"

"Let Us with a Gladsome Mind"

"Jesus Shall Reign Where'er the Sun"

Third Annual Youth Choir Festival of the Columbus Presbytery

The program included the following numbers:

Anthems:

"Jesu, Jesu, Gently Sleeping." Black.

"Brother James' Air." Jacob.

"Were You There?" Arranged by Burleigh.

"Fairest Lord Jesus." Arranged by Christiansen.

Hymns:

"O Come, O Come, Emmanuel"

"Rejoice Ye Pure in Heart"

"Lo How a Rose E'er Blooming"

"We Would See Jesus"

"All Glory, Laud, and Honor"

"Jesus Christ Is Risen"

Music for the 1954 Lynchburg, Virginia, Festival

"The Shepherd." Brook. Oxford University Press.

"The Snow Lay on the Ground." Sowerby. H. W. Gray.

"Ah, Dearest Jesus." Bach-Bitgood.

"Lord, Dismiss Us." Arranged by Kettring.

"We, Thy People, Praise Thee." Haydn-Curry.

"Savior, Blessed Savior." Edw. Mueller.

(The preceding four anthems are from *Anthems for the Junior Choir.* Westminster Press.)

193

"Here with the Ox and Donkey." Arranged by Couper   J. Fisher.

Psalm 150 in choric speech, followed by one stanza of "Praise to the Lord" (Lobe den Herren).

"The Lord Is My Shepherd." Round brought to Toronto from Cornwall over 100 years ago.

"We Will Be Merry." Marryott. H. W. Gray.

Hymns for choirs and congregation.
"O God, Our Help in Ages Past."
"Glorious Things of Thee Are Spoken."

Program for the Fourteenth Annual Children's Choir Festival

Lynchburg, Virginia

I

"Rejoice, Ye Christians, Loudly." J. S. Bach. Arranged by Glaser. E. C. Schirmer No. 2238.

"God of Youth." W. Glenn Darst. H. W. Gray No. 2147.

"A Festival Chime." Holst, Galaxy No. 8.

"Brother James' Air." Gordon Jacob. Oxford University Press. OCS 166.

II

"Christmas Song." Holst. G. Schirmer No. 8119.

"On Christmas Night." Arranged by Vaughan Williams. *Galaxy.*

"The Virgin's Slumber Song." Max Reger. Associated Music Publishers No. 91.

III

"Dona Nobis Pacem." *Rounds and Canons.* Robert Wilson. Hall & McCreary.

"His Beauty Now Appears." R. Deane Shure. Belwin No. 858.

"Worship." Geoffrey Shaw. H. W. Gray No. 1.

Hymns

"Hosanna, Loud Hosanna." Text: Threlfall. Tune: Ellacombe.

"Not Alone for Mighty Empires." Text: Merrill. Tune: Hyfrydol.

"God Be with You Till We Meet Again." Arranged Vaughan Williams.

Optional Number

"Two Christmas Carols." Arranged by Healy Willan. Frederick Harris Co. No. 1641. Jesous Ahatonhia" and "Old French Noel."

Includes Children in Cantatas and Oratorios

Mary Penick, Lexington, Virginia, writes the following article:

This idea may be helpful to some Guild members. When I choose an oratorio or cantata for performance, I usually do so with an eye to the Children's Choir having a part. The Primary children are too young for this, but I use the group made up of children from grades four through seven. They sing a soprano or tenor solo in unison, and the soprano part on any chorus which they may learn, supplementing the adult choir. Some of the music which is effective this way is:

THE MESSIAH, with children singing "Come unto Him" and the "Hallelujah Chorus."

ELIJAH, with children singing the tenor aria, "If with all your hearts."

ST. MATTHEW PASSION. Any of the lovely chorales.

BACH CANTATAS, No. 140. "Sleepers Wake," with children singing the chorale in diminution with the florid accompaniment and again at the end with the adult choir.

No. 80. "A Mighty Fortress Is Our God." The familiar chorale, which we do at the beginning with choirs and congregation, and again at the end.

No. 4. "Christ Lay in Death's Bonds." Tenor aria (verse 3) and chorale at the end, with the adult choir.

No. 142. "For Us a Child Is Born." Tenor aria, ("Lord, my thanks to Thee"), and the Alleluia Chorus with adult choir at the end.

The blessings from such participation have been as follows:

The children have learned and memorized some great music which I hope will carry over to their adult life. I am not much on feeding children what I call musical Gerber's Baby Food. Of course, there is much good music which is more suited to their age level than oratorio, but I do not think it does any harm to expose them to the latter.

It makes them feel important to be taking part in a "grownup" oratorio.

Since we import soloists for the solo parts, the children have a fine opportunity to hear fine singing demonstrated in a way which I, with my feeble voice, can never do. Of course they could hear the performance whether they participated or not, but for the most part, they do not come unless they are participating.

It gives me an opportunity to teach them something about composition, particularly in the Bach cantatas. After they have learned the chorale they can understand how Bach embroidered and embellished, gave the melody to parts other than the soprano, changed the rhythm, etc., even though the music itself may be too difficult for them to sing.

It gives the performance variety to have instead of always high-powered soloists, the children singing in unison. And, of course, the parents love it.

St. Matthew's Passion

Dr. Austin Lovelace, Evanston, Illinois, used his Juniors, Boys' Choir, Junior High Choir and the sopranos of his High School Choir for the six chorales in his presentation of Bach's *St. Matthew's Passion*.

Messiah, Easter Portion

Wesley Marquart's Junior Choir, Orange, California, sang the soprano air, "How Beautiful Are the Feet of Them," also the soprano line on "Lift Up Your Heads." They watched like hawks, didn't miss a cue, attacks and releases were something to hear, and their discipline was superb, they sat through the entire hour and a half and hardly moved a muscle. It is interesting to know the real potential of a youngsters' choir. The more you expect of them, the more you receive. Incidentally, there was not one absent.

Negro Spirituals

Cecil Lapo built the Holy Week Service for his Youth Choir on Negro Spirituals.

Sacred Folk Songs

Walter Davis, Middletown, Ohio, had a similar inspiration. He presented a Vesper Service of American Sacred Folk Songs and Spirituals.

Gymnafu-ganu

The members of the Lynchburg, Virginia, chapter of the Choristers Guild hold an annual Gymnafu-Ganu (the Welsh equivalent of hymn sing) for their youth choirs. They thought the name would appeal to the young people—and it did.

ANIMATED FAIRY TALES

There were so many inquiries about Bob McGill's "Animated Fairy Tales" that I asked him for a report. This is it:

We are acting three fairy tales that everyone knows or that are familiar stories to everyone. The first will be "The Shoemaker and the Elves," followed by "Little Black Sambo." The characters in this and in "Peter and the Wolf" all come from my Junior and Intermediate choirs (ages 9 to 13). The first two tales will be read aloud by an adult, and the boys and girls will act out the story as he reads. Sound effects in this will be supplied backstage by anything we can think of to do the trick. Costumes, for the most part, will be rented from New York. For "Peter and the Wolf" we are getting honest-to-goodness animal costumes with fur, hair, and all. We are using the record to tell the tale and provide music and sound effects.

Our staging is being done by the High School Choir, under supervision. We shall have real props, such as trees, small house, fence, etc. At the moment we are trying to devise a mechanism whereby the bird can actually fly; it is taxing the imagination and ingenuity of all of us. The children are most enthusiastic about this, and we are planning to make it nothing short of a professional job. A lady in the church who is good at such things is helping me direct it, and the rehearsal schedule is something to behold, but the parents now know that I'm a stickler for perfection and hard work, and that it pays off, so they are willing to let the kids come.

I got my idea from seeing "The King and I" in New York. In that, they acted out the story of *Uncle Tom's Cabin*.

Of course we are charging for this. We shall present an evening performance for adults and older children and a matinee for children 12 years old and younger. We are using the entire group of choristers.

Believe me, this is exciting. I who always vowed I would stick to "music in the chancel" am finding this great fun and something I shall *never* stop doing.

UNCLE REMUS

"The children of Joel Chandler Harris School in Atlanta dramatized the *Uncle Remus Tales* for the Story Book Fair at one of the large downtown stores. Margaret Kendrick and Dorothy Guy were in charge, but the children had a hand in planning the episodes and making the scenery. Some 90 children were transported to the store to take part in the performance.

197

OLD TESTAMENT DRAMAS

Mrs. Phillips of the First Baptist Church in Texarkana let her choir children create musical plays on Old Testament stories. Not only did everyone have a good time, but the plays were actually *good*.

TOM SAWYER

Mrs. Bruce Milligan, First Presbyterian Church, Pauls Valley, Oklahoma, presented the operetta "Tom Sawyer" by Grant-Schaeffer, published by the Raymond Hoffman Company of Chicago. She writes, "Our basement seats only 200; it was full both nights. We charged 50 cents for adults and 25 cents for children. We used all our children's choirs, from the first through the ninth grades. The boys really went for this, and it perked up their interest in choir. The teachers at school said that they were reading more—looking for Mark Twain books. Our choirs are included in our Youth Club program: 45 minutes of Bible, 45 minutes of choir, 45 minutes of craft or recreation. Supper is served by two mothers, and the children pay 25 cents for the meal."

Christmas

On Christmas Eve they filled the house, some fifty guests all told,
  (O little Lord of Christmas, were you left out in the cold?)

And ate and sang, played cards and danced till early morning light.
  (O little Lord of Christmas, did they think of you that night?)

Next morning came the presents on a glittering Christmas tree.
  (O little Lord of Christmas, was there any gift for Thee?)

The dinner was a Roman feast, and how the guests did eat!
  (O little Lord of Christmas, were you hungry in the street?)

Then came some teas, a movie, and at night the last revue.
  (O little Lord of Christmas, what had these to do with you?)

By midnight all were tired and cross and tumbled into bed.
  (O little Lord of Christmas, did they think that you were dead?)

They all woke up with headaches and no joy in work or play.
  (O little Lord of Christmas, did they mark your birth that day?)

The love, the joy were good, no doubt; the rest a pagan spree.
  (O little Lord of Christmas, let us keep the day with Thee!)

HENRY HALLAM TWEEDY

Symbols of Advent, Christmas, and Epiphany

 Lighted Candles. Symbolize Christ as the Light of the World. According to an old legend lighted candles placed in the window guided the Christ child in his wanderings on Christmas Eve.

Lighted Lamp. Symbol of the Word of God.

 Blossoming Rose. Symbol of Advent.

Star of Epiphany. Commemorates the visit of the Magi.

 Christmas Tree. Symbol of Christ as the Tree of Life. In the tenth century a beautiful legend began to spread all through Europe. The story said that on the night Christ was born all the trees in the forest, even those in the cold ice and snow, bloomed and bore fruit.

Laurel, Holly, and Ivy. In ancient Rome laurel was the emblem of peace, joy, and victory. Holly and ivy take its place in Christian homes to indicate Christ has entered.

 Yule Log. The custom of the Druids was to light fires during the Yule season to burn out the sins and evil of the past year. A huge log was cut and blessed by the Druid priest. In early Christian times the log became a part of the Christmas celebration. It symbolized for them Christ as the Light of the World.

Bells. In medieval times bells were tolled on Christmas Eve to warn the powers of Darkness of the approaching birth of the Savior. It was believed "the Devil died when Christ was born."

Mistletoe. Used by pagans to keep out evil spirits. Among Christians it has come to symbolize the healing powers of Christ.

Ships. An early legend and carol likens Mary to a ship bringing us her Baby "whose love shall make us free."

Gold, Frankincense, and Myrrh. The gifts brought by the Magi; gold signifying gold for the King; frankincense signifying High Priest; myrrh signifying Great Physician.

Copyright . . . Hall and McCreary Company.

CHRISTMAS ALPHABET

A. Advent, angels.
B. Babe, behold, Bethlehem, Bible, birth, birthday.
C. Christ, Christmas, camels, carol.
D. Donkey, doves.
E. East, Egypt, Emmanuel.
F. Firstborn, flocks, frankincense.
G. Gifts, gold, Glory to God, Good Will to Men.
H. Heavenly hosts, herald, Herod, holy.
I. Inn, innkeeper.
J. Jesus, Joseph, joy, Judea.
K. King of kings, Kings from the East.
L. Lambs, Lord, love.
M. Manger, Mary, midnight, mother, multitude, myrrh.
N. Nazareth, newborn, night, Noel.
O. Opened, ox.
P. Prince of Peace, praise.
Q. Quest, quietly.
R. Ruler.
S. Shed, sheep, shepherds, shine, sign, son, song, stable, star, swaddling.
T. Tidings, treasure.
U. Unto (us a child is born).

V. Virgin, visit.

W. Wake, watched, Wise Men, wonder, worship.

Y. Young child.

Can you write the story of Christmas, and use all the words in the Christmas alphabet?

(Copied)

It's Christmas

Things to Make:

A manger scene.

Christmas Carol Books.

Christmas cards and gifts for the family.

Christmas Services for the Whole Family:

Christmas Eve Carol Service.

Community Carolling.

Round-the-Table Carol Service.

White Gifts Service.

Christmas Customs and Carols of Many Lands.

Festival Processionals:

Stop while choirs are still in the aisles, sing first stanza of several familiar carols before resuming processional.

Candlelight processional. In one New England colonial church, candles are placed in all the windows, and these with the processional candles are the only light.

Use echo choir for alternate stanzas.

Christmas Films:

Christ Is Born (slides): Methodist Publishing House, Nashville, Tennessee.

Christmas Around the World (sound film): Methodist Publishing House.

Merry Christmas (sound film): Church Film Service, 2595 Manderson Street, Omaha 11, Nebraska, uses Vienna Choir Boys.

Shrine of a Nation (Westminster Abbey). Not Christmas, but of interest to the choir. Sound film. Church Film Service. Uses boy choir.

202

Christmas Games

Santa and his reindeer. The group stands in a circle, holding hands. One is chosen to be Santa; another his reindeer "Blitzen." Blitzen carries a small bell, which he must ring when Santa calls "Ho, Blitzen." Santa is blindfolded. They must stay inside the circle, and Santa must try to catch Blitzen. He may call "Ho, Blitzen," four times. If Blitzen is caught, two new players are selected. If not, Blitzen stays in the ring, and a new Santa tries to catch him.

Santa's Pack. The group sits in a circle. The leader says, "Santa is filling his pack, and he put in a ...." Everyone in the circle repeats the previous items, and adds another. The one who can repeat all the items in their correct order wins the game.

Christmas Carols. Divide the children into teams. The leader reads a line of a carol; the team that picks up the tune first and finishes it scores.

Sing Down. Divide the children into two groups. One side sings a carol. The other group must be ready with one as soon as they have finished. Keep up until one side repeats a carol that has been sung before.

Christmas Seal Hunt. The leader sticks a seal in plain sight on some child, while all close their eyes. The first one to see it, sits down. When all have sat down, the first one gets to place the seal.

Pinning on Santa's Pack. The children, blindfolded, pin a sack of toys onto a large Santa on the wall. The prize goes to the one who gets it most nearly in the right spot.

Christmas Gift. The children sit in a circle. A Christmas package is passed around until the music stops. The one caught holding the package is out. The last one in the game gets to open the package.

Christmas Stage Coach. The children sit in a circle. Each is assigned the name of something in " 'Twas the night before Christmas." As the object is mentioned while the poem is being read, each gets up and turns around. Whenever the leader says "Santa Claus" everybody must stand up and turn around, and the one in the center tries to get a seat.

Hidden Bell. The children are seated in a circle with a bell on a string. They slide their hands back and forth along the string to the tune of "Jingle Bells," thus passing the bell along the string while the leader tries to find it. Three times the leader may challenge a hand to see if the bell is underneath. If unsuccessful, he joins the circle and the person challenged takes his place.

Christmas Words. Give each child a piece of paper with "Merry Christmas and a Happy New Year" printed across the top. The prize goes to the one who in a given time has the longest list of words, using only the letters appearing in this phrase.

Christmas Literature

Christmas in the Country Church. Rural Institute, Barnes Hall, Ithaca, New York (pamphlet).

Christmas in the Home. Pilgrim Press. 14 Beach Street, Boston, Massachusetts.

Christmas. Edited by Robert Schauffler. Dodd, Mead and Co. (origin of celebrations; stories; legends, etc.)

The Christmas Book of Legends and Stories. Smith and Hazeltine. Lothrop, Lee & Shepard.

Christmas in the Church School

Use a different Christmas picture each Sunday for the worship center, with native greens and berries for the decorations.

Lighting the Advent Candles. Within a circle of greens place four candles, one for each Sunday of Advent. The first Sunday of Advent, a child lights one candle, saying: "All over the world men look to Bethlehem's King for light. The candle that I light reminds us that His light is for everyone who seeks it." The second Sunday two candles are lighted with appropriate statements. Such a service could be mimeographed and sent home with the children as a suggestion for a family altar.

Missions. Select one of your mission stations, write to them, find out what gifts would be most welcome, and make a Christmas box a department project.

Christmas For the Primary Choir

To Sing: Many of the simple, familiar Christmas hymns and carols. What could be more appropriate! But if you feel the need of some special octavo music, get "God bless the little things this Christmas-tide." Hatch. Published by Flammer.

To Hear: "Christmas Carols of Many Lands." Vienna Choir Boys. Victor C32.

To Do: I heartily recommend four little 20 cent booklets, published by the Department of Children's Work, Board of Education of

204

the American Baptist Convention, 1703 Chestnut Street, Philadelphia 3, Pennsylvania.

Christmas with Children
Christmas with Kindergarten Children
Christmas with Primary Children
Christmas with Junior Children

You would be wise to get all four of them.

To Make: Help your choir make a Christmas gift for the birds. Pour melted suet mixed with bird seed into the openings of a large pine cone, and hang it upside-down in a tree. If no cones are available, the food can be placed in a soap shaker, or in a branch with holes whittled in it. Some birds like a combination of peanut butter and melted suet.

And here is a design for name tags for your Christmas party. In our Primary Choir, we are hanging them on a little tree, and as each child performs some little musical stunt (things we have been working on during the rehearsal), he may take his name tag from the tree.

Christmas in the Church

The story, "Why the Chimes Rang," could be very simply dramatized with the characters coming from their places in the congregation to take their parts while a reader tells the story. A recording of a fine carillon could be used effectively for the chimes.

Everywhere Christmas Tonight, a series of tableaux of Christmas in different countries, using carols of many lands. Both carols and tableaux could be very simple.

Family Night Christmas, with members gathered around the tables in families. An informal carol sing with everyone participating is all the entertainment necessary.

Evergreen Breakfast. Mrs. Nancy Poore Tufts of Washington, D. C., invites her Youth Choir to her country home, where the members are permitted to cut all the trees and branches necessary for decorating the church. The morning in the open is followed by a substantial breakfast and cherry punch bowl around the fire in her living room, and then the load of greens is hauled to the church for an afternoon of decorating. It is the most loved tradition of the season for her choir.

Pictures to Illustrate the Christmas Story

Announcement to the Shepherds. Plockhorst. P 811
Madonna from Holy Night. Correggio. B 1907
Holy Night. Correggio. P. 367
The Nativity. Sinkel. P 3341
Star of Bethlehem. Pighleim. B 1024
Christmas Chimes. Blashfield. P 1020
Nativity. Hofmann. P 797C
Holy Night. Havenith. T. P.
Nativity. Muller. W 12
Arrival of the Shepherds. Lerolle. P 620
The Wise Men on Their Way to Bethlehem. Harper. U 101
Star of Bethlehem. Pighleim C 940. B 1024
Star of Bethlehem. Warren W 590
Magi on the Way to Bethlehem. Portaels B 1563
The Three Wise Men. Taylor. G 19
Worship of the Magi. Burne-Jones. P 963
Worship of the Magi. Hofmann. W 20

(Index to Abbreviations of Picture Companies publishing inexpensive prints)

B   George P. Brown, Beverly, Massachusetts
C   Cosmos Picture Company, 461 Eighth Avenue, New York
G   Erward Gross Co., New York City
P   Perry Picture Co., Malden, Massachusetts
RN   Reinthal and Newman, 106 W. 29th Street, New York
S   Soule Art Co., 101 Ferry Street, Malden, Massachusetts
TP   Tabor Prang Art Co., Springfield, Massachusetts
U   Union Press, 1816 Chestnut Street, Philadelphia, Pennsylvania
UV   University Prints, Newton, Massachusetts
W   W. A. Wilde Co., 120 Boylston Street, Boston, Massachusetts

Nativity Scenes

The practice of setting up a miniature manger scene at Christmas time is a very old and a very beautiful one. St. Francis, the gentle saint of Assisi, started the custom to make the Christmas story more real to the people of his little village. That was about the year 1200, and ever since then it has been an integral part of the festival season in the churches of Italy and France.

It seems natural to find some of the finest manger scenes in Oberammergau, the home of the Passion Play. It was there, after long years of searching, that I found carvings of Mary and Joseph and the Babe, and the gentle donkey, that are both beautiful and convincing. They have become the heart of our Christmas decorations.

There is a mountain village in North Carolina, where wood carving has been encouraged as a folk art. I am told that the wood carvers of Brasstown will make the sheep and the oxen and the donkey, but hesitate to touch the holy figures. It is Ben Hall, a gray-haired father with kind, deep-set eyes, who carves the shepherds and the wise men. And it is a young mountain mother who carves the Christ child.

If you would make the Christmas story meaningful to your children, why not let them create a manger scene. The experience of carving the figures, and reproducing the manger, will carve the story indelibly on their hearts. The results may be crude by all standards of art, but not to the children, if they have worked with sincerity and a sense of dedication like the carvers of Oberammergau and of Brasstown.

Christmas in the Family

Reserve one evening for trimming the tree. Have a festive supper in the preparation of which everyone has some share, sing carols, and let everyone have a hand in decorating the tree.

Spend a family evening preparing a Christmas stocking for some friend who is alone.

In our family the children always had a candlelight procession through the house and around the tree before the gifts were opened.

A Christmas Tree for the birds, with suet and seeds, and places where the family can enjoy watching the response.

Children's Records—As Christmas Gifts

1. A Child's Garden of Manners. Educational Record
2. Manners Can Be Fun. Educational Record
3. The Doctor Song. Educational Record
4. Herman Ermine in Rabbit Town. Educational Record
5. The Churkendoose. Educational Record
6. Little Red Riding Hood. Story
7. Alice in Wonderland. Story
8. Pinocchio. Story
9. The Little Engine That Could. Story
10. Winnie-the-Pooh. Story
11. The Flight of the Bumblebee. Musical Record
12. Raindrop Prelude (D-Flat). Chopin. Musical Record
13. Nutcracker Suite. Tchaikowsky. Musical Records
14. Carnival of the Animals. Saint-Saens. Musical Records
15. Pee-Wee the Piccolo. Musical Story
16. Tubby the Tuba. Musical Story
17. The Emperor's New Clothes. Musical Story
18. Said the Piano to the Harpsichord. Musical Story
19. Peter and the Wolf. Prokofieff. Musical Story
20. Sparky's Magic Piano. Musical Story
21. Rusty in Orchestraville. Musical Story
22. Lonesome Octopus. Musical Story
23. Grumpy Shark. Musical Story
24. Further Adventures of Tubby the Tuba. Musical Record
25. "Dance of the Comedians" from the Bartered Bride. Smetana. Musical Record
26. Gaiete Parisienne. Offenbach. Musical Record
27. German Dances. Mozart. Musical Records
28. "Golliwog's Cakewalk" from The Children's Corner. Debussy. Musical Record
29. "Polka" from The Age of Gold. Shostakovich. Musical Record
30. "Anitra's Dance" and "In the Hall of the Mountain King" from Peer Gynt Suite No. 1. Grieg. Musical Records
31. *The Toy Trumpet*. R. Scott and *Pavanne*. M. Gould. Both on one musical record.
32. Marches recorded by The Goldman Band. Musical Records
33. Thunder and Lightning Polka. J. Strauss. Musical Record
34. Bozo Series of Albums
   Bozo at the Circus
   Bozo on the Sea

208

Bozo and the Birds

Bozo in His Rocket Ship

35. Bugs Bunny Series of Albums
36. A 12-inch vocal record of the Nutcracker Suite by Fred Waring
37. Bible Stories for Children
38. Hymns for Children
39. Bambi
40. The Night Before Christmas
41. Johnny Appleseed
42. Little Black Sambo
43. The Three Little Pigs
44. Margaret O'Brien's Stories
45. The Little Red Hen

List assembled by Mrs. Haskell Boyter

CHRISTMAS GLEANINGS

Christmas Eve Family Service

Alvin Wooster, North Adams, Massachusetts. From the Minister's column in the church bulletin writes: "Last year when a Christmas Eve Family Service was proposed, there were some doubts. Out of the hurry and scurry, the dollars and ducats, the pressure and problems of last-minute Christmas shopping, would there be any energy left? Would more than a handful come? The service was prayerfully planned. We were prepared not to be disappointed, if only a few were there. But we were not prepared for what happened! The attendance was nothing short of thrilling. Best of all, many families came together—dad and mother and the children. They sat together. They sang together. They prayed together. Somehow when the benediction was pronounced at 8:30, the tinsel and the trinkets had taken their rightful place and we were gratefully aware of Immanuel—God with us. Now we know. A Christmas Eve Family Service is a *Must*. It will be held in the sanctuary from 7:30 to 8:30. God's people are invited to come to their Father's house, to worship Him in the simple but sublime faith revealed in Bethlehem's manger."

A Human Christmas Tree

Birchard News reports a school Christmas program in which the choir was placed on risers formed like a Christmas tree. Evergreen festoons were held by the children, and the whole was surmounted by a lighted star.

Our Savior and His Lady

Walter Davis, Middletown, Ohio, writes: "I am interested in your note about *ships* with regard to Christmas and their symbolism of Mary and Jesus. We sang the carol "I Saw Three Ships," and talked about it in rehearsal, speculating what "Our Savior Christ and His Lady" meant. Some thought it was simply reference to Mary, but one girl came up with the idea that it might refer to the Christian Church, as it has been symbolized as the Bride of Christ. This is an interesting interpretation and I am interested in knowing if it has any validity. Can anyone enlighten us?"

All-inclusive Christmas Bulletin

The First Methodist Church of Glendale, California, printed all of its Christmas programs in one booklet, under the title: "The Christmas Festival, for the Season of Advent and Christmastide." This is becoming increasingly the practice, and a fine one it is, making the services and the carol sings and the dinners and the Church School celebrations an integral part of one great Festival Season.

Choir Christmas Card

Mrs. Gladys Neuenschwander, Berne, Indiana, used a picture of her children's choir on her Christmas card.

Twelfth Annual Round-the-Table Carol Sing

Madeline Ingram, Lynchburg, Virginia, held her *twelfth* annual Round-the-Table Carol Sing with her five choirs.

Community Christmas Celebration

Howard Stampfli, reporting from Wheeling, West Virginia: "This year we are inaugurating what is to be known as the Wheeling Community Christmas Celebration. All the churches and schools are co-operating, and from December 10 on, we will have groups of singers at various bus stops, and on the main streets, singing carols. On the twenty-first, we are going to rope off one whole city block, where the singers from the whole city will congregate to sing carols, interspersed with the reading of the Christmas story, and ending with the Hallelujah Chorus. This is a big step for Wheeling in that it includes all denominations, faiths, and creeds."

Kodachrome Slides

Dorothy Guy, Atlanta, Georgia, used Kodachrome Transparencies in her Christmas program for the Joel Chandler Harris P. T. A.

In Our Image

Do you know the Portfolio of Biblical Portraits titled, "In Our Image" by Guy Rowe and published by Oxford University Press? It is a collection of magnificently human portraits of Old Testament Characters. Hubert Taylor of Atlanta, Georgia, has used six of these portraits for a series of short musical services for the Church Night suppers.

ROUND-THE-TABLE CAROL SERVICE

Wednesday, December 5, 1951

Grace

Festive Group

Usher in the
Christmas Season
By Attending
A Musical Treat
Given by the
Carol Choir
Chapel Choir
Chancel Choir

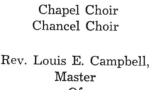

Rev. Louis E. Campbell,
Master
Of
Musical Feast
Of Songs,
Rounds,
Carols

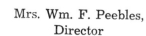

Mrs. Wm. F. Peebles,
Director

Bell Group

Pudding Group

Lullaby Group

Herald Group

The program will be given in the church social room, and is for the entire family and guests. A nursery will be provided for the very young. ERNESTINE PEEBLES, Delaware, Ohio.

A Very Simple Christmas Service

Margaret Dow, Meridian, Mississippi: "I am enclosing a copy of our Christmas program. There is nothing unusual about it, except possibly the fact that we hope to use every child in the Church school, from Beginners through Senior High. The Speech Choir will be composed of Juniors, Intermediates, and Seniors who are not in one of the singing choirs." (Most of the music in the program is familiar, and can be found in standard hymnals. R. K. J.)

A. Prophecy
   Isaiah 9 (selections). Speech Choir
   "O come, O come, Emmanuel." Chancel Choir. Sung in very
   Quempas Carol—Prelude
   Procession. All choirs
Carol
   "Lo, How a Rose." Praetorius. Men's Choir

B. The Angels and the Shepherds
   "O Little Town of Bethlehem." Congregation
   Luke 2: 8-14. Speech Choir.
   "Joseph Came Seeking a Resting Place." Willoughby. Chancel Choir
   "Rise up early." Kountz. All choirs
   "Angels and Shepherds." Bohemian Carol. Chancel Choir
   "The First Nowell." Congregation.

C. At the Manger
   Luke 2: 15-20. Speech Choir
   "What Child Is This?" Youth Choirs
   "Away in a Manger." Primary and Beginners' Departments
   "Lullay, Thou Little Tiny Child." Youth Choirs

D. "Then they offered unto Him gifts"
   "The Friendly Beasts." Bethlehem Choir
   Offertory Prayer. Offering
   "Sing We All Noel." York. Chancel Choir

E. "Everywhere, Everywhere, Christmas Tonight." Speech Choir

F. Recessional: "Joy to the World." Congregation and choirs

G. Closing Prayer and Benediction

H. Postlude

Service of Lights

Candlelight services. J. William Jones at Redlands University has developed a Service of Lights that combines music, drama, and pageantry, and makes use of all the faculty and student body. It attracts visitors from all of Southern California.

Edith Lovell Thomas has sent a copy of a Christmas Service prepared by Miss Gladys Gray of Geneva, New York. It appears to be an exceptionally fine and devotional service, and closes with the following service of lights:

THE SERVICE OF LIGHTS

(Immediately at the conclusion of the responses, the minister goes to the communion table, and the acolytes, carrying unlighted candles, stand behind him. The minister lights the single candle, using the vigil lamp.)

Minister: Come, Heavenly Child, and on this place
Shed the sweet halo of Thy grace.
O burning Love, O Heavenly Fire,
Consume me with Thy deep desire.

Congregation: As in the Holy Christ Child's name
This blessed wax shall feed the flame,
So let my heart its fires begin
And light the Heavenly Pilgrim in.

(Here the minister, using the single candle, shall light the candles of the acolytes, who in turn will light the tapers of those sitting at the end of each pew, and those in turn will pass the light to those beside them until all the candles are lighted.)

Choir sings "Silent Night" during candlelighting service.

The Benedictions

The benediction of silence

The Choral Benediction. Nunc Dimittis:

Lord, now lettest Thou Thy servant depart in peace according to Thy word,
For mine eyes have seen Thy salvation which Thou hast prepared before the face of all people:
To be a light to lighten the Gentiles, and to be the glory of Thy people Israel.

The Pastoral Benediction   Choral Amen

213

The Child, the Church the Home

WORSHIP

At a famous writers' club one day the discussion was on the relative merits of the great philosophic leaders. The general opinion was that Jesus was just a great leader among other great leaders. Then one of the men said, "Gentlemen, if Socrates or Plato were to enter this room, we would stand in respect, but if Jesus Christ were to enter, we would kneel." That's the difference that should be the crux of all our educational program in the church, including the music program. The church sanctuary is too commonly a social hall, and the class room a prize-fight ring. The church should be the place where the spirit learns to kneel, a place set apart for communications beyond the human. It is well enough to teach children to stand for the right, but it is when the spirit kneels that it gains strength to stand. We speak glibly of the art of worship, as if it were the process of fitting together a few prayers and readings and choral responses. These may encourage worship, but they quite as frequently intrude between worship and the worshiper. Worship is a sense of the presence of God and the commitment of one's own will to His. There must be intelligent Christianity, historically informed, but without worship it is only the portrait of reality.

A friend brought up in a non-religious home, and forced to consider the deeper meanings of life by the sudden death of her husband, said, "I'd like to know more about church, but I feel most at home in the Catholic church. You can go into the smallest chapel in the poorest Indian village of the southwest, and feel at home, and have a sense of peace."

But there are hopeful signs in the Protestant church. There are chapels that are open day and night; church bulletins encourage the congregation to bow the head in prayer upon entering the church. But the burden of responsibility rests on us who direct most of the corporate expressions of worship. If our children graduate from the choir without a consciousness that the church is a place for experiences and thoughts that transcend those of school and club; if they have not learned to expect quiet of themselves when they enter the church; if their participation in the service does not reflect a sense of obligation to their own and the congregation's higher aspirations, then we have failed. "Though I speak with the tongues of men and of angels" I may still be "as sounding brass or clanging cymbal."

Training the worship attitudes of our children is like tending a rare plant. The seed must first be planted, the soil in which it is planted kept in a condition that encourages growth; it must have a chance to weather adverse conditions, and any wild or abnormal growth must be pruned away.

The seed is best planted in the Primary Choir, before the sense of wonder has been dulled, and self-consciousness imprisons the child.

And once the seed has been planted, it requires patient care, until it reaches its full flower. But when it does put forth a bud fragrant with the richness of true worship, we may be humbly grateful for the privilege of having been the gardener.

SOME ASPECTS OF RELIGIOUS EDUCATION THROUGH CHILDREN'S CHOIRS

Dr. Whittlesey

The rehearsal periods for the Children's Choirs should contain some elements of religious education. Most children do not have much weekday religious training. The true minister of music, that is, one who uses music as a means of ministering to the people, will want to make the rehearsal hours count toward the enrichment of life and the development of Christian character.

216

For many years I have had a special project each season with the youth choirs—some study plan which could be a part, though often brief, of each rehearsal. Each season some subject was chosen for study, which was akin to the choir's main function but not directly related to the singing of anthems. Also I try to pick subjects that probably will not be covered in the regular church school curriculum.

The following paragraphs may give you some suggestions as to what may be done. I have used all these ideas during different seasons.

Every church has some Christian symbols in it. Acquaint the children with these symbols. Symbols came into being to (1) remind, (2) teach, (3) beautify. Make a study of the ecclesiastical symbols in your church. Handy books for your preparation for teaching are:

> The Sign Language of Our Faith. Griffith. Morehouse-Gorham, New York.
> An Outline of Christian Symbolism. Wilson. Morehouse-Gorham, New York.
> My Own Work Book on Christian Symbolism. Brookman. Morehouse-Gorham, New York.
> Christian Symbolism in the Evangelical Churches. Stafford Abingdon. Nashville, Tennessee.

A study of the art windows can be helpful. If your church does not have windows which picture Biblical scenes, you can still call attention to the ecclesiastical symbolism of the colors found in a window.

Another study can be made of the "Things we hear and see in church which help us to worship God." I used this project last season. Among the items discussed were: Message of the chimes; what makes a church Gothic—including carvings, arches, cross floor-plan; light shades which look like ancient towers; "A Mighty Fortress Is Our God," also Psalm 46; origin and use of "Gloria Patri" and "Doxology"; why vestments; symbolism of flowers in church; pulpit; open Bible; prayer, etc.

The book, "One God, The Ways We Worship Him," by Fitch (Lothrop, Lee and Shepard Co., New York), makes an excellent year's study. Through following this book and supplemental study material, you can guide the children along the pathway of understanding and brotherhood. Field trips to a synagogue and Catholic cathedral are valuable.

Hymnology is a helpful study. The children are interested in the stories back of the hymns. Many Christian truths can be taught

217

through hymns. The handbooks to the Hymnal will give much helpful material as will *Lyric Religion* by Smith. (The Century Co., New York.)

By all means build eternal values in the lives of the children.

Easter

Christmas is a joyous festival whose spirit even the smallest child can catch. Easter, too, is a joyous festival, but a more mature and profound joyousness. The joy of conquest over disappointment and fear, the joy of self-dedication to a great cause. There would have been no Easter without a Good Friday. If our presentation of the Easter message is restricted to the beauties of springtime, we are celebrating no more than a pagan festival. The Christian Easter is much more than joy in the nature's cycle of seasons. We can celebrate Easter only because Jesus, of his own volition, despite very human fears, chose death. The meaning—and the majesty—of Easter find reality only against the background of the Last Supper, Gethsemane, Golgotha.

It is not easy to help our Juniors and Intermediates find the deeper values of Easter. May I suggest that we start now to prepare ourselves for that task. Read the accounts of Holy Week in the four Gospels. Read them aloud, and suddenly you may become conscious of the depth of drama in those reports. Compare the four reports. If the events still seem remote, to you, and the language archaic, get a copy of Goodspeed's "Life of Jesus," and read it thoughtfully. It is simply and beautifully written, and completely authentic throughout. It will make you feel very close to someone to whom you have long given lip service. Then with that experience, read the gospel story again, and again, until your veil of complacency is lifted. Then perhaps you will be able to make Easter meaningful to the children.

Rather than teaching them only a succession of Alleluia and Easter Flower anthems, let them hear the story of Holy Week, and let them help tell that story through familiar hymns. Using as a basis the Bible and "Hymns for Junior Worship," let us attempt to plan a Christian Easter service. The readings must be done with an understanding of the profound drama of the events, and the children must be thoroughly familiar with the hymns. Then if you can get from your denominational headquarters fine slides of each episode to throw on the screen during the reading, your children may begin to have a dawning realization of the majesty of Easter.

Life of Jesus. Goodspeed. Harper and Brothers
Hymns for Junior Worship. Westminster Press

CHILDREN'S BEHAVIOR AT THE MEETING HOUSE

DECENTLY walk to thy Seat or Pew; run not, nor go wantonly.

Shift not Seats, but continue in the Place where your Superiors order you.

Lend thy Place for the easing of anyone that stands near thee.

Talk not in the Meeting House, especially in the Time of Prayer or Preaching.

Fix thine Eye on the Minister, let it not wildly wander to gaze on any Person or Thing.

Attend diligently to the Words of the Minister: pray with him when he prayeth, at least in thy Heart; and while he preacheth, listen, that thou mayest remember.

Be not hasty to run out of the Meeting House when the Worship is ended, as if thou wert weary of being there.

Walk decently and soberly Home, without Haste or Wantonness; thinking upon what thou hast been hearing.

(From a book published in 1787, in Worcester, Massachusetts, by Isaiah Thomas.)

Just after Easter is a good time to reflect on children's behavior in the Meeting House—1955. Probably every children's choir in the country took part in one or more Easter service. I wonder about their behavior. I wonder what they contributed to the service besides movement and color. And I wonder, too, what the service contributed to their fund of impressions regarding the Meeting House.

The Lincoln Memorial in Washington does what a church should do. Guards say that without exception visitors speak in a whisper, if at all; and many show signs of being deeply moved by the sense of the presence of the great emancipator. Do we honor less the presence of God? The behavior of the choir reflects the behavior convictions of the director. How did your children behave?

Obtain a copy of the May, 1951, issue of *Better Homes and Gardens*. It contains two articles of particular value to the children's choir director. "Make Music Fun Instead of a Struggle" stresses an important factor of music education.

The other article, "What Are You Going to Tell a Youngster." If your children have faith in you, they will ask you questions. If you would retain that faith, you must answer honestly and intelligently. "Strangely enough, parents who spend hours studying the problems of their youngsters' physical health, schooling and diet, are apt to spend no time at all on the kind of answers they should give to important questions raised by the same boy or girl. A thoughtless, off-the-cuff answer may really foul a youngster up. So can complicated answers, and white lies that are found out later to be untrue. Be honest, yet be sure your answers don't exceed the limit of your child's understanding."

Recently I took a walk with my four-year-old nephew. We passed an abandoned little cemetery and he asked what that was. I said it was a cemetery where they put people when they died, and then drew his attention to something else. When I told my 21-year-old daughter about the incident, she said: "Why didn't you just tell him they were stones? That would have satisfied him." We were both right, but she was *wise*.

Evaluation of the Influence of Music

A group of choir directors and public school music teachers in Atlanta were asked to list the values of music experience for which they had the proof of personal experience. The returns are thought-provoking and should encourage a more careful evaluation of the sort of experience our choir provides.

"A child that seemed to be a misfit mentally and socially was found to have musical talent. Succeeding in music, he became interested in achievement in the fields that seemed impossible before."

"In working with palsy children, music has aroused an interest to do things they haven't tried before, and has developed co-ordination."

"A school somewhat drab in outlook: music changed entire spirit of school and of student body."

"Study of music introduces a child to all arts, to history, to religion, and to all the better things of life."

"I can walk into a room full of chattering children and begin to sing a song in a very soft voice. Immediately the atmosphere clears, and the children are singing with me. Peace is restored."

"I have noticed that the children who have an opportunity to develop an interest in music become happier and over a period of time it has given them greater interest in doing other things well."

"A problem boy, after joining a boys' choir, became better adjusted. By the end of the year his entire attitude had changed."

"What I have seen music do! Interest a boy who isn't interested in much else; give many children the great privilege of making their parents come to hear beautiful music; give some children a chance to shine that they would never have otherwise; bind a grade together that was a troublesome class. This and much more."

"*I know* that music can bring joy and fun to a child in school— many times the only joy a poor home-neglected child can really experience with a true sense of accomplishment."

"I've never seen a group singing under a good leader that did not look happier than the average audience under a speaker."

"Music correlates the spiritual ideas with the practical so that a child who tends to be shy has a way of expressing his thoughts and aims through music. Children active in extra-curricular organizations keep away from the corner drug store crowd."

"A high school boy I know was material for the chain gang until he started singing. His voice has earned his own self-respect as well as that of his fellows."

"It has restored calm and quiet, harmony and peace in a room of noisy, excited children."

"Physical well-being from correct posture and breathing; discipline to self and constituted authority; mental alertness and sensitivity; give and take of ensemble work; use and control of emotions; pride of accomplishment and independence of thought and action."

"Opportunity for release of the emotional states, desires, ideas that underlie words but cannot be expressed by them alone; provides sense of belonging—here I rise above myself, this is my contribution; provides avenue for developing craftsmanship—growing sense of achievement; sense of continuity, connection with the past and the future."

WHAT INFLUENCE DO YOU INTEND YOUR CHOIR TO HAVE ON THE CHILDREN?

WHAT ARE YOU DOING TO ACHIEVE THOSE RESULTS?

ARE YOU CONSISTENT AND INTELLIGENT IN YOUR EFFORTS?

IS YOUR OWN PERSONALITY GROWING THROUGH YOUR CHOIR WORK?

A Spontaneous Class-room Prayer

This happened in a public school music class in Texas. A little girl came to her teacher at the beginning of the period and told her that her grandmother was to be operated on at that very hour. The teacher said "Go back to your seat and say a little prayer for your grandmother." Then she thought better, and said to the class, "Rachel is worried because her grandmother is very ill, and is being operated on right now. Suppose we all stop for a minute and say a prayer for her." Lillian Thompson, the teacher, told me later that she had never seen any group of people as quiet and as sincerely in prayer as that class of children.

A Singing Religion

(Condensation of a sermon preached by Dr. W. C. Newman, May 23, 1954, First Methodist Church, Memphis, Tennessee.)

Christianity is a singing religion. Christianity is the only singing religion. There are other powerful religions in the world and always have been, but no great religion has ever been a singing religion except Christianity, and its ancestor, the Hebrew religion.

For, as we have done in many other realms, we have inherited from the Jews a rich treasure of Christian worship. And among the finest is the Book of Psalms, the hymnbook of the Jewish Temple in Jerusalem.

A singing religion differs from any other very largely, I think, in spirit. A singing religion indicates a happy religion. A singing religion implies beauty of worship rather than grimness of worship.

Other religions have made much of bloody sacrifices—Christianity has made much of song. Other religions have made much of gloomy prayers—Christianity has made much of great praise. And I suspect that we modern Christians, more than any others who have lived for a long time, have missed the melody of our faith. We sing, to be sure, but we do it almost as if it were an arduous duty. And as I watch you sing, Sunday after Sunday, I see in your faces, not only reluctance to sing some of the hymns that may not be familiar to you, but often a lack of the joyousness, the gaiety, the high praise that belongs to a singing religion.

This singing of our religion began far back in the dim past of the Jewish people. The oldest religious song recorded for us in the Bible goes back to the time of the Judges, but that song did not resemble Christian singing. It was grim and forbidding, a song of battle and

222

blood, a song of vengeance and hatred. It missed the whole point of Christian happiness.

But as the years came and went—and particularly as the Hebrew prophets got their great insights about God, and revealed them to the people—the songs took on a different character, until at last in the Book of Psalms, which covers a period of about 600 years of Jewish history, we have the highest hope, the noblest aspirations, the most eloquent praise and thanksgiving to be found in all literature.

This book of devotions, which has fed the spirit of man ever since the Bible came into the possession of the people, is much neglected in our day, largely because you have little time for Bible reading; and those of you who go through the motion of daily devotions prefer a little digest of a prayer and a Scripture that can be quickly read at the breakfast table. And while none admires such digests more than I do, I would be the first to say that they can never substitute for the deep and profound insights of the Bible itself. And in that Bible, no portion of it can so feed your spirit as can the Psalms.

Let me draw you a picture of a Sabbath Day in the Temple in Jerusalem. The people have gathered there from all about in a vast congregation; for to the Jews the Sabbath Day was indeed a holy day, meant for just one thing—the pilgrimage to the Temple, there to meet God and to adore Him.

This congregation waited with eager hearts, because they believed that at every service in the Temple, they would meet God—that God would be there and reveal himself to them.

Suddenly upon the silence that had prevailed, there would burst forth the sound of music. The three choirs of the Temple began their stately procession to the altar, singing as they went, to the accompaniment of harp and cymbal and flute and lyre, played by the chief musicians. They were followed by one hundred and twenty priests blowing upon their ram's horns.

Choir, musicians, and priests were dressed in robes of gorgeous colors and elaborate decoration. But this was something more than a formal ritual; this was not a performance. Music was not used for music's sake, but only for the purpose of praising God. Robes were not worn for the sake of dignity or show, but as a symbol of dedicated lives. And as the music caught hold of the hearts of the congregation, the Scriptures say, "The glory of God filled the temple."

How far we have departed from that high expectation, I do not need to tell you. When we come to church—let's be honest—you do want a beautiful and interesting service. You do want an exciting and

223

brief sermon. You do want to get out at twelve o'clock. You do want us to sing hymns that are easy and singable, whether or not they praise God worthily. But you would be most amazed if "the glory of God should fill the church."

It was not always so, and it ought not to be so at any time. The only purpose of coming to the house of God is to meet God, and have a revelation of Him, and let His glory fill the Temple and cling to us. The only purpose of music is that we shall find a more adequate expression of our adoration and thanksgiving, of our praise, of our needs, and of our hunger. To the extent that we have lost that purpose we have lost the radiance of our faith.

If you read the Book of Psalms carefully, you will find the most amazing variety of songs. There are songs for weddings, and songs for funerals. There are songs for days of planting, and days of harvest. There are songs for the dedication of the Temple, and the dedication of a child. There are songs of sorrow, and songs of joy. Any mood that ever comes to your heart in all your life can be matched by one of those wonderful songs of Israel.

Read the First Psalm, in which the psalmist draws a vivid contrast-picture of the ultimate end of the righteous and the unrighteous, in an astonishingly unique way. He does not say that men ought to be good because the Bible says so or, as some men suppose, because the good prosper. What he does say is that goodness is everlasting, and wickedness is perishable, that men ought to be good because by being good they themselves become sturdy and durable "like a tree." Is that a truth about life? If so, we had better grasp it.

When Abraham came into Palestine with his tents, and camels, and his people, men would have supposed that his name would never be widely known. A wandering gypsy, he never wrote a book, or conquered a nation, or acquired a monument. In that day, Egypt to the south, Babylon to the east, and Assyria to the north, were already ancient civilizations, and great states. In the next few hundred years, Egypt first, then Babylon, then Assyria, then Persia, then Greece, then Rome, arose to world power. Now all of them lie in the dust, impotent and forgotten except for the historian.

But Abraham and the First Psalm have proven to be more durable than the pyramids of Egypt, the giant statues of Babylon, the armies of Assyria, the classics of Greece, even the mighty empire of Rome. How can that be? It can be only because there is something that was enduring, something not "chaff which the wind driveth away."

I am interested in the psalmist's description of an ungodly man, because too often we think of a sinner as some sort of criminal. But see how deftly the psalmist paints the portrait of a sinner. A sinner is a man who walks in the counsel of the ungodly. By ungodly, he means only those who do not worship God. He is not talking about murderers or drunkards or reprobates; he is talking about upstanding and decent people who have no faith.

A sinner, he says, is one who stands in the way of wicked men; that is to say, having started out to walk in the companionship of the ungodly, he advances one step farther in his deterioration, and stops and talks to them, so that the association is fixed more tightly. And then at last, he sits down to talk with the scoffers.

The first class of people who help him to deterioration are the people without faith in God, harmless folk apparently, maybe very attractive people, maybe fine and honorable citizens, but nevertheless ungodly in the sense of having no faith, no God. The second class are the wicked, those who do positively evil things. And the third class are the people who not only do evil things, but have so lost conscience that now they scoff at goodness, scoff at God, and scoff at those who try to be good. This kind of man, lightweight, shallow-brained, with no depth of character, and with no nobility of aspirations, says the psalmist, is wafted away on the first wind that comes by, disappears, is gone. He is not burned up; he is just blown away, too light to last.

And over against that, he sets the righteous man. He is not a man who just keeps all the laws and goes to church and makes a prayer. He is a man who "delights in the law of the Lord," a happy man. No grim and arduous duty performer here, no joy killer, no puritan frowning upon the foibles of his fellows; but a man with a happy heart, and a glad faith, who delights in the law of God, and who day and night meditates in that law and joyfully obeys it.

His is the radiant faith, the singing religion. He has in his heart such joyous praise, such gay faith, that he goes to the business of being a Christian as one would go to a festival. A singing religion!

Music and Morals

Fritz Kreisler's conception of art: "To my mind, it all comes back to the conviction that musicianship is the most direct expression of personality. Thus, one way of perfecting musicianship is to conquer oneself, to rid oneself of meanness, to live the sort of life one can admire. The 'artist's life' in its best manifestation is anything but a round of fun, parties, and gaiety. It is a constant problem of values, a constant desire to be the person one wants to be. Certainly no one ever reaches his ideal, but the act of striving does something to the spirit that can never be lost."

The Music Program Reaches into the Home

There are very few homes without music, if it is no more than the indiscriminate blaring of the radio. But there are very few homes where music is used to strengthen the family ties. A family does not need to sing or play to be a musical family. Simply enjoying music together has value, and there is a great deal of music available for family enjoyment. Some of the best of it God gave us, and needs no radio or television for transmission. The song of birds, thunder, the wind in the trees, the rhythm of waves, of falling leaves, of waving branches—these are the musical birthright of all. Eyes that see, and ears that hear are the only requirement for enjoyment.

Couldn't your Primary Choir learn to recognize the birds of their area, and their songs? Couldn't they learn to recognize melodies by imitating bird calls? Couldn't you find pictures of the birds to paste in a scrapbook, or mount for the bulletin board?

Have you noticed that different species of trees make distinctive sounds when the wind blows through them? Wouldn't the children enjoy trying to recognize trees by their sound?

Shortly after I left for my first year in college, there was one of those rare phenomena—a thunder storm in California. My little brother ran into the house and announced to my mother, "They're moving trunks in heaven. I heard them." Perhaps the new arrivals were saints who on earth had helped children to hear and see.

Yes, there is plenty of music in the home, but mighty little "together music." The teen-agers dial the throb of jazz, the little tykes hunt out the gallop of westerns, and mother's favorite music is silence. Do you know of one program the family could enjoy together? If so, tell them about it, and help them to develop the fine art of occasional togetherness. Call their attention to the program, tell them something interesting about it, ask the children something about it at the next rehearsal. Give the choir advance information whenever possible, and encourage them to be the program commentator at home.

One of the most polished hosts I have ever known always has a background of very quiet, rather remote music for his dinner parties. There is just a chance that it might also have a commendable effect on the family dinner hour. What would you recommend to your church families for meal-time music?

226

In families where some or all of its members sing or play, there is no end to the opportunities for group enjoyment. The Trapp Family is a shining example of a large family united by music. The Larry Clarks of Anderson, Indiana, make car travel enjoyable by singing rounds. Before the two children even started school, they could hold their own in a four part round. One of the most delightful memories I have is of these two little tykes singing "Dona Nobis Pacem" in canon form before the summer school class in Green Lake.

Singing the familiar Christmas Carols together should be a part of the tradition of every church family. If no one plays, they can sing along with a recorded group. You might even make inexpensive recordings with your choir, and let the children take them home to use in the family celebration. Our daughter loved pageantry, and when she was little our celebration always started with a solo procession. She would light a candle and march about the house and around the tree with an expression of exaltation on her face, while we all sang the familiar carols. That is long since past, but it is a part of her heritage that she will never shake off, and one her parents will always cherish.

Is there any more restful pleasure than singing around an aromatic campfire in the darkness?

Those of our members who have carried the Festival of the Singing Church through consistently have found that the most gratifying response came from families that made a family project of learning the hymns.

A harmonica was the only instrument my father could play. It is a good instrument to have in the home. It has a good many simple virtues; it is inexpensive, easy to learn to play, can be carried around in the pocket, never needs to be tuned, is informal and homey, and serves adequately to accompany group singing. It is a good fireside instrument. If one is lying around the house, someone is sure to learn to play it.

A musical saw is fun, too. That is the instrument for the country home. Anchor the handle on the chair with your leg. Strike the steel with a soft hammer and holding the tip of the blade bend it to create the desired pitches. The more the saw is bent, the higher the pitch. It is the country cousin of the steel guitar.

There is one instrument that has more influence on the happiness of the home than all the others combined—the human voice. Tin horn and violin voices are definitely reflected in the family atmosphere. And that is an instrument every one of us is obligated to make as musi-

227

cal as possible. There are endless opportunities for the use of this instrument, if only in calling the children in from play. A familiar call or whistle will carry farther, and get better results than yelling.

An eight-year-old child struck near the truth when she wrote:

> "There is music in the swaying of the trees,
> There is music in the whispering of the leaves;
> Oh, all the world has music in it
> But there are very few who sing it."

As directors of children's choirs, shouldn't we be among the "very few who sing it"?

For help in improving the speaking voice, read "Put Your Best Voice Forward" in Reader's Digest of April, 1955.

For further suggestions on Music in the Home, read Chapter III in Edith Lovell Thomas' *Music in Christian Education*. Abingdon.

Are You Timid About Insistence on Regular Attendance?

Then fortify yourself with these statements by J. EDGAR HOOVER

Shall I force my child to go to Sunday School and Church? Yes! And with no further discussion about the matter!

Startled? Why?

How do you answer Junior when he comes to the breakfast table Monday morning and announces rebelliously, "I'm not going to school today." You know, Junior goes!

How do you answer when Junior comes in very much besmudged, and says, "I'm not going to take a bath." You know, Junior bathes!

How do you answer when Junior, threatened with illness, says, "I'm not going to take medicine." You know, he takes it!

Why all this timidity, then, in the realm of his spiritual guidance and growth? Going to let him wait and decide what church he'll go to when he's old enough? Quit your kidding! You didn't wait until he was old enough to decide whether or not he wished to go to public school and get an education; or until he could make up his mind as to whether he wished to be a clean person or not; or whether or not he wished to take the medicine that would make him well.

Afraid he'll succumb to the old wives' tale about "too much religion when he was young . . . parents made me go" sort of gag! Look about you; the story is demonstrably and obviously false, despite its currency. Do you suppose that because you insist over his protests that Junior take his bath tonight, he will turn into a "Bathless Groggins" when he's twenty-one?

Do you suppose that because you insist he take his medicine, he'll take up Christian Science ten years from now?

What shall we say when Junior announces he doesn't like Sunday School or church? That's an easy one. Just be consistent!

"Junior, in our house we all attend Sunday School and church, and that includes you." Your firmness and example here will furnish a bridge over which youthful rebellion may travel into rich and satisfying experiences in personal religious living.

The parents of America can strike a most effective blow against the forces which contribute to juvenile delinquency, if our mothers and fathers will take their children to Sunday School and church regularly.

From the *Church News* of the National Avenue Christian Church, Springfield, Missouri.

Parent Education—Indirect Method

A certain Junior department leader uses a committee of four children to help plan and present the weekly worship service. Membership rotates; each week one member is dropped and another one added. The leader collects the three experienced members in her car and takes them to the home of the new member for the committee meeting. She calls the mother beforehand and arranges for her to be present at the meeting. Sometimes the father drops in, too. This very simple plan accomplishes a great deal. Each week the leader becomes acquainted with the parents, the home, and the surroundings of one of her children. The parents have a chance to see how the church works with their children; frequently through this experience they become actively interested.

What works for a Church school department should work as well for a choir.

No Sundays?

Did you ever stop to think what life would be like without Sundays? It would be like forever pulling the heavy load of living up a steep grade without any downhills to rest you. Surely God must have made the Sabbath not only for rest for the body, but to give the better part of our nature a chance to grow.

Along country lanes the sounds of the Sabbath seem much different. Even the old rooster—with his crowing—seems to know the day is different. The birds in their music seem to sing a different key. There are sounds to delight the ear, which those who spend the day sleeping never come to know.

There are even those who till the soil that do not recognize Sunday as a day of rest. They go right on plowing, sowing, reaping, driving nails, hunting, or whatever comes to hand. Some even tell you, "The better the day, the better the deed."

But it does something to them. They lose so much more than they gain. They do not take time to obey the admonition, "Be still and know that I am God."

The parson tells the story of a farmer, writing a letter to the editor of a religious paper, saying that he plants, tills, and harvests his crops on Sunday, while his neighbors are at church, and yet he has better crops than they do. He challenged the editor to come up with an honest answer to that one.

And the editor placed his footnote below the letter: "Dear Sir: God does not balance His books in October."

So we may discover when we least expect it, that we have been robbed of something beautiful when we pass up a chance to make use of Sunday for "spelling" ourselves, as we used to do the heavily-laden horses while they were going downhill. Somehow the books always seem to get balanced.

From *Ozark Plain Tales* by FRED STARR

Tipping and Tithing

Now it came to pass on a day at noon that the Editor was a guest of a certain rich man. And the lunch was enjoyed at a popular restaurant. And the waiters were very efficient. And the food was good.

Now when the end of the meal was at hand, the waiter brought unto the host the check. And the host examined it, frowned a bit, but made no comment.

But as we arose to depart, I observed that he laid some coins under the edge of his plate. I know not what denomination the coins were, howbeit, the waiter who stood nearby smiled happily, which, being interpreted, means that the tip was satisfactory.

Now this parable entereth not into the merits or demerits of tipping, but as I meditated on the coins that become tips throughout our

230

nation, I began to think of tips and tithes. For the proverbial tip should be at least a tithe, lest the waiter turn against you.

And as I continued to think on these things, it came unto me that few people who go to church treat their God as well as they honor their waiter. For they gave unto the waiter a tithe, but unto God they give whatsoever they think will get them by.

Verily, doth man fear the waiter more than he feareth God? And doth he love God less than he loveth the waiter? Or doth the waiter do more for him than his God?

Truly, truly, a man and his money are past understanding!

Cadenza

One of the blessings of ignorance—I have much to be thankful for—is that many things wise folks have known for years come to you as an amazing, joyous surprise. I have just discovered one of the loveliest words in the dictionary. It is a beautiful word, with a beautiful idea set in it like a jewel. It is the word "cadenza" which I learn from the dictionary means "that portion of a concerto where the soloist is permitted to build some fanciful improvisations upon the straight musical facts that confront him."

I do not know how we could live without cadenzas, especially when the facts we are confronted with are pretty bare.

The cadenza is the refuge of childhood against a dull world of facts. Children as a tribe do not lie. They make cadenzas, "improvisations on the facts that confront them." On the street they see a bus or a dog. But what sort of food is that to nourish the emotional life of a child? So they do a little cadenza; they report seeing two grizzly bears, or on red letter days, a deer. With highly gifted children there is even sometimes an elephant. That adds to the joy of life.

Some foolish parents punish their children for such improvisations. They should be reported to the Society for the Prevention of Cruelty to Children.

Too many people seem to take as their life motto the words of the poker-faced detective in the Dragnet television program: "I want the facts, ma'am, just want the facts." So they live on facts and never bring any music out of life more thrilling than Chop Sticks.

There is an old story with a lot of wisdom to it about two cowboys who were snowbound for the winter in the mountains. Each had one book which he read continually. One had "One Thousand and One Interesting Facts." The other had Omar Khayyam. When spring came,

231

they went down to Texas and both courted the same girl. One would say, "Miss Louisa, did you know that the Brooklyn Bridge is 5,678 feet long?" The next night the other, drawing on his winter's study, would say: "A book of verses underneath the bough, a jug of wine, a loaf of bread and thou beside me singing in the wilderness—oh, wilderness were paradise enow!" Louise plunked for Omar. And wisely. He could do a cadenza on the facts.

Many people have lived in a town that was a collection of dreary facts—from the car window. But they have made improvisations, and have brought excitement and romance to life that was a lot truer than "the facts." Others have made lilting music that was not in the score of a grim and rugged job. Charles Lamb might have written the story of his life under the title, "Thirty Years on a Stool in the East India Office." Instead, he improvised on the facts and wrote immortal cadenzas.

Faith is really a cadenza. Here are the facts of St. Paul's life: "Often at the point of death . . . five times have I got forty lashes, three times have I been beaten by the Romans . . . once pelted with stones . . . starving many times, cold, and ill-clad . . . ."

Bleak facts! Here is the improvisation he made on the facts: "He makes my life a constant pageant of triumph!"

(If you would enjoy a whole book of interesting, amusing, thought-provoking cadenzas on life, I heartily recommend *Like a Mighty Army*, by Halford Luccock, published by Oxford University Press.)

Declaration of Faith

By DR. WARREN JOHNSTON, pastor of the First Methodist Church of Baton Rouge, Louisiana.

ONE of the things about my church that brings me the most satisfaction is its interest in young people. I like young people, and feel that they are the hope of the church. It is fine for a church to manifest interest in its youth and to make adequate provision for them; but it is equally important to understand the many ways in which they make a contribution to the church.

PERHAPS the most significant thing about them is the power of their idealism. No one takes a more vigorous outlook toward the Christian faith than they do. Once they have committed themselves to the Christian way of life, they have no patience with littleness and petty things. They help to keep the church Christian in spirit and idealistic in action.

232

ALSO HIGH on the list of their contributions are enthusiasm and a forceful way of taking hold of things. They see a Christian idea that ought to be put into practice, and they want to do it right away, whether it is practical at the moment or not. I admire their zeal even when I might not agree with their judgment.

YOUNG PEOPLE give to the church the fine gifts of friendliness and laughter.

I AM GRATEFUL for their naturalness, their straightforwardness, for their directness that borders on rudeness. I am glad that this generation has no time nor inclination for pretense or affectation. One of the evidences of their wholesomeness is that they have so few inhibitions in their religious practices.

THEIR ACTIVITIES remind me that the program of the church is a full-time business, something that should be going on all the time, not just on Sunday. Throughout the week, our Youth Center is abuzz with craft classes, choir rehearsals, devotionals, planning groups, Church school classes, inter-church and inter-faith meetings, parties, sports, and many other activities.

YOUNG PEOPLE also make a very personal contribution to ministers, teachers and other leaders. They bring them the tremendous sense of satisfaction in seeing youth develop as Christian persons. They keep them on their toes, and alert to responsibility. They keep the minister from becoming a stuffed shirt.

SUNDAY AFTER SUNDAY it stirs something deep within me to see the young people kneel for our Altar Prayer Service. I have a renewed sense of their basic goodness, of their almost unlimited possibilities. To me, this voluntary act is a very real demonstration of the reality of their Christian faith and life.

Ten Little Choristers

Ten little choristers, standing in a line,
One didn't like the leader, then there were nine.
Nine little choristers stayed up very late,
One slept Sunday morning, then there were eight.
Eight little choristers on the road to heaven,
One took the lower road, then there were seven.
Seven little choristers got in an awful fix,
One didn't like the music, then there were six.
Six little choristers seemed very much alive,

But one lost her interest, then there were five.
Five little choristers, wishing there were more,
But they quarreled with each other, then there were four.
Four little choristers, cheerful as could be,
But one lost his temper, then there were three.
Three little choristers knew not what to do.
One joined a sporty crowd, then there were two.
Two little choristers—our tale is almost done—
Differed with each other, and then there was one.
One lone chorister won his neighbor true,
Brought him to rehearsal, then there were two.
Two earnest choristers, each won one more,
That doubled their number, then there were four.
Four sincere choristers worked very late,
But each won another, then there were eight.
Eight splendid choristers, but nothing rhymes with sixteen.
So simply note that in seven more jingles there would be one
thousand and twenty-four choristers—which would be
quite a choir!

Apologies to V. L. Smith, and the *Bulletin* of the Pine Street Methodist Church, Williamsport, Pennsylvania.

Hymns and Hymn Study

Another New Year

Whatever other objectives we may have, let us during this season adopt the universal one of stimulating congregational singing. Starting *now*, let us all lead our congregations into the habit of hearty and meaningful singing. By directing our efforts intelligently and consistently, we should by the close of the season be able to celebrate a "Festival of the Singing Church." The hymns to be used in this nation-wide project were the ones most frequently to appear in your lists of ten basic hymns.

Great periods in church history have always been characterized by great hymn singing. The general inertia of present-day congregational singing is significant. Whatever the cause, as church musicians we have a share in the responsibility for attempting a cure. Unless singing is a joyous, stimulating, unifying experience, it might better be eliminated from the service.

But with our united efforts we may be able to make the congregational singing of good hymns a reality, and a vital factor in church life. *Let's try!*

The Festival of the Singing Church

This is an educational project in which every one of us can share. Whether your people sing well or poorly, you can encourage active participation and family interest in hymn singing. The emphasis should be enjoyment rather than obligation. As each hymn is intro-

235

duced, give the children bright colored mimeographed folders including the words of the hymn, or the hymn itself (if it is not copyrighted), and the hymn information and quiz similar to those suggested elsewhere.

Perhaps it could be arranged to have a short hymn sing before the regular Church school session. Appointing a hymn leader for each department would make good use of much talent that may now be unused or unrecognized.

Churches that are accustomed to open the evening service with a hymn sing would profit by a definite program of learning.

Have a poster contest, and encourage classes, choirs, departments, families, to enter the contest. Use impartial judges: the city librarian, an advertising man, a newspaper man, or an artist. Put a different poster on display every week.

Plan for a family night in late spring when the posters will all be on display and the prize awarded.

Look for anthems and organ pieces based on the Festival hymns.

Use the church bulletin to maintain and increase congregational interest. Each week use a short paragraph on the order of the two suggested here:

"It is a fine art to say 'Thank You' graciously and sincerely. We have many reasons to say 'Thank You' to God. *Last Sunday* you sang 'For the Beauty of the Earth' together. Some of you recognized it in the organ prelude. *Today*, let us use it as a responsive service of thanks to God for His boundless gifts. Perhaps you will hear the tune (Dix) once again before you leave the church."

"Open your hymnal to No. . . . . . It is the second of our Hymns of the Singing Church. When the choir enters the sanctuary, throw back your shoulders and sing with them, 'May Jesus Christ Be Praised.' Hearty singing is the ideal Sunday exercise—for the body, for the mind, and for the spirit, too. May Jesus Christ be praised through *me*."

Making Hymn Learning Church-wide and Year-long

Learn One Hymn a Month

Teach it to the children.
Use it in various ways in the service—
Hymn prelude; call to worship; call to prayer; anthem; offertory.
Publish interesting bits about it in the church bulletin.

Encourage Church-wide Interest

Ask the adult classes to use the new hymn.
Organize an essay contest.
Encourage families to learn the hymns together.
Send copies of the hymns home with the children.
Plan a family night; have fun with games and contests based on the hymns.

Climax the Year with a Festival

Use all the hymns learned.
Use all the choirs and the congregation.
Join with other churches that have shared in the hymn study.
Plan a festival service that will sweep people into joyous participation.

Keep a Record

Of organ music based on these tunes.
Of ways families have used the hymns.
Of original ideas you have had on learning the hymns or popularizing the project.
Of reaction of the congregation.

> Blest is the church whose people join in song,
> Harmonious hearts make congregations strong;
> Music, God's gift, to God's own uses bring,
> Let every soul rejoice, rejoicing sing!

Evaluation of Our Hymn Study Program	Yes	No
Does it reach the whole of the church school?		
Does it encourage a love of singing?		
Does it encourage the church to think of hymn singing as an act of worship?		
Does it train the children to sing with physical and mental vigor?		
Does it follow a well-planned learning program?		
Does it start at the level of the children's appreciation?		
Does it make the historic background of the hymns interesting?		
Does it make the learning of hymns a guide to Christian living?		
Does it capture the imagination of the children?		
Does it make opportunity for varied use of the hymns learned?		
Is the plan carried out with originality?		

Let's Have a Festival Week for the Singing Church

Morning Worship Service—
> Use as many of the hymns as possible
>> Hymn Prelude
>> Call to Worship
>> Call to Prayer
>> Anthem setting
>> Special Setting for the Offertory
>> Select all congregational hymns from the festival list

For the Bulletin
> Have an essay contest: "How our family learned the festival hymns," or, "I Like a Singing Church."
> Offer a prize for the best essay by an adult; by a child.
> Present a harmonica to the child who learned to play the most hymns with one finger or otherwise.
> Present a hymnal to the family that produces the oldest hymnal, or the largest variety of hymnals.

For Family Night
> A Spelldown. Divide into two sides; each family has one representative. One side starts with the first line of a hymn, other side must carry on with the second line, and so on. Person missing must drop out.
> A Display of Hymnals.

238

A Hymn sing. Each table in turn starting a new hymn.

Table covers: Paper, with a border of hymn tunes, put on with crayons.

Name It. Have organist play one phrase of a hymn (other than the first phrase). Contestants must write or sing the first line of that hymn. Prize to the person having the largest number correct.

Read prize essays, and award the prizes.

Contest: Most original family performance of a selected hymn.

Take flash pictures for release to papers.

Sunday Evening

A Festival combining the choirs of all the churches that have shared in the Festival of the Singing Church. Make it as brilliant and joyous as possible, using instruments, choirs, and congregation.

Rules for Congregational Singing

By JOHN WESLEY

Learn *these* tunes before you learn any others; afterwards learn as many as you please.

Sing them exactly as they are printed here, without altering or amending them at all; and if you have learned to sing them otherwise, unlearn it as soon as you can.

Sing *all*. See that you join with the congregation as frequently as you can. Let not a slight degree of weakness or weariness hinder you. If it is a cross to you, take it up, and you will find it a blessing.

Sing *lustily*, and with good courage. Beware of singing as if you are half dead or half asleep; but lift up your voice with strength. Be no more afraid of your voice now, nor more ashamed of its being heard, than are those who sing the songs of Satan.

Sing *modestly*. Do not bawl, so as to be heard above or distinct from the rest of the congregation, that you may not destroy the harmony, but strive to unite your voices together so as to make one clear melodious sound.

Sing *in time*. Whatever time is sung, be sure to keep with it. Do not run before nor stay behind it; but attend close to the leading voices, and move therewith as exactly as you can; and take care not to sing *too slow*. This drawling way naturally steals on all who are lazy; and it is high time to drive it out from among us, and sing all our tunes just as quick as we did at first.

239

Above all, sing *spiritually*. Have an eye to God in every word you sing. Aim at pleasing Him more than yourself, or any other creature. In order to do this, attend strictly to the sense of what you sing, and see that your heart is not carried away with the sound, but offered to God continually; so shall your singing be such as the Lord would approve of here, and for which He will reward you when He comes in clouds of heaven.

Waldo Seldon Pratt on Standards of Church Music

The following statements are by Waldo Seldon Pratt, one of the first American scholars to have a concern for Protestant church music.

"Sacred music can never exercise its full functions among those who are never more than passive listeners to it."

"It is far better to spend money for a skillful player of tunes, and limit the music to hymn singing, than to sacrifice the latter for elaborate choral work or organ recitals."

Standards for an organist:

He should be sensitive to the text, if possible studying it in its original format as a poem.

He must cultivate all the techniques for adequate rendition of the tunes.

He must be a leader, as opposed to an accompanist.

He should know why he is playing it at one or another tempo.

Organ Music Based on Hymn Tunes

Ten Hymn Tune Fantasies. McKinley. H. W. Gray.
Italian Hymn, "Come, Thou Almighty King."
Melcombe, "New Every Morning Is Thy Love."
Mendon, "Great God of Nations, Now to Thee."
Hamburg, "When I Survey the Wondrous Cross."
St. Catherine, "Faith of Our Fathers."
St. Theodolph, "All Glory, Laud, and Honor."
Munich, "O Word of God Incarnate."
Dominus Regit Me, "The King of Love My Shepherd Is."
St. Clement, "The Day Thou Gavest, Lord, Is Ended."
Amsterdam, "Rise My Soul and Stretch Thy Wings."
Seven Chorale Preludes. Purvis. Carl Fischer.
Ton-y-Botel; Forest Green; Liebster Jesu; Austria; Tallis Canon; Mercy; In Babilone.

240

Chorale Preludes on Hymn Tunes. T. Tertius Noble. Arthur Schmidt.
St. Ann, "O God, Our Help in Ages Past." Rockingham.
Dundee.   Stracathro.
Picardy, "Let All Mortal Flesh Keep Silence." St. Kilda.
"Fairest Lord Jesus." Greener. Ed. Schuberth Co., 240 W. 55th St.,
New York.
"A Meditation on Brother James' Air." Drake. Oxford University
Press.

Sample Letter to Be Sent to All Church Families

Dear Friends:

Will you accept this personal invitation to become a part of our
plans for a Festival of the Singing Church? We are joining with
churches from coast to coast to revive the fine art of congregational
singing.

The children in the Church school are planning to learn a dozen
well-known hymns by heart. The choir children are competing to see
how many more than twelve they can learn during this season. Can
you sing twelve hymns through without once referring to your hymnal? If so, you can easily learn twelve more. If not, you will never
start younger. No excuses! When we are too old to learn, we are too
old to live.

Does your family sing together? If you have never tried it, you
might be surprised to find it a happy practice. A priest coined the
phrase, "The family that prays together, stays together," but we would
like to add: the family that sings together, *enjoys* staying together.

The first memory hymn in our Festival of the Singing Church
will be introduced next Sunday. If you listen closely, you will hear it
in the prelude. Later in the service we will sing it, and the children
will have copies to bring home. Perhaps you can sing it together at
the breakfast table. And even if you can't carry a tune in a basket,
you can add to your treasury of uplifting thought by learning the
poem.

It is as true of churches as it is of families: The Church That Sings
Together Clings Together. Will you help make this year for our
church a Festival of Joyous Song?

Cordially yours,

FOR THE BEAUTY OF THE EARTH

"But, Mommy, why do we thank God for our food? I helped you wheel it in the Super Market." In a way Bobby is right. The first time most boys and girls see food is in a can or box in a big store. But youngsters who live on thousands of American farms know better. Back of the can and the box, back of the manager and the clerks, are God's helpers in the natural world: sun, rain, soil, air, seed; as well as human helpers like the farmers. Sometimes we take being thankful for granted. Sometimes boys and girls in some churches say a "General" Thanksgiving, a prayer for all God's goodness. But I know a hymn that helps you remember all the wonderful definite every-day things for which we are thankful. Maybe you know it too. It is by an Englishman with an odd name: Folliet Pierpont. Just say together:

"Lord of all, to Thee we raise
This our hymn of grateful praise."

Let your choir director or your father say the stanza beginning:

"For the beauty of the earth,
For the glory of the skies,
For the love that from our birth
Over and around us lies."

Look it up in your Hymnal. There are usually seven (or less) stanzas. Count how many different things Mr. Pierpont mentioned that we ought to be thankful for. I found twenty-eight in my Hymnal. Have one of the choir members say each stanza, then all join in singing the lovely refrain. This is fun at a picnic as a sung grace. Or maybe your pastor will use this hymn as a pastoral prayer some Sunday. He will SAY all the stanzas as his part of the prayer, and we will all sing the responses. You will like the moving, singable tune called DIX. Perhaps for your notebooks, you will have a guessing contest and see who can be first to discover what the author meant by the words about the church:

"Offering up on every shore
Her pure sacrifice of love."

He had something very definite in mind. Can you guess what it was?

A. H.

It takes two to make a good hymn: the poet and the composer. Did you know that a hymn always has two names: the word name and the tune name? The tune name of this hymn is ....

Make a list of the things for which this hymn gives thanks.

. . . .

. . . .

. . . .

. . . .

. . . .

How many are there? . . . .

Is there something else for which you are especially thankful?

Can you express it in a stanza of your own?

. . . .

. . . .

. . . .

"When Morning Gilds the Skies"

Did you ever watch mother bake a cake? She follows a rule book and uses what we call a recipe. If she uses baking soda instead of baking powder the chocolate cake will taste funny. Or if dad is building something in the carpenter's shop, he must follow the pattern carefully. A good hymn has a pattern, too. Sometimes you can see it on the printed page without singing it. Look up that stirring German hymn you all like: "When Morning Gilds the Skies." Do you see the pattern? Of course, there it is, the repeated phrase, "May Jesus Christ Be Praised." You can lift out the two places where they come in each stanza and sing them all by themselves. One time it is made up of short notes. Then come the white notes, each held for two counts. Either sounds nice. This hymn makes you get up with a smiling face, even in the early morning. Just hum it the next time you get up on the wrong side of the bed. I like the stanza about the church bell. Isn't it fun to lie in bed and hear the bells calling some Christians to early church? There's a big bass one way over in town . . . Boom . . . Boom . . . Boom; then an alto one near by: Bong . . . Bong . . . Bong . . . Bong. If you are fortunate enough to live near a carillon, you can hear all the bell voices singing out a joyous anthem: "May Jesus Christ Be Praised." Ask your organist to play the bass and tenor parts. How they march along, never stopping. Always sing the hymn with clear voices, don't drag it. It makes a grand processional. The original German hymn had 14 stanzas and appeared in 1828. Try this one for grace at meals:

> Be this at meals my grace
> In every time and place:
> May Jesus Christ be praised.

243

Or to begin choir practice, sing.

> My tongue shall never tire
> Of chanting in the choir
> May Jesus Christ be praised.
>
> This song of sacred joy
> It never seems to cloy,
> May Jesus Christ be praised.

Note how the tune, Laudes Domini (you Latin students may translate) moves up like the rising sun with brightness and strength. You see, even a good hymn tune has its own pattern.　　　　A. H.

Do you know where to find the tune name of a hymn? You will find it right under the title. The name of this tune is Laudes Domini, and means ....
....
There are several words dad or the dictionary will have to help you understand.

"To Jesus I *repair*" means ....

"In this your concord find" means ....

"My canticle divine" means ....

"O Beautiful for Spacious Skies"

Miss Bates taught English at Wellesley College, and she kept a parrot. But we keep her memory alive because of one hymn she wrote. It is almost as popular as "America." In school or church you have probably joined in singing: "O Beautiful for Spacious Skies." How wonderfully clear the chorus swells:

> "America, America, God shed His grace on thee,
> And crown thy good with brotherhood
> From sea to shining sea."

Miss Bates had no idea that her poem would be used at the Inauguration of President Eisenhower, marched to by thousands of service men, and sung over a national hookup to celebrate Fourth of July. She was just a quiet teacher, but she taught us all something about unselfish patriotism. She went on vacation; she saw the amber waves of grain and the Rocky Mountains, and she never forgot them. They lived in her memory until they inspired this poem.　　　　A. H.

A. H. stands for Rev. Alfred B. Haas, Associate Professor in the Department of Practical Theology, Drew Theological Seminary, Madison, New Jersey, and member of the Hymn Society of America, who makes these hymn reviews his generous contribution to the *Festival of the Singing Church*.

"Rejoice, Ye Pure in Heart"

Rejoice on one note! In my hymn book it is a D. The sopranos lift it up and hold it, while the basses climb up the scale. I like that one note chorus. Who said Christians were grumpy people? Certainly not choir members, who have more fun than most anyone else, and learn while having fun. Choir practice reminds me of a recent movie, "The Happy Time." It can be, and usually is. Well, this hymn of the Rev. Edward Plumptre was written for a church parade, or perhaps we had better call it a procession. It was to be sung at a choir festival at Peterborough Cathedral in England in 1865.

Why should the firemen have all the parades? Think of a lovely May in England. Out of the Choir School near the Cathedral come many men and boys. In the front are the national and church flags. Then comes the crucifer (boy carrying the cross), proudly carrying a large beautiful brass cross. Hear the words, "Lift high the cross of Christ. . . . Your glorious banner wave on high, The cross of Christ your King." You may not have a processional cross, but you do have a church flag, with the red cross on the blue field. Use it on special days, and sing this great hymn of joy. The man who wrote the music was an Englishman, too, only he adopted America by becoming organist and choirmaster at Trinity Church, New York. It's the grand old church at the head of Wall Street. Mr. Messiter's tune, Marion, is always used for this hymn, and I think you will enjoy practicing a processional with it. How about a grand processional *outside* the church on a sunny day in June to close the year's work? Let your town know you have a wonderful group of choirs. Let's have a parade!   A. H.

How will you introduce these hymns to the congregation?

Make a list of the different ways they can be used in the service

Do the children know the meaning of the texts?

How many of the beauties of America are familiar to them?

How will you present the thought that America's "good" should be "crowned with brotherhood"?

Can you create an opportunity to use "Rejoice, Ye Pure in Heart" in a festive procession?

What have you done to arouse a congregational interest in the learning and singing of new hymns?

Have you managed to make the whole church conscious of this program?

245

"O Come All Ye Faithful," "Silent Night"

One wonderful quality of hymns is that they unite people rather than divide; they belong equally to everyone. "O Come All Ye Faithful" is at home in all churches, whether Catholic or Protestant; it is as comfortable in the mission church as in the cathedral. Nobody knows who wrote either the words or the music. The original poem was Latin, and there have been at least 38 translations. The tune appeared out of nowhere, and got its name—Portuguese Hymn by mistake. In 1785 the Duke of Leeds, who was a director of the "Concerts of Ancient Music," heard it in a chapel in Portugal. Thinking it was known only in that country, he programmed it in his next concert as "Portuguese Hymn." Long before the words and music ever appeared together in print, they were copied by hand for use in church homes. And at Christmas time Christian families still continue the custom. O come, let us adore Him, Christ the Lord.

Suppose our organ should refuse to play on an important Sunday? It happened in St. Nicholas Church in Oberndorf, Austria, in 1818, just when a new song was to be learned by the congregation at the Christmas Eve service. The young priest of the church had written the words. His friend, the village school teacher and organist at St. Nicholas, had composed the music. But it did not matter too much that the organ could not be used. Herr Gruber had written the music for two solo voices, chorus, and guitar—and that is the way it was first sung that Christmas Eve. Visitors to the village heard it, and carried the simple tune throughout Germany. Like a stone thrown into water, the circles of "Silent Night" widened until it is today heard around the world—the present of a young priest and his friend, the village organist. There is a profound simplicity about the music of "Silent Night." More than any other hymn or carol, it suggests the lowly birthplace, the lowing cattle, humble shepherds, the watching mother, the sleeping Infant. The thoughtful singing of "Stille Nacht, Heilige Nacht" will help you understand what Christ's Mass really means, and you will begin to know what the One whose birth we celebrate meant when He said, "Unless you become as little children. . . .   A. H.

Imagine a little church in a little German village on Christmas Eve. Everything was ready for the Christmas celebration; the minister had written a beautiful new song and the organist had written the music for it. And then suddenly the organ just wouldn't play. Do you think that stopped the celebration? No, sir. The organist played the song on his guitar, and everybody learned the song and loved it. And ev-

246

erybody has loved it ever since. "Silent Night, Holy Night" was the song. Most people call it their favorite Christmas song. Is it yours, too?

"O Little Town of Bethlehem"

Though the newspapers at times belie it, Philadelphia is the City of Brotherly Love. When Christmas warms our hearts, this is more noticeable, even in Philadelphia. The young rector of Holy Trinity Episcopal Church in Philadelphia was sent to Palestine in 1865 and on Christmas Eve of that year, stood outside the little town of Bethlehem. On his return to his church, he wrote for the Sunday School Christmas celebration this hymn which has become America's gift to the songs of Christmas. The superintendent of the Sunday School was also the church organist, Lewis Redner. Between Phillips Brooks, the young rector, and Lewis Redner there was a perfect understanding, and a strong friendship, just as there is a perfect understanding between the words and the music of "O Little Town of Bethlehem." During December, the last stanza—the prayer—will be used as our choral introit. Learn it by heart. Sing it from the heart. It is the perfect collect prayer for Christmas, and one will never tire of hearing it if he *prays* it as the choir sings it.   A.H.

How would you like to spend Christmas Eve far away in Bethlehem, where Jesus was born? That is just what Phillips Brooks did, and when he got home he wrote a song about what he felt and saw. Read "O Little Town of Bethlehem" carefully.

Can you tell what he saw? ....

How did he feel to be in that holy place at that holy time? ....
....

Have the words of the three hymns and the following notes mimeographed on an attractive folder for the children to take home.

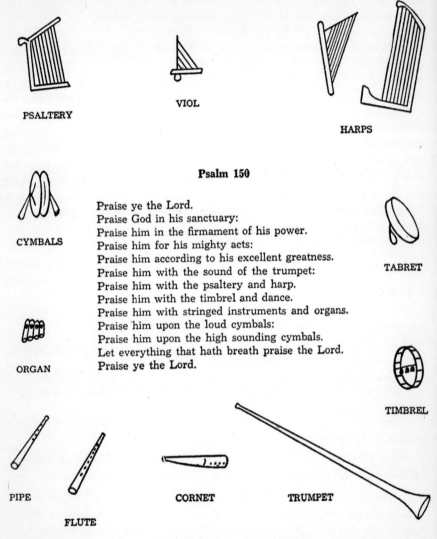

PSALTERY

VIOL

HARPS

CYMBALS

ORGAN

TABRET

TIMBREL

PIPE

FLUTE

CORNET

TRUMPET

Psalm 150

Praise ye the Lord.
Praise God in his sanctuary:
Praise him in the firmament of his power.
Praise him for his mighty acts:
Praise him according to his excellent greatness.
Praise him with the sound of the trumpet:
Praise him with the psaltery and harp.
Praise him with the timbrel and dance.
Praise him with stringed instruments and organs.
Praise him upon the loud cymbals:
Praise him upon the high sounding cymbals.
Let everything that hath breath praise the Lord.
Praise ye the Lord.

Long, long ago, when King David wanted to sing his praises to God, he wrote Psalm 150. Notice how every line begins with "Praise him." And when the Hebrews sang Psalm 150 in the Temple at Jerusalem, they used all the instruments they knew, along with a choir of several hundred voices.

248

"Joyful, Joyful, We Adore Thee"

When Beethoven wanted to praise God in a very special way, he wrote the Ninth Symphony, using all the instruments of the orchestra. Then for the very end he added a choir of many voices.

Joyful, joyful, we adore Thee, God of glory, Lord of love;
Hearts unfold like flowers before Thee, Praising Thee their
sun above.
Melt the clouds of sin and sadness; Drive the dark of doubt
away;
Giver of immortal gladness, Fill us with the light of day.

All Thy works with joy surround Thee, Earth and heaven
reflect Thy rays,
Stars and angels sing around Thee, Center of unbroken praise;
Field and forest, vale and mountain, Flowery meadow, flash-
ing sea,
Chanting bird and flowing fountain, Call us to rejoice in Thee.

Thou art giving and forgiving, Ever blessing, ever blest,
Well-spring of the joy of living, Ocean-depth of happy rest!
Thou our Father, Christ our Brother, All who live in love are
Thine:
Teach us how to love each other, Lift us to the Joy Divine.

Mortals join the mighty chorus, Which the morning stars
began;
Father-love is reigning o'er us, Brother-love binds man to
man.
Ever singing march we onward, Victors in the midst of strife;
Joyful music leads us sunward In the triumph song of life.

Henry Van Dyke wrote these words that we sing to Beethoven's music. It is called the "Hymn of Joy." Can you tell why?

On page 248 you have pictures of the instruments in David's orchestra. Can you find pictures of modern instruments?

When you sing this "Hymn of Joy," imagine that all these instruments are playing it with you. If you use it for a processional hymn, march tall and straight, and sing as the hymn tells you to—*joyfully.*

TRUMPET	PICCOLO	CLARINET	FLUTE
OBOE	BASSOON	ORGAN	
HARP	VIOLIN	CELLO	BASS VIOL
CYMBALS			DRUMS

249

"O Worship the King"

Sir Robert Grant wrote a dozen hymns. We sing only one of them, and it is both beautiful and popular. Based on the majestic account of God's creative power in Psalm 104, "O Worship the King" is filled with moving poetry and vivid imagery. Note the account of the rain in stanza 3 which is good science as well as lovely poetry. Sir Robert was born in India, and became Governor of Bombay in the era of Britain's power of Empire. A member of a famous Aberdeen family, he was not Presbyterian but Anglican, and came under the warm evangelical influence of the Methodist movement.

Lyons is a fitting tune by the brother of Joseph Haydn. Dr. H. A. Smith in *Lyric Religion* says this tune should be sung in a style akin to the free rhythm of the old plain-song. "They should not be sung with hurry-up, catch breath liveliness, but in the free, hearty traditional style."

Note how Sir Robert calls God names in the last stanza, working into a moving Christian climax. "Our Maker" that's seen in the Creed, maker of heaven and earth; "Defender"— that's evident in the Old Testament accounts of a Covenant God caring for His people, defending what He has created; "Redeemer"— here enters the New Testament with its emphasis on the love of God Who "buys back" what has been lost; "and Friend"— think of Jesus' words in John 15: "I have called you friends." Into this noble word the Christian tradition pours even greater meaning. The God we know in Christ, "the King all glorious," is unto us an understanding Friend.   A. H.

"Where Cross the Crowded Ways of Life"

"In 1737 a Saxon clergyman published a universal song book in which songs were to be found for christenings, marriages, and other family events; others appropriate for difficult lawsuits, for lameness, blindness and deafness, or for the affliction of having too many children, and for noblemen, ministers; for the officials, lawyers, barbers, bakers, fishermen, teamsters, merchants, apprentices, and many other professions and requested songs for clowns, tight-rope walkers, magicians, thieves and rogues." From *The Chorale Through Four Hundred Years* by Lieohn. Muhlenberg Press.

But today we have become a brotherhood of man, and our hymns have meaning for all, whether magician, fisherman, teamster, or lawyer.

250

Take any fair-sized city in America, stand at the busiest intersection in town, and read the words of Frank Mason North's hymn. They seem to fit any center of teeming life. Dr. North wrote this hymn while working in New York. Every day, enroute to work, he passed Union Square. Here in the region close to the garment center and the Eastside tenements he watched the throngs of hurrying people, and heard the harangue of soapbox orators. He recalled Jesus weeping over Jerusalem, the New York of His world. He saw wretched families crowded into small rooms, selfish merchants "selling the needy for a pair of shoes," as Amos put it. Read the hymn with the eye of your imagination, and you can see the sordid life of a great city pass before you in parade. But note the last two stanzas; they intercede on behalf of all. They call out to the Christ who knows what is in men's hearts, and still loves them. They call to us also, so to live that Christ's kingdom may grow in human hearts.

Though other tunes have been used, William Gardner's tune, Germany, seems to fit best. In that fascinating book on hymns by H. Augustine Smith, *Lyric Religion,* there is a picture of William Gardner, the stocking manufacturer: "He was a funny little figure, and had a funny way of going half shambling and half trotting, and he seemed in a crablike fashion always to be following his nose, that member being twisted out of the straight. But in his love for great music, he was a prophet calling out of the darkness, and I think there must be living some amateur musicians who owe their first acquaintance with the works of the great masters to Billy Gardner."   A. H.

"O Master Let Me Walk with Them"

Have you ever noticed that most of our hymns are prayers? They invoke God, or Christ, or the Holy Spirit. They teach us to pray together, and may often be read as prayers in group meetings. Close choir practice by reading a stanza of a profound prayer-hymn. Use selected stanzas as prayer responses or introits (sometimes I call them prayer vestibules, introductions into the Holy of Holies). Dr. Washington Gladden wrote such a prayer. This American pastor, whose church, First Congregational, still ministers to the people of Columbus, Ohio, was a farm boy, born in the little town of Pottsgrove, Pennsylvania. He said this hymn was "an honest cry of human need, the need of divine companionship." Note how the abstract theological virtues of patience, faith, trust, hope, peace are made warm and understandable by Dr. Gladden's description of what they bring to life. The line, "Work that keeps faith sweet and strong," has profound significance.

The tune Maryton was written by Canon Smith for "Sun of My Soul." The music quietly adores the text, reveals the words, is not ostentatious, and helps us to pray this prayer in humility and sincerity.

A. H.

For the Children

Give the children mimeographed copies of the words of "O Master let me walk with Thee" and "Where cross the crowded ways of life."

On the blackboard write the rhythmic patterns of the two hymns:

Play the melody of "Where Cross the Crowded Ways of Life"; ask the children to tell which one of the two patterns on the board it matches.

Let one volunteer point out the rhythm, and all clap it while you play it through a second time.

Read the words together, or let individuals read one stanza each.

Now let's see how the words and the music fit each other. Sing first stanza only.

What is the time signature of that tune?

How about the other one? Both ¾.

Who can tap the second one? Look at it carefully, then raise your hand if you think you can do it without a mistake. (One or two volunteers tap.)

Let all clap the rhythm while the most proficient one taps it on the board.

252

Now I am going to play a tune, and I want you to tell me if it is exactly like that pattern, or different in spots. Watch carefully.

Read for the children the first stanza of "O Master, Let Me Walk with Thee. Now suppose we all read those words while I play the music that belongs to them. (Read the words in the rhythm of the tune.)

I believe you almost know that tune already. Let's see if we can *sing* the words to the music now.

When you get home, ask mother and daddy if they know these hymns.

I wonder who is going to get a star for memorizing one of them by next rehearsal. (This should take 15 minutes at the most.)

Can You Name it?

Each week, either write on the board, or clap the rhythm of one or two of the hymns already studied. Who will be first to recognize the hymn. The first to guess it may clap another familiar one.

"When I Survey the Wondrous Cross"

Tune: Hamburg

Sir Thomas Abney was a wealthy member of the Mark Lane Congregational (Independent) Chapel in London. He liked the pastor of the Chapel, the Reverend Isaac Watts, and invited him to dinner at his country seat. Mr. Watts came to dinner and stayed thirty-six years! It was rather similar to the patron idea, the wealthy person providing the facilities for literary work. Sir Thomas made the right choice, for Isaac Watts not only has a memorial in Westminster Abbey, but a living memorial in the singing churches of the Christian world. This little man, in ill health most of his life (though one would never guess this by reading his hymns) made it possible for you and me to sing hymns instead of the Psalms. Under the influence of John Calvin, English churchmen were permitted to sing only the Bible words of the Psalms in metre. While some noble metrical psalms resulted, it was a severe limitation. Watts believed Christians ought to sing not only the praise of God as revealed in the Old Testament, but His glory as revealed in Christ. What was worse, the tunes were abominable. At the early age of 15, Watts rebelled against them. When he complained about the singing in the church service, his father urged: "Give us something better, young man." He did, that very day, by writing a hymn. He became the bridge over which English singing passed from

253

the Psalms in metre to the hymns we inherit today. Some have said that the amazing work of the Wesleys in the field of hymn writing could never have been accomplished without the foundations laid by Dr. Watts. As a child Watts often spoke in a versifying manner. When scolded by his father who said he would whip him if he continued, the lad replied:

> "O father do some pity take
> And I will no more verses make."

But we are thankful that he did make more verses, and Christmas never arrives without Watts singing with us:

> "Joy to the world, the Lord is come!
> Let earth receive her King."

to Handel's stirring tune.

We can never have a festival celebration thanking God for His goodness except Watts helps us with his:

> "O God, our help in ages past,
> Our hope for years to come."

Take up any good book on hymnody and read about Isaac Watts. You will be amazed at the richness of his life, and be moved to exclaim: "There were giants in the earth in those days."

As Lent approaches, you will be asked to use the hymn we chose for our study: "When I Survey the Wondrous Cross." Another English poet, Matthew Arnold, called it one of the greatest poems in the English language. Watts wrote it at the age Jesus died on the cross— 33. Its original line is stronger as Watts wrote it: "Where the Young Prince of glory died." It is so profoundly simple that, like the New Testament account of the crucifixion, it stirs one deeply, not by a superficial sentimentality, but by genuine emotion aroused by contemplating the tragedy that became the world's hope. It becomes a master sermon on a great theme, done very quietly in four stanzas.

"All Glory, Laud, and Honor"

Tune: St. Theodulph

Give the children a copy of the words for their notebooks. In rehearsal, sing first half of each line, and let them finish it. On Palm Sunday, use as processional hymn, with trumpet fanfare interludes, or as an anthem, with violin or flute on the second stanza (as in the original Bach setting). Oxford University Press, Church Music Reprints number 17a.

254

"Praise the Lord, Ye Heavens Adore Him"

Tune name: Hyfrydol
Composer: Rowland Pritchard (1811-1887)
Text: Foundling Hospital Collection, 1796

Praise the Lord, ye heavens adore Him,
Praise Him, angels in the height;
Sun and moon, rejoice before Him;
Praise Him, all ye stars of light.

Praise the Lord, for He hath spoken
Worlds His mighty voice obeyed;
Laws which never shall be broken
For their guidance He hath made.

Praise the Lord, for He is glorious;
Never shall His promise fail;
God hath made His saints victorious,
Sin and death shall not prevail.

Praise the God of our salvation,
Hosts on high, His power proclaim;
Heaven and earth, and all creation,
Laud and magnify His name.

Text: The immensity and the complexity of nature is the surest proof of God. The birds follow the laws of migration; trees, of growth and fruiting. What would happen if the sun and moon failed to follow the laws of the universe?

Composer: Rowland Pritchard came from Wales, a hymn-singing country. Those of you who have seen "How Green Was My Valley" have a picture of Pritchard's background. He wrote this hymn while he was still in his teens. All his life he was a choir singer, first as a choir boy, and then as a preceptor of the boys. The name Hyfrydol was undoubtedly given this tune because of its Welsh origin.

The choir room should be equipped with a large world map for the study of hymns. Let the children locate Wales. Explain that hymns have names, just as boys and girls do. The composer is like the father, and the tune names are the names of his children. Have the children look in the Hymnal for other Welsh tune names. They will look for rather long names with lots of consonants.

Author: Foundling Hospital was an orphans' home, founded in London by a sea captain in 1739. In those days there were no laws protecting children, and many of them were abused and deserted. At one time there were 600 children at the Foundling Hospital. Many

255

wealthy people helped to support it, and the king gave $15,000 to help build a chapel. Handel gave them the organ, and every year until he died conducted a performance of his "Messiah" to raise funds for the school. The chapel was generally so crowded that the ladies (this was the day of hoop skirts) were asked to wear small hoops, and the men to come without swords, to make room for more people. This hymn was pasted in the back of the chapel hymnal that the boys and girls used. No one knows who wrote it.

The films, "The Mudlark" or "Oliver Twist" paint a realistic picture of the neglected children of England in earlier days. There are thousands of unhappy children in the world today, too—the homeless in Korea, the war orphans in Europe, the poor in our own cities, and the children with so much that they never learn how to say "Thank You." Children with good homes and thoughtful parents should not only be grateful, but show their gratitude. What can they do? Encourage specific suggestions. Is there something that the children of the choir can do together as an expression of their gratitude? Could we remember this week to thank our parents and friends for the many kind things they do for us?

Memory Verse: "O Lord, how manifold are thy works! in wisdom hast thou made them all. The earth is full of thy riches."

First Week: Learn the tune; give the children copies of the words and the memory verse.

Second Week: Discussion of tune name, and composer.

Third Week: Discussion of author.

Fourth Week: Use as an anthem. An arrangement by Malin, published by Birchard, is available in S.A.B., also S.A.T.B. with children. C. Fischer also has an arrangement, number OCS—1557.

"For the Beauty of the Earth"

In England, it used to be the custom on a special Sunday in late summer, to hold a flower service. Everyone brought the loveliest flowers from his garden to the church. The whole church was decorated with flowers, and the choir boys carried an armful of them in the procession. After the service the flowers were taken to hospitals and to old people who had no gardens of their own.

Some of our Choristers' Guild choirs are bringing this custom to our country. The boys and girls in the choir each plant and care for some spring flowering bulb. Then, about Easter time, when all the bulbs are in bloom, they hold a special service, carry their own flowers in the procession, and after the service take them to some friend or invalid. They have had the fun not only of bringing pleasure to someone, but of helping God to create the beauty of the earth.

Folliet Pierpont wrote this hymn for such a service. He mentions many of the things for which we can thank God, just as we would, if we were to make a list here in rehearsal. We would mention things just as they came into our minds; read the words of the hymn, and notice all the things for which we raise our hymn of grateful praise.

Can you add others? Suppose you keep your eyes open this week to the beauty of the earth, and at the next rehearsal bring one little thing that you have noticed. We will have a large table just inside the door, and you may arrange your exhibits there in any way you like. Who would like to paint the motto to go over the table?

The tune we use was adapted from a chorale tune. Now chorale is a word every choir member should know, because it was the first music created by the Protestant church. When Martin Luther was a young priest, several hundred years ago, the music in the Catholic Church was so difficult that only a very good choir could sing it. Luther thought the people should have a chance to sing, too, so he and some of his friends thought of and wrote hymns that would be easy to learn and to sing, and that would sound good if lots of people were singing them together. They called these hymns chorales, and the people loved singing them so much that some of them are in almost every hymnal even today. Some of the best known chorales are: "Now Thank We All Our God"; "Praise to the Lord, the Almighty"; "O Sacred Head, Now Wounded"; A Mighty Fortress." You can imagine how they would sound with several hundred people singing for all they are worth, and the organ adding still more.

When you sing the words "Lord of all, to Thee we raise this our hymn of grateful praise," shut your eyes and imagine yourself in a big, big church full of people all singing joyously along with you.

"All Creatures of Our God and King"

Tune: Lasst uns erfreuen

This hymn was written by a man who probably was more nearly like Jesus than any other person who has ever lived. His name is Saint Francis of Assisi. He gave up his fortune, his beautiful home, his friends, and his life, to help the poor and the sick and the people that nobody else cared about. He wandered about the country, just as Jesus did, preaching and comforting the sick, and loving the people that nobody else loved. He was one of the poorest, and the happiest, men that ever lived.

Saint Francis wrote this hymn, all about praise and happiness and thankfulness, when he was almost blind, and so sick that he could hardly sit up. When Saint Francis died, it is said that even the song of the birds was sad. The people of Assisi, his little hometown in Italy, built a beautiful big church in his honor. And if you should ever visit Italy, you could worship there, because it is still standing, although it was built more than seven hundred years ago.

The name of the tune is German. It means "Let Us Be Glad." It is a happy tune, because it was written as an Easter Alleluia. About the time that the Pilgrims were coming to America, this Easter tune was printed in a German hymn book. When people were looking for a tune that would be able to express the happiness of Saint Francis' words, they chose "Let us be glad" (Lasst uns erfreuen). I don't think they could have found a better one. Do you?

Make a list of the things in nature mentioned in this hymn.

....
....
....
....

Saint Francis believed that animals, and clouds, and stars, and flowers all praised God. How could they?

....
....

You can praise God too. How?

....
....

258

"Now Thank We All Our God"

Now thank we all our God
With hearts and hands and voices,
Who wondrous things hath done,
In Whom His world rejoices,
Who from our mother's arms
Hath blessed us on our way
With countless gifts of love,
And still is ours today.

O may this bounteous God
Through all our life be near us,
With ever joyful hearts
And blessed peace to cheer us;
And keep us in His grace,
And guide us when perplexed,
And free us from all ills
In this world and the next.

All praise and thanks to God
The Father now be given,
The Son, and Him who reigns
With them in highest heaven:
The One eternal God,
Whom earth and heaven adore;
For thus it was, is now,
And shall be evermore.

This is a hymn of thankfulness. It is one of the best known and best loved hymns. Many churches use it regularly in their Thanksgiving services. In Germany it is sung on all great occasions, such as the dedication of a new church, or a great public building. I suppose every Sunday School boy and girl in Germany knows it by heart, and in many homes it is sung as a grace at table. If your mother and father know this hymn, or if you can teach it to them, you could sing it together too sometime, perhaps when you sit down to your Sunday dinner.

If you think that Martin Rinkart wrote "Now thank we all our God with heart and hands and voices" because he had everything he could possibly ask for, you are mistaken. I wonder if we could sing this hymn and mean it, if we had the kind of life Martin Rinkart had.

When he graduated from school, he went back to his home town, Eilenberg, to be the minister. He had hardly gotten settled when war broke out. Because Eilenberg was surrounded by thick walls and heavy gates, people from all the villages around fled to it for protection. People had no place to live, and before long the food supply gave out. Finally people were not only hungry, but starving, and would fight like wild animals for a crust of bread. With starvation came a plague, and in one terrible year, Martin buried more than 4,000 people. He was the only minister left alive. He and his family were starving, too, but instead of yielding to complaining, Martin was the one to whom everyone turned for courage and comfort. And when, at the end of the Thirty Years' War, peace was finally declared, Martin wrote this hymn. Sometimes it is the people who seem to have the least, who know best the meaning of thankfulness.

"The God of Abraham Praise"
Tune: Leoni

Nobody knows where this tune came from, but you can find it hiding in Jewish and in Russian music, and in the music of Spain. When the Czech composer, Smetana, wanted to describe the Moldau, a beautiful river in his country, he used the tune in this rhythm:

In Jewish synagogues the Hebrew doxology, always sung at the beginning of the morning service, and at the close of the evening service, uses the same tune, but in sounds like this:
The Precentor sings:

and the congregation answers:

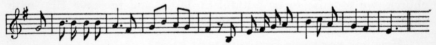

One time Thomas Olivers visited a great synagogue in London. He heard the Hebrew doxology sung by a precentor named Meyer Leoni, who had a big, beautiful voice that filled the whole sanctuary. Thomas thought, "What a wonderful hymn that would make," so he made an English poem out of the Hebrew words. The tune was called "Leoni" in honor of the singer who inspired Thomas.

"The God of Abraham Praise" is a wonderful hymn for a festival; the more people singing, the better it sounds.

260

Do you know what these words mean?

Doxology ....

Synagogue ....

Precentor ....

"Rise Up, O Men of God"

Rise up, O men of God! Have done with lesser things,
Give heart and soul and mind and strength To serve the King of kings.

Rise up, O men of God! His kingdom tarries long.
Bring in the day of brotherhood And end the night of wrong.

Rise up, O men of God! The Church for you doth wait,
Her strength unequal to her task; Rise up, and make her great!

Lift high the cross of Christ! Tread where His feet have trod;
As brothers of the Son of Man, Rise up, O men of God!

This hymn is about courageous Christians. When we join the church, we promise to be faithful to Jesus, and to serve Him with "heart and soul, and mind and strength."

How will you serve Him with your *heart?* ....
....

How can you serve Him with your *mind?* ....
....

A boy spends his Saturday mornings getting the groceries, and cleaning the yard for an invalid neighbor. He is serving Jesus with

his ....

261

There are lots of courageous Christians today, living exciting and happy lives because they are doing what they think Jesus wants them to do.

There is a couple that adopted seven Korean orphans, and are bringing them up in their own home.

A very rich young man has studied medicine, and is building a hospital for the poor people of Cuba.

If you keep your eyes open, you will learn of other people who find being a Christian an exciting experience.

It could be that something special has been waiting for *you* to come along, and do it.

"Ye Servants of God"

Ye servants of God, your Master proclaim, and publish abroad His wonderful Name; The Name all-victorious of Jesus extol; His kingdom is glorious and rules over all.

God ruleth on high, almighty to save; and still He is nigh, His presence we have; The great congregation His triumph shall sing, ascribing salvation to Jesus, our King.

Then let us adore, and give Him His right, all glory and power, all wisdom and might, All honor and blessing, with angels above, and thanks never ceasing for infinite love.

These are the four phrases of this hymn tune. Do any of the four have the same melody?

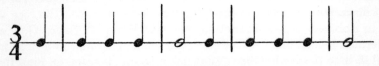

This is the rhythm of the first phrase.

Make just one change and you have the rhythm of the second phrase.

262

Write the rhythm of the third phrase on this line. . . . .

Is the fourth the same as the third, or different? . . . .

What do we mean by the *infinite* love of Jesus? . . . .

In gratitude for the infinite love of Jesus for us, what does this hymn say we should give Him?

Then let us adore, and give Him His . . . . ,

All . . . . and . . . . , all . . . . and . . . . ,

All . . . . and . . . . with angels above,

And . . . . never ceasing for *infinite love.*

"In Christ There Is No East or West"

In Christ there is no East or West, In Him no South or North,
But one great Fellowship of Love Throughout the whole wide earth.

In Him shall true hearts everywhere Their high communion find.
His service is the golden chord Close-binding all mankind.

Join hands, then, Brothers of the Faith, Whate'er your race may be!—
Who serves my Father as a son Is surely kin to me.

In Christ now meet both East and West, In Him meet South and North,
All Christly souls are one in Him Throughout the whole wide earth.

It is very easy to think that we are better than other people. It is hard to feel at home with people who live on the other side of the world, or the other side of town, and perhaps speak a different language. But we can learn. A young American paratrooper in the last war learned the hard way to be grateful to all kinds of people. He was shot down over enemy country. His legs were crushed. His face was cut to ribbons. A poor French farmer found him. A Negro G. I. and a German helped him. A Catholic priest smuggled him to a field hospital in time to save his life. A Jewish surgeon operated on him, fixed his leg, and rebuilt his face. He came back to himself in an English hospital. And that is why he says his home will always be open to all kinds of people—every day, not just on special occasions.

Jesus had little patience with people who considered themselves better than others.

Read Matthew 5:43-48. What did He mean?

Read Matthew 9:9-13. Why did the Pharisees criticize Jesus?

Read Luke 10:30-37. What did the priests and Levites think of the Samaritans?

Read Luke 18:9-14. What was the difference between the prayer of the Pharisee and the tax collector?

Do you have any foreign students in your school? Have you invited them into your home? Do you keep people out of your gang just because they are different?

"O Come, O Come Immanuel"

Before Jesus was born, the Jews were constantly at war with their neighboring countries. Many times they were conquered and taken away as captives. For a long time they were kept as slaves in Egypt. Their prophets kept telling them that sometime there would come a leader who would rescue them from their captivity.

The Jews thought that this savior would come soon, and prayed every day, "O come, O come, Immanuel, And ransom captive Israel." Israel was the name they called their country. So sure were they that their prayers would be answered, that after their prayers they would say to each other, "Rejoice, Immanuel will surely come."

There are several things you will be interested to know about this hymn.

1. It is called an ADVENT hymn, because it is about the coming of Jesus. Christmas hymns are about His birth.

2. In some hymnals, you will find this sign above the hymn: 8,8,8,8,8,8. That means that it has six lines of poetry, and there are 8 syllables in each line. Let's see if the numbers are right. Count the syllables in each line.

O come, O come, Im-man-u-el	. . . . . .
And ran-som cap-tive Is-ra-el	. . . . . .
That mourns in lone-ly ex-ile here	. . . . . .
Un-til the Son of God ap-pear	. . . . . .
Re-joice, re-joice, Im-man-u-el	. . . . . .
Shall come to thee, O Is-ra-el	. . . . . .

3. The first two stanzas were written in Latin, about 800 years ago. The third stanza was added much, much later. Only in modern times have people begun to think of the *whole world* as one family. We are just beginning to realize that God cares for all people, all

264

races, all nations, and that we must learn to do so, too. Fill in the missing words of this stanza.

> Bind ...... nations in ...... heart and mind; bid
>
> envy, strife and ...... cease; fill the ....
>
> with heaven's ....

4. The tune of this hymn is almost as old as the Latin words. In fact, it comes from the time when music had no tune at all. It was called *plain* song, because it was almost like talking on one pitch. If you sing the first stanza very slowly, you will notice that at the end of each line there is something like a little melody on just one syllable. That was the way our church music began, by adding a little melody at the end of a very *plain* phrase. In your hymnal, you will probably have a sign like this: ⟋ to mark the end of the chanting and the beginning of the melody.

RIGHT OR WRONG

1. This is a Christmas hymn. ....

2. All three stanzas were written in Latin. ....

3. The tune is very old. ....

"O Lord of Heaven and Earth and Sea"

1. O Lord of heaven and earth and sea, To Thee all praise and glo - ry be,
2. For gol - den sun-shine, ver - nal air, Sweet flowers and fruit Thy love de - clare;
3. For peace-ful homes, and health-ful days, For all the bless - ings earth dis - plays,
4. To Thee, from whom we all de - rive Our life, our gifts, our power to give.

How shall we show our love to Thee Who giv - est all?
Where har-vests rip - en, Thou are there Who giv - est all.
We owe Thee thank - ful - ness and praise Who giv - est all.
O may we ev - er with Thee live Who giv - est all.

There are only two words in this hymn that you may not know.

Vernal means ....; *derive* means ....

265

The first stanza is a question. How would you answer it?

....

....

Can you imagine what kind of world this would be, if nobody ever wanted to share anything with anyone else?; if God had not given us "the power to give"?

If no one were willing to give, would there be any churches? Any hospitals? Any missionaries? Any homes? Make a list of things that depend on our power to give.

....

....

....

....

....

....

This melody is built around one note, which is called the *key-note*.

Draw a red line *under* it, whenever it appears in the alto line.

Draw a red line *over* it, whenever it appears in the soprano line.

How many times does it appear in the song? ....

On what note does the melody end? .... What is this note called? ....

"Faith of Our Fathers"

Faith of our fathers! living still In spite of dungeon, fire, and sword,
O how our hearts beat high with joy Whene'er we hear that glorious
word:
Faith of our fathers, holy faith! We will be true to thee till death.

There were Christians who were thrown into dungeons because they would not be untrue to their faith. Can you name one?

....

266

There were Christians who were burned alive because they would not deny their religion. Can you name one?

. . . .

There were Christians who died by the sword, rather than give up their religion. Can you name one?

. . . .

You, too, are a Christian. Do you think you could be as courageous as these?

Faith of our fathers, we will strive To win all nations unto thee;
And through the truth that comes from God Mankind shall then indeed be free.

What are some of the things that Jesus taught that would help to bring peace and freedom to the world, if we really practiced them?

. . . .

. . . .

Faith of our fathers, we will love Both friend and foe in all our strife,
And preach thee, too, as love knows how, By kindly word and virtuous life.

Is there someone at school whom you dislike? Could you make yourself be as good to him as you are to your best friends?

Can you make yourself say something kind, when you would much rather be nasty?

What does it mean to live a virtuous life? . . . .

. . . .

Why is it hard to live a virtuous life? . . . .

. . . .

When we sing this hymn we are making a promise to be true to our religion, no matter what people might say about us, or do to us. It is a hard promise to make. It is a hard promise to *keep*.

"Come Ye Thankful People, Come"

Here are three 4/4 rhythmic patterns.

No. 1 is very easy. CLAP IT.

No. 2 is just like No. 1 except for one place. Underline the place that is different. CLAP IT.

No. 3 is just like No. 2 except for one place. Underline the place that is different. CLAP IT.

Can you clap all three without a mistake?

Our hymn, "Come, Ye Thankful People, Come," is made up of these three phrases.

As your pianist plays each phrase slowly, see if you can tell whether it is No. 1, 2 or 3.

Write the number in the box beside the phrase.

1. ☐ Come ye thankful people come

2. ☐ Raise the song of harvest home

3. ☐ All is safely gathered in

4. ☐ Ere the winter storms begin

5. ☐ God, our Maker, doth provide

6. ☐ For our wants to be supplied

7. ☐ Come to God's own temple, come

8. ☐ Raise the song of harvest home.

Write the rhythmic pattern of the first two phrases on this line.

Write the rhythmic pattern of phrases 5 and 6 on this line.

What have you discovered? ....

Now compare 3 and 4 with 7 and 8. They are: the same.........
different .... Now compare the first half with the second half.

They are: the same .... different ....

268

This hymn is found in almost all hymnals. On what page is it in your hymnal? ....

In the *New Hymnal for American Youth* (Appleton-Century Company) there are a second and third stanza you will want to learn; also a descant you might try.

"Now The Day Is Over"

Now the day is over, Night is drawing nigh,
    Shadows of the evening Steal across the sky.

Jesus, give the weary Calm and sweet repose;
    With Thy tenderest blessing May their eyelids close.

Grant to little children Visions bright of Thee;
    Guard the sailors tossing On the deep blue sea.

Comfort every sufferer Watching late in pain;
    Those who plan some evil From their sins restrain.

When the morning wakens, Then may I arise,
    Pure and fresh, and sinless In Thy holy eyes.

Sir Robert Jones was a very fine orthopedic surgeon. His home was in Liverpool, England. He loved children, and they all loved him in return. The children on whom he had operated would wait patiently for his evening visit at the hospital, and when he left they would sing this hymn, with an extra stanza that they had made up especially for him.

"Give the children's doctor calm and sweet repose;
    With the children's blessing may his eyelids close."

Have you ever noticed how quiet nature becomes just as the sun goes down? The tune of this hymn is very quiet too.

This tune has only 5 different pitches.
How often is this one repeated?
This is almost a one-note hymn.

Sing the first two measures. Now sing the last two.

When you have learned the whole tune, see if you can sing it alone while your director plays the alto part. It makes an interesting duet.

This is the alto melody. Perhaps you could teach it to someone at home.

Doxology

Praise God from whom all blessings flow;
Praise Him, all creatures here below;
Praise Him above, ye heavenly hosts;
Praise Father, Son, and Holy Ghost. Amen

The Doxology is sung in most churches every Sunday.
Is it sung in your church? .... At what point in the service?.....
The words are adapted from Psalm 148.
Which verses of the Psalm speak of:

all creatures here below ....

ye heavenly hosts ....

THESE TWO SINGING GRACES ARE SUNG TO THE SAME TUNE

Be present at our table, Lord,
Be here and everywhere adored;
Thy children bless, and grant that we
May live in fellowship with Thee. Amen

For all the glories of Thy Way,
For Thy protection night and day,
For roof and warmth, and bed and board,
For friends and home, we thank Thee, Lord. Amen

Grace: "A short prayer, in which a blessing is asked, or thanks rendered at a meal." Webster's dictionary.

There are many ways of saying grace.

The Roman Catholic crosses himself.

Others bow the head, and say grace silently.

Sometimes the father or mother says grace for the family.

Sometimes the members of the family take turns.

Sometimes the whole family sings a grace.

Sometimes they join hands around the table, and sing a grace.

What is the custom in your family?

Can you write an original Grace to this same tune? Try it.

It would be easier if the whole family helped.

. . . .

. . . .

. . . .

. . . . Amen

The Spirit of the Leader

GREAT ENTHUSIASM, GREAT DEVOTION

It is not the critic who counts; not the man who points out how the strong man stumbled, or where the doer of a deed could have done better. The credit belongs to the man who is actually in the arena; whose face is marred by dust and sweat and blood; who strives valiantly; who errs and comes short again and again, because there is no effort without error and shortcoming. It is the man who does actually strive to do the deeds, who knows the *great enthusiasm*, the *great devotion*, who spends himself in a worthy cause, who at the best knows in the end the triumph of high achievement, and who at the worst, if he fails, at least fails while daring greatly, so that his place shall never be with those cold and timid souls who know neither victory nor defeat.

THEODORE ROOSEVELT from *The Liberator*

Great enthusiasm and great devotions. What are yours? Do you respect them, or apologize for them? Some people are sure to laugh at the thought of attempting the impossible. But there is always someone else who needs just such an example to start him climbing after his own ideal with renewed devotion.

My enthusiasm is to live to see a national Children's Choir Center with a training school and a beautiful little chapel, and a model children's choir to record music that will be available at minimum cost to all churches and all directors; a place where children's choir directors

273

can come for a few days or a few weeks any time in the year to renew their devotion and rekindle their enthusiasm. Impossible? Perhaps so, but—perhaps *not.*

Happiness Is Not a Gift

Happiness is not a gift; it is an achievement.

"What a Great Privilege Is Mine"

Albert Schweitzer says, "If you are called on to play or sing at a church service never forget that you are accorded one of the greatest privileges, one more beautiful than to attend the most brilliant concert.

"Your attitude should be a deeply religious one, otherwise there will be neither piety, appeal nor sympathy in your harmonies—your music will be dead.

"Do not permit anyone about you to converse in church, neither should you yourself hold conversation.

"Every Sunday on awakening, say to yourself, 'What a great privilege is mine.' "

Discouraged?

Have you lost that enthusiasm that kept you going last fall? Is the indifference of the choir parents pulling you down? Are the children becoming careless?

Is that little trouble maker getting the best of you?

Doesn't the church appreciate you?

Do you wish you could drop the whole business?

Sooner or later, we all feel like that, but luckily most of us get over it. And so will you! If not, the choir is better off without you. No situation is without its problems; there is no growth without some pain. And there is no problem without some solution.

Why have you lost your enthusiasm? Probably because you have lost sight of your objective. You must always have something to get excited about, and you must always be wholeheartedly enthusiastic about something. If you have no such objective, create one. Without exception, the choir's attitude is the reflection of the director's attitude. So if the children are apathetic and you are discouraged, look to yourself. Look for some all-engrossing, some challenging, new purpose.

Are the parents indifferent? What have you done to challenge their interest? Do they know how much you depend on their co-operation, or do you just expect them to know. Do you consult the

274

parents when the children enter the choir? Do you call them when the children are absent? Do you ask their assistance in promoting choir projects? Do you give them the responsibility and the credit for specific tasks? Do you set the enthusiastic ones to influence the indifferent ones? Do you work consistently and intelligently at the job of maintaining interest?

And those problem children? Isn't it usually the children you like least who cause you the most trouble? We claim that we dislike them because they are so unruly. But could it be that they are unruly because we dislike them? Children are clairvoyant. They know what your heart says, no matter what your lips say. They want to be sure of three things: that you expect the best they have to offer; that you have faith in them; that they can count on you. On that basis, there is always a solution.

Doesn't the church appreciate you? "Fame and accident are seldom synonymous. Those people in any walk of life who enjoy popularity over a prolonged period of years have invested vitality and energy, with their fullest measure of intelligence and talent, in careers which a willing public accepts as gifts. *As long as that vitality* continues to nourish the mind and spirit of the great audience, it will stay in a prominent position."

Do you want to drop the whole business? Maybe what you really want is a little vacation to respark your spiritual batteries. Take a day off, or a week, and do that extra special something you never quite found time for. Go out in search of *happiness,* and when you find it, share it with your choir. But if you can't take a vacation from your responsibilities, Dr. William L. Stidger has another plan:

"Here is a formula for happiness which is unfailing. I found it in an old musty book I picked up in a secondhand book shop in Boston. Alice Freeman Palmer, the second president of Wellesley College, tells it:

One hot July morning I left my country home and went into a hot Settlement House in Boston, where I found a crowd of poor girls from the slums, each caring for a baby with a few to spare.

The temperature was around one hundred with a heavy, humid atmosphere. Every child was disheveled and dripping with sweat; so was I. I wondered how I could possibly say anything that would interest them that hot morning.

"Now," I said, "what shall I talk about this morning, girls?"

Up spoke a small, pale-faced, heavy-eyed child with a great fat baby in her arms: "Tell us how to be *happy*." The tears rushed to my eyes, and a lump to my throat.

"Well," I replied, "I'll give you three rules for being happy; but mind, you must all promise to keep them for a week, and not skip a single day."

So they all faithfully promised.

"The first rule is that you will commit something good to memory every day. It needn't be much, three or four words will do; a pretty poem, or a Bible verse. Do you understand?" Yes, they understood.

"The second rule is: Look for something *pretty* every day: a leaf, a flower, a cloud—you can find something. Isn't there a park somewhere near here where you can all walk? (Yes, there was.) And stop long enough before the pretty thing to say: 'Isn't it beautiful?' Can you do it?" They promised to a girl.

"My third rule is: Give something of yourself; or do something for somebody every single day—and never miss a day."

What a trilogy for happiness: To commit something beautiful to memory every day; to look for something beautiful every day; to give something to somebody every day: yourself, your material things, your talents, as Mrs. Palmer did on those hot mornings; as those young girls did. That is an unfailing formula for happiness."

Take Time for Ten Things

(From a Church Bulletin)

1. Take Time to Work.
   It is the price of success.

2. Take Time to Think.
   It is the source of power.

3. Take Time to Play.
   It is the secret of youth.

4. Take Time to Read.
   It is the foundation of knowledge.

5. Take Time to Worship.
   It is the highway of reverence, and washes the dust of earth from our eyes.

6. Take Time to Help and Enjoy Friends.
   It is the source of happiness.

276

7. Take Time to Love.
   It is the one sacrament of life.
8. Take Time to Dream.
   It hitches the soul to the stars.
9. Take Time to Laugh.
   It is the singing that helps with life's loads.
10. Take Time to Plan.
    It is the secret of being able to have time to
    take time for the other nine things.

And then—take time to express your thanksgiving for your ability to work, and think, and play, and read, and worship, and help and love, and dream, and laugh, and plan.

"Mirror, Mirror, Tell Me True"

Are you enthusiastic?

Do you really enjoy your work?

Are most of your pupils interested and eager?

Do you set a definite goal for each pupil and work toward it?

Do you have a sense of responsibility toward your pupils?

Do you encourage them to ask questions and express themselves?

Do you help and encourage creative work?

Do you always praise or reward sincere effort of any sort?

Do you go out of your way to help and to advise pupils?

Do your pupils voluntarily come to you for advice and conference?

Do you especially like children?

Are you genuinely interested in your pupils?

Are you acquainted with the parents of your pupils, and do you occasionally visit their homes?

Do you receive parents' co-operation in securing adequate preparation for lessons?

Do you greet your pupils with a cheerful smile?

Do you often laugh and joke with them?

Are you fair minded, giving every pupil a square deal?

Are you sympathetic?

Do you honestly try to see things from the pupil's viewpoint?

Do the lesson periods pass quickly?

Do you accept obstacles and hard knocks as a challenge?

When your path is blocked by some difficulty, do you devise a way of overcoming it?

Are you constantly on the alert for new teaching material and new methods?

Do you spend at least an hour a day in study and practice?

Do you take advantage of master classes or workshops that come to your region?

Do you take at least one music course each year on subjects in which you need brushing up?

Do you honestly try to hold your interest in the less talented pupils, working with them as hard as you do with the more gifted ones?

Are you a member of any organization of music teachers, or do you have teacher friends with whom you discuss mutually helpful matters?

Do you constantly vary the teaching material you use?

Is your rehearsal room neat, clean, attractively and conveniently arranged?

Is it well lighted?

Are windows and doors adjusted to give the best possible ventilation?

Is your general appearance—posture, dress, and so on—good?

Is your voice musical, and do you enunciate clearly?

Do you maintain an even disposition during the rehearsal?

Are you there in time to arrange all materials before rehearsal?

Do you start on time, and dismiss promptly?

Do you avoid all interruptions during rehearsal?

Do you have the right size chairs for the children?

Do you keep your records, reports and roll book up to date?

Do you have a bulletin board, well filled at all times with attractive and interesting material?

Does each child have a notebook?

Do you keep good books and magazines on music in a prominent place, always accessible to the children?

Do you subscribe to one or two music magazines?

Does your enrollment steadily increase?

Does your work advertise itself?

Do you plan your rehearsal one week in advance?

Do you try to find the individual needs of your students; or put them all through the same routine?

278

Do you teach convincingly, authoritatively, being able to back up your statements with sound reasons?

Do you insist on musical quality, whether in exercise or song?

In your criticism, do you first speak of the good features, and when pointing out defects, show clearly how they can be remedied?

Do you emphasize the imaginative qualities of the music, by frequent word-pictures of the mood of the piece?

Do you make it a point to teach some musical fact or term at each rehearsal?

Do you devote a part of each rehearsal to some musical activity or rhythmic game?

Do you originate or try out new methods of teaching—do you experiment?

Do you let your children *hear* good music at each rehearsal?

Do you insist that all anthems sung publicly be done as musically as possible, and from memory?

Do your pupils attend class regularly, and on time?

Is the routine of passing music, etc., so organized as to be done without delay or confusion?

Do you make use of your blackboard at each period?

Do you keep each child busy *all* the time?

Do you give some ear training, harmony or rhythmic drill at each period?

Do you call on children frequently for their own criticism of the work?

Do you pleasantly insist on strict discipline and good behavior in class?

Do you give time outside the class to pupils who need extra help?

Is your procedure so carefully planned that all the necessary work is covered in each period?

Adapted from Guy Maier's personal evaluation test for piano teachers. The *Etude.*

Do It Well

Teaching is becoming increasingly simple, and at the same time increasingly complex, for the emphasis is changing from the teaching of assorted specific facts, to the teaching of children. Facts to be learned are not isolated in a vacuum of experience, but childhood experiences are made the anchor to which necessary knowledge is fastened. Intelligent choir directors are adopting the same techniques with their choirs. Children learn best when they are most interested, and they are most interested when all their resources are brought to focus upon a given project. Learning becomes enjoyable when it provides an opportunity to do, to feel, to see, to hear, to create, as well as to sing.

Such an approach demands a great deal more time and thought in preparation, but the response is worth it. The old adage, "When a task is once begun, Never leave it till it's done; Be the labor great or small, Do it well or not at all," may be old-fashioned philosophy, but it still holds true for our day. We are helping to build a new world. It can't be done in our off hours.

What Teaching Is

Education does not mean teaching people what they do not know. It means teaching them to behave as they do not behave. It is not teaching the youth the shapes of letters and the tricks of numbers, and then leaving them to turn their arithmetic to roguery, and their literature to lust. It means, on the contrary, training them into the perfect exercise and kingly continence of their bodies and souls. It is a painful, continual, and difficult work to be done by kindness, by watching, by warning, by precept, and by praise, but above all—by example.   JOHN RUSKIN

A Fresh Start

It may be true that "All's well that ends well," but any venture that *begins* well has a better chance to end well. With September, choir directors will all be determined to start the new season intelligently. A successful season demands enthusiasm, but it also requires that enthusiasm have intelligent direction. If we are to be intelligent about our plans, we will take into consideration the factors that govern our situation, and will direct our efforts accordingly. Whatever our problems are, we cannot ignore them, nor expect them to solve themselves. Our job is more than selecting music and teaching it to a group of children for occasional performance. That is only a part of our basic purpose: to be an influential factor in establishing high standards of church music and participation, developing strong Christian character, and strengthening the church as a whole.

There is more than one road to Rome, and if you have your destination clearly in mind, you will get there, even if you have to detour from time to time.

280

You are not the only traveler on the road. Sometimes it helps to know that others get travel weary, too. Why not have occasional meetings with other directors this winter?

Rome was not built in a day—but it can be destroyed in a day. You are building a generation; that takes time, and consistent courage.

You are working with people—not things. Others may have just as many and as strong convictions as you have. Try to see their point of view. You accomplish more by winning than overpowering. Are the children indifferent; do the church school teachers, or the parents, or the minister fail to co-operate? Why not discuss the situation openly with all those who should share the responsibility of the music education of the church?

Dr. Whittlesey invited his pastor, organist, music committee chairman, a layman and a parent to such a meeting. Everyone was free to speak his mind. Out of that meeting came the following valuable suggestions, which a number of other directors have copied for distribution in their churches.

IF I WERE A PASTOR I WOULD:

1. Know the names of every member of my adult choir. These people are my co-laborers in leading people in worship, and really to work with them, I must know them.

2. Pay an occasional visit to rehearsals of each of the choirs. This lets them know that I am interested in them and appreciate what they are doing.

3. Realize that many anthems are prayers, and use phrases from them in my own prayers.

4. Give an occasional word of honest appreciation of the music program.

5. Work closely with director and organist in planning all programs—not to dictate—but to give them a very definite knowledge of my intense interest in such programs.

6. I would occasionally want the choirs to have a large part in the Sunday morning service, for that is when the most people are present.

7. Realize that music can either make or break a service. "Religion and music are twin doors that open to the soul."

IF I WERE AN ORGANIST I WOULD:

1. Realize that I was the most heard musician in my church. The people hear me more than any other single musician. I guide their musical destiny, and would plan the best music possible.

2. I would put only English titles on bulletins.

3. I would study how to play hymns so that I could really lead a congregation.

4. I would learn how to modulate and transpose.

5. I would study the psychology of public worship. Playing is not to show off but to lead in worship.

6. I would not have a lot of music cluttered on the console.

IF I WERE A MEMBER OF THE MUSIC COMMITTEE I WOULD:

1. Get musicians for my church who were prepared spiritually and otherwise.

2. When I got a person, give him active support and help. Get him the best possible tools—good room, piano, money for new music. My job is not just to get a person, and then sit down and do nothing till that person resigns and I have to get another.

3. Learn all possible about church music. Ask my director for some books on the subject.

4. Encourage the musicians and attend rehearsals occasionally.

5. See that my director has a Sunday off occasionally (besides his vacation) to visit other churches and see what they are doing.

6. Make it possible for my director to attend refresher courses— and see that the church pays for it.

7. Be the go-between for the music department and all other departments of the church.

IF I WERE A LAYMAN WORSHIPING IN THE PEW I WOULD:

1. Realize that it takes the composer, singer, and reception to make music. If I am not trying to be a part of the music and worship through it, I am missing something. It is something offered to God, into which I should enter.

2. Do my best to be in my place when the music starts so I can be receptive to the mood of the prelude. Not read the bulletin or *talk*.

3. If I could sing, do so lustily.

4. Listen to those around me, and if I heard someone I thought could sing, speak to him, suggest that he try out (not join—that is for the director to decide) for the choir, and if necessary take them to the director.

5. If the choir had *helped* me through their music, tell them so.

282

IF I WERE A MEMBER OF A CHOIR I WOULD:

1. Give my very best to being a part of leading people to wor-ship. The choir deals with eternal values. I would let *nothing* avoiaable interfere with my being there for rehearsals and on Sundays to sing.

IF I WERE A PARENT OF A CHILD IN A CHOIR I WOULD:

1. Encourage the child and see that he gets the training he should have. Never make fun of his singing.
2. See that my child attends rehearsals.
3. Not plan trips that would interfere with the choir schedule.
4. Help the child at home with his music.
5. Always be there when he sings.

IF I WERE A DIRECTOR OF MUSIC:

At this point Dr. Whittlesey said, "But I am a director—and I realize that my very best is totally inadequate." His last remark was to the effect that when he thought of the great privilege and the great responsibility that was his he could only go to his knees in prayer to God.

The Joy of Life

A great deal of *the joy of life* consists in doing perfectly, or at least to the best of one's ability, everything which he attempts to do. There is a sense of satisfaction, a pride in surveying such a work—a work which is rounded, full, exact, complete in all its parts, which the superficial man, who leaves his work in a slovenly, slipshod, half-finished condition, can never know. It is this conscientious completeness which turns work into art. The smallest thing, well done, becomes artistic.

WILLIAM MATHEWS

Participating or Passive

Many of the criminals interviewed by Senator Kefauver in his crime investigation blamed their failure in life on the lack of church influence in their childhood. I wonder what a difference a choir would have made in the course of their lives. Think of the tremendous character influence your combined choirs represent. We work with two of the greatest influences known: religion and art; we work through the strongest moral force in society—the Christian Church. And as Choristers' Guild associates, we work with a keen awareness of our personal obligation to the present and to the future, to others and to ourselves. If we have that awareness, we will constantly be improving our methods, enlarging and deepening the meaning of the choir, and supporting the Guild's efforts to bind together in one universal movement the scattered seeds of growth. It is the *participating*, not the passive members who will bring that goal in sight.

Peace on Earth, Good Will to Men

This is the message of Christmas expressed in carols, anthems, and special services. The message will be "as sounding brass, or a tinkling cymbal" if it does not actually exist within the church family. Too often the minister and church musician view each other with mutual distrust. One time at a dinner meeting, at which the ministers were the obviously wary guests of their music directors, the speaker, sensing the cautious atmosphere, discarded his notes, and asked everyone present to write on a slip of paper the qualities he desired most of all in his minister or minister of music, and to pass the paper in unsigned.

This is the summary of the ministers' desires:

Good horse sense.

Understanding of the minister's total task, and how music is a part of the *total program*.

Deep appreciation of the ultimate aim and purpose of the worship service.

One who has had a deep spiritual experience.

Keen interest, co-operation, and progressiveness.

Ability to co-operate, and work as a teammate in the total program, and not see his task as separate from the whole.

Stable and dependable; not too emotional.

Ability to see the importance of music participation for the entire congregation, and to work toward greater participation.

Knowledge of the boundary of the respective fields, with ability to advance or retreat as the case may warrant.

This is the summary of the desires of the ministers of music:

A *real* interest in the music, with constructive criticism and approval.

Understanding of the problems involved in choir work.

An awareness of service music as opposed to "special music."

Encouragement and inspiration to the choirs; willingness to show interest in the music program.

Intelligent co-operation, a patient attitude, musicality.

Willingness to talk things over together.

Willingness to be truthful.

Opportunity to develop active participation in the congregation.

Complete understanding of the responsibilities and obligations of the director.

The ice was broken when they discovered that they had the same misgivings, and the same aspirations.

Perhaps our share of the responsibility for peace on earth, and goodwill, is to have more faith in the good intentions of our working partner.

_____

"Teach us, O Lord, to do little things as though they were great, because of the majesty of Christ who does them in us, and who lives our life; and to do the greatest things as though they were little and easy because of His omnipotence."   PASCAL

> "Four things a man must learn to do
> If he would keep his record true:
> To think without confusion clearly;
> To love his fellow men sincerely;
> To act from honest motives purely;
> To trust in God and heaven securely."

Anonymous

Turn, sometime, to the index of your hymnbook and discover how many of the hymns were written by that great poet, Anonymous. It is a rather stirring exploration.

Every hymnbook will list at least twenty-five or thirty hymns to the credit of this unknown figure. Some of them, surprisingly enough, are the great hymns of the Church. "Come, Thou Almighty King" was written by Anonymous. So was "Adeste Fideles," both words and music. So were "Fairest Lord Jesus," and the great Easter hymn, "The Strife Is O'er, the Victory Won."

Think of launching into eternal remembrance such great hymns as those which have just been named, among the many! What a debt the church and the world owe to the writer whose name has been forgotten.

If we start out on this line of thought, and let our imagination run freely, we will have an exciting journey. How many of the great gifts of life have come from Anonymous! Who invented the wheel? Who first made use of fire? Who first pried loose a great stone with a lever? Nobody knows. His name was Anonymous.

Consider the New Testament. How many of those who served greatly the cause of Christ were without name?

There was the man, for instance, who made possible the Last Supper by allowing it to be held in his house. We do not know his name, but he was a vital part of all it has meant to the world.

There was the town clerk in Ephesus who saved the life of Paul by a flash of inspired common sense amidst hysteria. We know his position but not his name.

Two things emerge from our remembrance. One is that no one can set a limit to the amount of good a person can do if he does not care who gets the credit. The second is that if our world is ever to be truly saved, to be made secure and livable, it will be done by Anonymous.

That is, it will be done by those who do not leave their names on the great rolls of history, but who are part of the forces making for public opinion that will ultimately make a better world. That means you and me.—Anonymous.

Halford E. Luccock in *Unfinished Business*. Harper & Brothers.

Thumbnail Sketches

A lot of people are like wheelbarrows—not good unless pushed.

Some are like canoes—they need to be paddled.

Some are like kites—if you don't keep a string on them, they fly away.

Some are like kittens—they are more contented when petted.

Some are like footballs—you can't tell which way they will bounce.

Some are like balloons—full of wind and ready to blow up.

Some are like trailers—they have to be pulled.

Some are like neons—they keep going on and off.

Selected

Sanctuary

On the coast of Southern California, where the Palos Verdes Drive follows the edge of the sea to the fold in the land known as Portuguese Bend, stands a church. It is a contemporary structure of sun-warmed redwood rising from native stone foundations. The big light of California streams through the glass walls; the worshiper whose thoughts lift his head toward heaven can see the blue vault of the sky through its glass roof. Beside it rises the admonishing finger of a white sandstone campanile, and when the soft floodlighting bathes it at nightfall, the fishermen working the waters off Santa Catalina Island murmur, "Ah, the candle of God." The church is the Wayfarers' Chapel. This is a place in beautiful context with an age prone to confuse motion with progress, likely to find aimless panic in what could be fruitful leisure hours. It is a spiritual oasis ministering to one of the major needs and one of the greatest of all possible blessings of increased personal time, the need to "Be still, and know that I am God." Here, at any hour, when the swallows dart at dawn over the tawny hills, or when the sun stains the Pacific at dusk, comes the fundamental realization that for all men life is a journey. It is a trek from forgotten darkness to a destination of deep mystery and sublime promise. There is no need for a headlong rush. The end is the same; let the pace be worthy of the dignity of the journey; let quiet restore serenity and courage. And here, too, in the Wayfarers' Chapel, when the breeze is fitful over the pews, remindful of lupines on the hills and the coppery touch of sun, it is easy to know that *all travelers carry within themselves some form of chapel, and there is time to sit within it."*

By Carl L. Biemiller. Reprinted by special permission from *Holiday,* copyright 1956 by The Curtis Publishing Company.

THANK GOD

When you first open your eyes in the morning, look up and thank God for the tasks that await you. Thank Him for even the difficult tasks. Try to imagine how dull the day would be if you had nothing to do. When you force yourself to work, and to do your best, you grow in mental and spiritual stature. If you did only that which you like to do, you would become morally weak and flabby. If God gives you a difficult job, He is complimenting you. He apparently thinks that you are strong, and capable, and dependable. Don't fail Him.

The difficulty with too many of us is that we live only in the middle range of the scale of life. We never know the full range of living because we seek only those areas of life which we can have without pain, and with as little effort as possible.

One never stands so straight as when one stoops to help someone who needs one's help.

The Parson's Pen, *St. Paul's Outlook*

PRAYING HANDS

By Albert Durer

As a young man, Albert Durer left his home in Nuremburg, Germany, to study art with a great teacher. Because he was very poor, it was exceedingly hard for him to study and make a living at the same time. He found a friend, a man older than himself, who also had a desire to become a great artist, and the two shared a room.

One day when the struggle for food had discouraged them both almost to the point of giving up their dream, Albert's friend made a suggestion—let one of them make the living for both while the other continued to study, then when the paintings began to sell, the one who had worked would have his chance. Albert's friend cheerfully insisted on being the first to earn the living, and he labored long hours for many days washing dishes in a restaurant, sweeping, and scrubbing.

At last came the day when Albert Durer sold a wood-carving for enough money to buy food and pay rent for a long time. Now his friend could return to art study. But, tragically, the days of hard work had done something to his friend's hands—the knuckles were enlarged, and the finger muscles stiffened from long hours with the scrub brush. He would never again be able to use a brush as an artist!

Young Durer was heartbroken at the tragedy. One day he returned to the room unexpectedly to hear his friend's voice in prayer, and, entering softly, saw the work-worn hands folded reverently in prayer. Albert Durer, with tears in his eyes, then made a vow that his masterpiece of art would be a painting of those work-worn hands, that the world should know of the beauty of hands that toiled for others and remember with devotion, on seeing his picture, the hands that had toiled for them.   *Selected*

AN AFFIRMATION OF EASTER FAITH

I believe that life everlasting flows from the
    Fatherhood of God as a stream from a spring.
        (A Moment of Silence)
I believe that the risen Christ is witness to
    the truth that death is not the end of man.
        (A Moment of Silence)
I believe that immortality is something to be
    lived rather than something to be proved.
        (A Moment of Silence)
I believe that the world is God's and that we
    may live in many different rooms therein.
        (A Moment of Silence)
I believe in living as God intended we should—
    as though we are a part of eternity with Him.

Selected

Challenge

Some of the most effective teaching is for unworthy causes. The principal of a Christian school in Indonesia, now on leave and studying for his doctorate, recently said that their greatest problem is the many Communist schools, where all the students are artfully trained as Communist missionaries. They are sent out in groups of four to propagandize homes and visit business houses. Each student makes a secret report on his teammates. The pressure is so great that the average "voluntary" contribution by the business houses of the city is forty per cent of their income.

As he spoke, I could not help but think how difficult it is for avowed Christians to give just ten per cent of their income to the cause of Christianity.

And I wondered, too, what power could be developed, if the thousands of children in our Guild choirs were trained as purposefully as the children in those Communist schools. The children's choir is the seedbed of Christian leadership. The conditions are ideal: the children come voluntarily; it is an activity that requires active participation; words and thoughts are sealed to the walls of the mind by the adhesive of music. But too often we are blind to our larger responsibility. The choir is a routine job, and we do it in a routine way.

Here and there, however, there is a director who has a sense of urgency in his work, who is as consumed by faith as is the Indonesian

Communist. It is such to whom the rest of us look with either envy or admiration, not realizing that whoever gives himself over to a powerful directive faith is bound to reflect a measure of that power. His mind becomes sensitive to all stimuli, his ability to create, adapt, to understand and to project, is tapped and he is able to go far beyond his own unaided ability. With gratitude he can say with St. Paul: "I can do all things in him who strengthens me."

Believe that your choir can help children to become self-reliant, informed adults, guided by Christian principles they understand and personally accept. Realize that you have but fleeting minutes of time to direct that course of character unfoldment; then permit everything you experience, read, hear, or think, help to mold you into the kind of director that will make those minutes meaningful.

But They Won't

A Methodist minister fell into conversation with his seat mate on the streetcar. The young man said that he used to be a Methodist, too, but became impatient with their lack of interest in bringing in the kingdom of God. "So I joined the Communist Party, that is really working to bring peace to the world. I have scheduled my day, and allow eight hours for sleep, eight for work, and the other eight I give to the party. And that's no more than any of the others do. Why, if the Methodists alone worked as hard for their religion, there wouldn't be any need for Communism or anything else." And then, as he got off to go to his cell meeting, he looked back with a knowing smile, and said, "But they won't."

Methodists, Christians, Presbyterians, Episcopalians, Baptists, Lutherans—but they won't?

> Would you set your name among the stars?
> Then write it large upon the hearts of children
> They will remember!
> Have you a vision of a finer, happier world?
> Tell the children.
> They will build it for you.
> Have you a word of hope for poor, blind, stumbling
>   humankind?
> Then give it not to stupid, blundering men.
> Give it to children.
> In their clear, untroubled mind it will reflect
>   itself a thousandfold
> And some day paint itself upon the mountain tops.

CLARE TREE MAJOR

290

In the Vanguard

In 1951, Howard Swan, a very successful Los Angeles church musician, predicted that the time would come when the determining factor in getting a church position would be one's ability to work with children. Very few people believed him then, but from the vantage point of the Guild office, we can see that time coming—and coming rapidly. And here is some of the evidence.

1. The increasing number of children's choirs, and youth choir festivals throughout the country. *Diapason,* the official publication of A. G. O., has frequent reports on such events, whereas, only a few years ago, there was seldom a mention of children's choirs.

2. The increasing demand for full-time ministers of music, capable of working with children as well as adults.

3. The interest in special training courses in children's choir methods. The Guild summer schools, devoted entirely to youth choirs, attract both volunteer and professional directors in increasing numbers.

4. The interest and the sense of destiny of those attending is steadily mounting.

5. One denomination, the Southern Baptist, has appointed a national music director with a staff of assistants, and has full-time music supervisors in 13 states.

6. The yeast-like growth of the Guild. Without publicity or advertising, we have grown steadily.

As a member of the Guild, and a children's choir director, you are in the VANGUARD. But unless you constantly improve your methods, and increase your knowledge, the procession will overtake you, and pass you by.

You must give increasing time and thought to your work.

You must base your work on sound educational principles.

You must be willing to experiment—and to share.

You must widen your circle of related interests.

THE CHURCH IN THE UNITED STATES AND IN BRITAIN

Twelve British ministers who visited the United States have returned home thrilled and impressed by the "enthusiasm for religion" in the United States. Some of their observations follow.

"You are not faced by a cold front of seeming defiance, which one sometimes meets in this country. No wonder every preacher from Britain feels the thrill of preaching in America today."

"Religion is taken much more seriously in America than in Britain. Nearly 60 per cent of Americans are church members. The figure for Britain is under 10 per cent."

"In America the churches are packed; in Britain they are usually half empty, especially on a rainy Sunday."

They made special mention of the enthusiasm in American churches, especially professional choirs. It is quite normal to have two or three choirs for a church and one had seven.

They made special mention of the warm friendship they felt in American churches as compared to the strange coldness in the English churches now.

Ye Call Me Master

Ye call Me Master and obey Me not,
Ye call Me Light and see Me not,
Ye call Me Way and walk Me not,
Ye call Me Life and desire Me not,
Ye call Me wise and follow Me not,
Ye call Me fair and love Me not,
Ye call Me rich and ask Me not,
Ye call Me eternal and seek Me not,
Ye call Me gracious and trust me not,
Ye call Me noble and serve Me not,
Ye call Me just and fear Me not;
If I condemn you, blame Me not.

Author Unknown

The Meaning of Excellence

A fundamental principle of education should be to make the pupil realize the meaning of excellence, of the first-rate, and to send him out of school and college persuaded that it is his business to learn what is first-rate and pursue it—not only in the job in which he earns his living, but in all the great fields of life, and above all, in living itself. And I would also try to give the pupil at school a better idea than he sometimes gets of what is first-rate in literature, architecture, music, art—and above all, what is first-rate in conduct and life. Then we might get nearer to creating a democracy which believes in, desires, and recognizes, where it cannot achieve, excellence in all the noblest activities.   SIR RICHARD LIVINGSTONE

Are You Ready for a Real Job?

PHYSICALLY?

Good health? Full of energy? Good posture? Attractive appearance?

EMOTIONALLY?

Can you hold your tongue? And your temper? Do you get along with people?

Do you know how to laugh? At the right time? Are you a worrywart? Can you accept criticism? Do you use both head and heart in your decisions?

INTELLECTUALLY?

Do you hunt and find new ideas? Do you finish what you start? Are you convincing?

Have you read any new books and articles? Have you planned your program?

SPIRITUALLY?

Is your religion real? Do you read your Bible purposefully? And contemporary religious books? Do you know the history and the tenets of your church?

Have you studied your Church school literature?

MUSICALLY?

Have you found interesting new material? Have you studied it? Decided how to present it? Set new standards of tone and musicianship for your choir?

Discovered improved rehearsal methods?

Every choir situation presents some problems. Whether they are caused by conditions, or by personality friction, they will not be solved by running away from them. Too often we succumb to the temptation of finding "the easy way out." But the easy way is seldom the courageous way. Leadership demands the power to see a personal problem with the eyes of an impartial judge, and to act with equal impartiality; to recognize disappointments as an inevitable part of life, and to find some wise solution; to refuse to accept opposition, and to convert it into friendship. These are the demands of honest leadership. He who accepts them will truly become a leader. And that is the quality of leadership the Children's Choir movement requires of you.

Materials

BOOKS

CELEBRATIONS

Christmas. Ed., Schauffler. Dodd, Mead and Co.
    A splendid collection of material, interestingly presented.
Christmas Book of Legends and Stories. Smith and Hazeltine. Lothrop, Lee and
    Shepard.
Christmas in the Country Church. Rural Institute. Barnes Hall, Ithaca, New York.
Christmas in the Home. Pilgrim Press. 14 Beach St., Boston.
Christmas Pamphlets. American Baptist Convention. 1703 Chestnut St., Phila-
    delphia.
    "Christmas with Children."
    "Christmas with Kindergarten Children."
    "Christmas with Primary Children."
    "Christmas with Junior Children."
Easter Pamphlets. American Baptist Convention. 1703 Chestnut St., Philadelphia.
    "Easter with Nursery Children in Church and Home."
    "Easter with Kindergarten Children in Church and Home."
    "Easter with Primary Children in Church and Home."
    "Easter with Juniors in Church and Home."
    "Easter in the Town and Country Church."

CHRISTIAN EDUCATION

At Work with Children in the Small Church. (Pamphlet size.) Judson Press.
Better Home Discipline. Cutts. Appleton-Century.
Can I Teach My Child Religion. Stewart. Doubleday.
Christian Teaching in the Church. Schisler. Abingdon.
Faith of Our Children. Jones. Abingdon.
Guiding Children in Christian Growth. Jones. Abingdon.
Heaven in My Hand. Humphrey. Methodist Publishing House.
How to Help Your Child Grow Up. Patri. Rand McNally.
Living with Our Children. Gilbreth. Norton.
New Ways in Discipline: you and your child today. Baruch. McGraw.

Pamphlets. National Association for Mental Health. 1790 Broadway, New York 19.
   A Pound of Prevention. Hymens.
   Helping Children Develop Moral Values. Montague.
   How Would You Help a Child Like This.
   Self-understanding for Teachers. Menninger.
   Teacher Listen, the Children Speak. Hymens.
   The Primary Teacher. Trager.
   This Is the Adolescent. Frank.
Teaching Junior Children. Judson Press. Philadelphia.
Teaching Primary Children. Judson Press. Philadelphia.
The Happy Family. Levy and Munroe. Knopf.
The Strategy of Handling Children. Laird. Grosset.
The Church School Teacher's Job. Eakin. McMillan.
Understanding Children. Lewis Sherrill. Abingdon.
Your Child and God. Trent. Harper.
Your Child and His Problems. Teicher. Little.
Your Best Friends Are Your Children. Benedict. Appleton-Century.
We the Parents. Gruenberg. Harper.
Your Part in Your Child's Education. Lane. Dutton.

CHURCH MUSIC

The Choirmaster's Workbook. Nordin. Augustana Book Concern.
Church Music, Illusion and Reality. Davison. Harvard University Press.
Lyric Religion. Smith. (The stories of hymns and hymn tunes.) Century Co.
The Chorale through Four Hundred Years. Liemohn. Muhlenberg Press.
The Gospel in Hymns. Bailey. Scribners.
The Story of Our Hymns. Ryden. Augustana Book Concern.

MUSIC AND CHRISTIAN EDUCATION

Music in Christian Education. Thomas. Abingdon.
Music in the Religious Growth of Children. Shields. Abingdon.
The Use of Music in Christian Education. Morsch. Westminster Press.

AIDS TO MUSIC EDUCATION

Flash Cards. Lyon and Healy.
Games for Children. National Recreational Assn., 315 Fourth Ave., New York.
Junior Music Quiz. Burch and Ripperger. Summy.
Maestro. Gamble-Hinge.
Music Time (singing games). Bampton. Birchard.
Music Bingo. Melody Card Co., Milbrae, California.
Music Fun: Books I-IV. Kenworthy Educational Service, Buffalo.
Note Speller. Thomson. Willis Music Co.
O Say Can You Hear: Vol. I-III. House. Mills Music Co.
Rhythm Fun for Little Folks. Renstrom. Pioneer.
Rhythms for Children. Wilcox. 175 Fifth Ave., New York.
Twice 55 Games with Music. Birchard.
Theory Is Fun. Castelli. Boston Music Co.
Thirty Rhythmic Pantomimes. Gaynor. Church.

CHOIR TRAINING

Boy Choirs. Nicholson. Paterson Publications, Ltd., 35 W. 32nd St., New York.
Correct Pronunciation of Latin, according to the Roman Usage. St. Gregory Guild,
   1705 Rittenhouse Square, Philadelphia.
Training the Boy Chorister. Noble. G. Schirmer.
Training the Boy's Changing Voice. McKenzie. Rutgers University Press.

DRAMATICS

Amateur Producer's Guide. Jackson and Forsyth. Paxton.
Handbook of Acting. Alberti. French.
How to Make Historic American Costumes. Evans. Barnes.
Preparation and Presentation of Operettas. Beach. Ditson.

TEACHING MUSIC

Children and Music. Landeck. Sloane Assn.
Discovering Music. Wadley and Allison. Boston Music Co.
It's Easy to Make Music. Leeming. Franklin Watts.
The Child's Unfoldment Through Music. Knapp. Willis Music Co.

RHYTHM BANDS

How to Teach the Rhythm Band. Diller and Page. G. Schirmer.
Rhythm Band Collections. Boston Music Co.
  Eighteen Folk Tunes. Churchill.
  Folk Tune Book. Diller and Page.
  North American Tunes for Rhythm Bands. Gest.
  Rote Pieces for Rhythm Bands. Diller and Page.
  Toy Orchestra Tunes. Jobson.

MUSIC FOR CHILDREN UNDER EIGHT

All Through the Year. Whelan. Hall and McCreary.
Complete Nursery Song Book (for preschool). Bertail, Lee, and Shepard.
Father, Hear Thy Children Sing. Hall and McCreary.
Follow the Music. Coit and Bampton. Birchard.
God's Wonderful World. Mason and Ohanian. Random House.
Hymns for Primary Worship. Westminster Press.
It's Fun to Sing. Ruff. Hall and McCreary.
Singing Fun (activity songs). Webster Publishing Co.
Song Wings Books I and II. Birchard.
Songs and Pictures. Foresman. American Book Co.
Songs for Children. Nordgren-Lekberg. Augustana Book Concern.
Songs for the Little Child. Baker and Kohlsaat. Abingdon Press.
Tiny Tot Songs. Warner Press.
Tone-matching Tunes. Coit and Bampton. Flammer.
The Whole World Singing. Thomas. Abingdon.
When the Little Child Wants to Sing. Westminster Press.

RELIGION

Christ and the Fine Arts. Maus. Harper.
In Our Image (paintings of Old Testament characters). Guy Rowe. Oxford University Press.
Life of Jesus. Goodspeed. Harper.
Like a Mighty Army. Luccock. Oxford University Press.
One God, the Ways We Worship Him. Fitch. Lothrop, Lee and Shepard.
The Story of the Bible. van Loon. Perma Book.

MISCELLANEOUS

Bells. Coleman. Rand McNally.
Getting the Most Out of Life. Reader's Digest Compilation.
Vestment Cutout Kit. S. Theodore Cuthbertson, Inc., 2013 Samson St., Philadelphia.
    (Vestments, cut out and packaged, with easy to follow sewing instructions.)

297

RECREATION

Junior Party Book. Bernice Carlson. Abingdon.
Family Fun Kit. Service Department Board of Education, Box 871, Nashville.
Handbook for Recreational Leaders. Superintendent of Documents, U. S. Printing
    Office, Washington 25, D. C.
Leadership of Youth. Ben Solomon. Youth Service, Inc., Putnam Valley, New York.
Playground Guide for Summer. National Recreation Assn., New York.
Recreational Pamphlets. Methodist Publishing Co., Nashville.
    "Family Pleasure Chest."
    "Handy I and II."
    "Lift Every Voice" (fun songs).
    "The End of Your Stunt Hunt."
    "The Children's Party Book."
    "The Pleasure Chest."
    "Skits and Stunts."
    "Promenade All."

CHORIC SPEECH

An Approach to Choral Speech. de Banke. Bakers Plays.
Choral Reading for Worship and Inspiration. Brown and Heltman. Westminster
    Press.
Musical Speech and the Making of Personality. King. Birchard.

STORIES

Call It Courage. Sperry. MacMillan.
Chimes and the Children. Bowie. Fleming H. Revel.
Favorite Stories. Cooper. Southern Publishing Co., Dallas.
Modern Parables. Ousler. Doubleday Doran.
Peter, the Boy Chorister. Nicholson. MacMillan.
See Where Jesus Lived. (Magic slate activity for small child.) Strathmore Co.
    Aurora, Illinois.
The Christmas Story. (Magic slate activity.) Strathmore Co. Aurora.
Sunny Windows. Bowie. Revell.
The Child Jesus, Told by Matthew and Luke. Doubleday-Doran.
Thoughts of God for Boys and Girls. Walker and Barber.Harper.

Symbolism

An Outline of Christian Symbolism. Wilson. Morehouse-Gorham.
Christian Symbolism in the Evangelical Churches. Stafford. Abingdon.
My Own Workbook of Christian Symbolism. Brookman. Morehouse-Gorham.
The Sign Language of Our Faith. Griffith. Morehouse-Gorham.

ANTHEMS

CODE OF SUITABILITY

1. Primary Choir: 6 to 8 years of age
2. Junior Choir: 9 to 12 years of age.
3. Junior High or High School: treble
4. Junior High and High School: mixed
5. Adult Choir
6. Combined Choirs

GENERAL

A Child's Thanksgiving. Baynon. Oxford University Press 1138, 1-2.
Alleluia. Mozart (simplified). Lorenz 8551, 2-3.
America (from symphony America). Bloch. Birchard 2-3-4. (For patriotic occa-
sions.)

298

An Awakening. Robson. Novello 1837, 2-3.
All Things Divine. Mueller. Edwin Morris 4073, 2-3. (Chorale tune.)
Be Thou My Vision. Gillette. Kjos 2-3.
Come together let us sing. Bach. E. C. Schirmer Choral Songs 1001, 2-3.
Come Christians, Join to Sing. Mueller. C. Fischer CM 6326, 3-4.
Dear Christians, Praise God Evermore. Kindermann. Concordia LD 503, 2-3. (Two
    violins.)
For the Blessings of Our Day. Krones. Kjos 4218, 2-3-4. (Spirited.)
Golden Grain, Harvest Bringing. Muzet-Whitehead. Boston Music Co. 2.
Glory to the King of Kings. Thompson. Lorenz 8543. 2-3-4.
Hymn of Praise. Larson. Proart CH 1397, 2-3.
If with all your hearts. Mendelssohn. G. Schirmer 2-3.
I Will Sing of Thy Great Mercies. Mendelssohn-Protheroe. Gamble-Hinge 2-3.
Lead Me, Lord. Wesley. Gray 2-3-4-5. (Original key rather low for children;
    otherwise good.)
Let All Things Now Living. Davis. E. C. Schirmer 1819, 2.
Let Us Praise God. Olds. Hall and McCreary, 2-3-4-5-6. (With readings, or speech
    choir.)
Now Thank We All Our God. Krones. Kjos, 3-4.
O Lord of Heaven and Earth and Sea. Larson. Schmidt 209, 2-3.
O Lord How Manifold Are Thy Works. Barnby. G. Schirmer, 2-3.
O Come, let us sing unto the Lord. Douglas. Hall and McCreary 2550, 2-3.
Praise to the Lord the Almighty. Mueller. C. Fischer CM6326, 2-3.
Praise ye the Lord the Almighty. Olds. Hall and McCreary, 6. (SAB with children.)
Prayer of Thanksgiving. Kremser. G. Schirmer 7950, 2-3-4-5.
Prayer of St. Richard of Chichester. White. Oxford University Press E43, 2-3-4.
    (Unusually fine.)
Psalm 150. Curry. H. W. Gray CMR 2129, 6. (Children sing Doxology in original
    form.)
Song of Praise. Thiman. Schmidt 40, 2-3.
Sing Thanksgiving. Ohanian. Flammer 86094, 2.
To God All Praise and Glory. Larson. Birchard 2095, 6. (Very easy.)
The Corn Song. Holst. E. C. Schirmer, 2.
The Knight's Song. Thiman. Edward Arnold, 2.
The Shepherd. Brooks. Oxford 149, 2-3. (Interesting imitative parts.)
Through All the Year. Pitcher. Birchard 30, 2. (Descant.)
We Gather Together. Netherlands Folksong. E. C. Schirmer 1579, 2, (Descant.)
We Come with Voice of Gladness. Larson. Proart 1138, 2. (SA)
With Happy Voices Ringing. Rossel. J. Fischer 8596, 2-3. (SA with violin.)
With Verdure Clad. Haydn. Arr. Reed. Birchard, 2-3. (Simplified version of the
    aria from Creation.)

CHRISTMAS

A Carroll. Jacobson. Birchard 965,2-3. (Unison with flute; middle section (SSA)
    can be omitted.)
A Catalan Christmas Song. McKinney. J. Fischer 6662, 2-3. (SSA. Not difficult.)
Bethlehem. Dickinson. Gray. (SA. Easy.)
Carol of the Messenger. Whitehead. Galaxy GM-1777-3, 2-6. (Baritone solo, for
    children, and SATB.)
Christ and the Children. Dickinson. Gray 258, 2-6. (SA with baritone solo.)
Carol of the Little King. Caldwell. Gray CMR-2260, 2-3. (SA)
Carol of the Singing Reeds. Johnson. J. Fischer, 2-3. (Unison, unusual and lovely.)
Carillon. Briel. FitzSimons, 2. (Contrasting sections; good for boys and girls
    divided.)
Christ is here. Richard. Birchard, 2. (Unison with violin.)
Christmas Song. Holst. G. Schirmer 8119, 2-3-4. (Easy and effective.)
Christmas Long Ago. Dunhill. C. Fischer 470, 2.
Chrystmasse of olde. Bartlett. Flammer, 2-3. (Melody has interesting archaic
    flavor to match the text.)
Good Christian Men Rejoice. Mueller. C. Fischer CM-6304, 2-3. (SA)

299

How Far Is It to Bethlehem. Gritton. Galaxy 15, 2. (Lovely simplicity.)
In Yonder Manger. Dickinson. Gray 51, 2-3.
In Bethlehem's Lowly Manger. Williams. Flammer 89085, 2-3. (SSA)
It Came upon the Midnight Clear. Dunhill. Edward Arnold Co. 2-3. (Unison with
    descant.)
Long, Long Ago. Nagle. O. Ditson, 2-3. (SSAA. Melody alone can be used.)
Long, Long Ago. Rawls. Gray, 2-3. (SA with flute.)
Little Christ Child, Sweet and Holy. Williams. Flammer, 2-3. (Descant.)
Lullaby, Little Jesus. Magney. Gray, 2. (SA)
Little Jesus. Williams. Flammer 86097,2. (Good range. Three melodies with first
    repeated. Easy accompaniment.)
Lantern Bright. Aulbach. C. Fischer CM-6754. (SATB, but melody can be used
    alone. Easy, straightforward.)
Mary's Lullaby to the Infant King. Warner. Birchard 1611, 2. (Very easy. Based
    on German folk tune.)
On a Morning Long Ago. Davis. G. Schirmer 7355, 2-3.
Noel. Wells. Presser 312-40107, 2-3-4-5-6. (Easy and useful. SATB, but can be
    used in many combinations.)
Puer natus in Bethlehem. Hales. Birchard 1241, 2-3. (Use antiphonally, first choir
    sings Latin, second sings English equivalent.)
Rise Up Early. Kountz. Galaxy, 2-3-4. (SA. Easy, joyous.)
Sleep, Little Jesus. Anderson. British-American Co., 2-3. (Quiet, atmospheric. Ac-
    companiment completely independent.)
Sleep, Holy Babe. Snow. R. D. Rowe, 2-3. (SSAA)
Sweet Marie and Her Baby. Niles. G. Schirmer, 3-4. (Sensitive. SA.)
Star Candles. Head. Boosey MFS-153, 2-3. (A rare find, but not easy.)
Softly the Stars Are Shining. Torovsky. 1317 G. St. N. W., Washington, D. C.
    (SATB. Very popular with the children's choirs of Washington.)
The Animals' Carol. Dunhill. British-American Co., 2. (Good for 4th and 5th
    grades. Imaginative.)
The Little Lord Jesus. Slater. British-American Co., 2. (SA. Alto part essential,
    but could be taken by cello.)
The Christ Child Lay on Mary's Lap. Tatton. Birchard 1213, 2-3. (Flowing phrases.
    Accompaniment written for piano.)
The Little Jesus. Holler. Gray 2042. (Easy.)
The First Mercy. Warlock. Boosey and Hawkes, 2-3. (Unison.)
The Snow Lay on the Ground. Sowerby. Gray CMR-2238, 2-3. (Descant. Grateful.)
The Sleep of the Holy Child. Anderson. Birchard, 6. (Solo with SATB.)
The Shepherds Sing. Young. Gray CMR 2256, 2. (Unison.)
The Shepherds Found Thee by Night. Shaw. Novello, 2-3.
The Savior of the World. Holst. Arthur Schmidt, 2-3.
Thou Child Divine. Voris. Gray 834, 2-3-4-5. (SATB)
Venite adoremus. Wright. Canyon Press, 3-4-5. (SATB)
Watching o'er His Manger Bed. Williams. Flammer 86116, 2-3. (Easy. Descant in
    canon form.)
What Strangers Are These. Purvis. Birchard 969, 6. (Question and answer form.)
Welcome, Welcome, Jesus, Hobbs. Canyon Press, 6. (SATB; with children.)
When the Shepherds Were Watching. McLain. Flammer, 2-3. (SA)
When Christ Was Born of Mary Free. Williams. Birchard, 2-4-5. (SAATB)

CAROL COLLECTIONS

Children's Favorite Christmas Carols with Pictures for Coloring. William. British
    American Co. 1. (Charming for small children.)
Christmas, Its Carols, Customs and Legends. Heller. Hall and McCreary. 2-3-4.
Christmastide (a medley of 9 carols). Bourdon. Flammer. 3-4. (SSA)
Christmas Carols for Treble Voices. Hall and McCreary. Auditorium Series 56. 2-3.
    (15 carols with good accompaniments.)
Christmas Carols for Secondary Schools. Ward and Mooney. Flammer. 3-4.
Descants for Christmas. Krones. Kjos Music Co. 2-3-4-5. (Singable descants for
    fourteen Christmas carols.)

300

Descants on Christmas Carols. Hall and McCreary Auditorium Series 47. 2-3-4-5. (Twenty unison and SATB carols with descants and accompaniments.
Five Christmas Carols. Arr. by Mansfield. Arthur Schmidt. 2-3. SA; all interesting.
Junior Choir Christmas Collection. Arr. by Lynn. Ditson. 5 carols for unison or SA. 2-3.
The Christmas Caroler. Arr. by Cookson. FitzSimons. 3-4-5. SATB. (Good for community sings.)
The Ditson Christmas Carol Book. Ditson. 2-3-4-5. (Forty-seven carols; many unusual ones.)

NATIVITY PLAYS

Christmas Carol Pageant. Diller and Page. G. Schirmer. 2. (Simple and charming; full instructions for presentation.)
The Finding of the King. Broome. Oxford University Press. 4. (In the medieval manner; interesting music; requires good acting; excellent for a good High school choir.)
The Holy Night. Kate Stearns Page. G. Schirmer. 2. (Words and music adapted from old French Christmas Songs based on the legend that on Christmas Eve the beasts could talk.)
There Was One Who Gave a Lamb. Ham. J. Fischer. 2. (Action, music, costuming, simple and effective.)

CHRISTMAS CANTATAS AND CHORAL SERVICES

A Ceremony of Carols. Britten. Boosey and Hawkes. 3-4. SSA; (Beautiful, but too difficult except for exceptional choir of high school girls.)
Childe Jesus. Clokey. Birchard. 2-3-4. (Simple and effective.)
Christmas Messiah. Handel. Lorenz. (The Christmas portion of The Messiah arranged for SSA.)
Christ Is Born. Clokey. Birchard. 2-3-4. (Easy and attractive; SATB)
Christmas-Tide. Bourdon. Flammer. 2-3. (Good continuity of familiar carols.)
In David's Town. Kirk-Kennedy-Sherman. Birchard. 2-3-4. Based on Latin American carols; several for SATB but can be adapted for children's voices: very attractive and different.)
The Story of Bethlehem. Willan. Concordia. Text is Luke 2:1-14. 3-4. (Longer work in recitative style, for a superior group of Junior High or High school girls. Requires an experienced and sensitive organist. SSA.)
The Story of Silent Night. Westervelt. Elkan-Vogal Co. 2-3. (Choral program for treble voices with descant, and narrator; attractive and easy.)

HOLY WEEK

Alleluia. Perry. Presser 21647. 1-2. (Very simple.)
Alleluia, Alleluia. Cain. Flammer 89114. 6. (SSA with children.)
Alleluia, Christ Is Risen. Gillette. Kjos 5085. 6. (Fine effect with simple means.)
Alleluia of the Bells. Marryott. Gray 1904. 3-4. (SAB, spirited.)
All Glory, Laud and Honor. Gillette. Kjos. 6. (Children sing the familiar hymn.)
All Glory, Laud and Honor. Bach. Oxford University Press. 17a. 2. (Uses the organ accompaniment of Bach Cantata No. 95.)
All Hail to Christ Our King. Rawls. Fischer 8533. 3-4.
An Easter Antiphon. Candlyn. Gray 683. 5-6. (Brilliant.)
An Easter Carol. Holler. Gray CMR 1946. 2. (Easy, with descant.)
Awake Thou Wintry Earth. Davis. E. C. Schirmer 1550. 2-3. (SA)
Carol of Joy. Walker. Gray 2329. 3-4. (Good effect with simple means.)
Come Ye Faithful. Thatcher. Oxford University Press. Ea 11. 2. (Easy.)
Choruses for Eastertide. Arthur Schmidt Co. 2. (Five easy SA numbers.)
Easter Bell Carol. Davies. Flammer 86101. 1-2. (Unison with descant. Easy.)
Easter Carol. McLain. Edwin Morris Co. 3-4. (SA, minor but joyous, broad alleluias, ends in major.)
Easter Chimes. Neidlinger. O. Ditson 332-11510. 1-2. (Very easy, comfortable range.)

Easter Joys. Baynon. Novello ss-1794. 2. (Unison, good text, fine phrase line.)
Jesu Do Roses Grow so Red. Webbe. Gray 1363. 2-3. (SA or unison. Unusual.)
Legend. Tschaikowsky. Kjos 8258. 2-3. (Good translation.)
One Early Easter Morning. Marryott. Ditson 14814. 2-3. (Very easy.)
Praise to the Lord Who Lives on High. Olds. Witmark 5W3244. 6.
O Sing Ye Alleluia on This Day. Sala-Bedell. Boston Music Co. 5-6. (Let a fine
    tenor take the text; the children the alleluias.)
Sing All Ye Christian People. Olds. Hall and McCreary 1606. 6.
Sing to the Son of David. Rawls. Fischer 8277. 6.
Song for Easter. Eichhorn. H. W. Gray 2057. 2-3. (Easy and happy.)
Spring Bursts Today. Thompson. Gray 1321. 2-3-4. (Several sudden changes of
    key.)
Nature's Eastertide. Baines. Presser 21137. 3-4. (SA, alternates 3/4 and 4/4.)
The Whole Bright World Rejoices Now. Hill. Gray 1861. 2. (Easy, bright.)
The Bird of Christ. Ross. Gray 1626. 2-3. (Omit the solo; takes a sensitive choir.)
The World Itself Is Blithe and Gay. Marryott. Gray. 2-3.
The Robin and the Thorn. Niles. G. Schirmer 9326. 2-3. (Unison, not easy,
    sensitive.)
This Glad Easter Day. Dickinson. 2-3.
This Joyful Eastertide. Somervell. Boosey and Hawkes. 15, 2-3. (Easy and joyous.)
To Zion Jesus Came. Williams. Gray 2330. 6. (Simple and effective.)
We Will Be Merry Far and Wide. Marryott. Gray 1273. 6. (Let children take the
    melody.)
Ye Watchers and Ye Holy Ones. Davis. E. C. Schirmer 1561. 3-4. (Descant.)

EASTER CANTATAS

The Builders. Clokey. H. W. Gray. 2. (Unison service, or pageant.)
The First Easter. Ada Richter. Presser. 2. (A story with music; music simple, much
    of it familiar hymns, suitable for either children or small volunteer choir.
    Would be effective with slides, or good tableaux.)

MOTHER'S DAY

A Prayer for Motherhood. Norman. Lorenz A-131. (SATB, or SA)
Carol for Mothers. Lovelace. Gray. 2-3-4-5. (SA; SSA; SATB)
Mother's Day Anthem. Ohanian. Flammer. 2-3. (A simple unison anthem with a
    worthy text.)
Mother's Day Hymn. Barnes. J. Fischer 8087. 2-3-4-5. (SATB)
Now Thank We All Our God. Bach. E. C. Schirmer. 2-3.
Responsive Service for Mother's Day. Voris. Ditson 14171. 2-3-4-5. (Would have
    to be adapted for children.)
We Thank Thee, Lord, for Mother Love. Flammer. (From Junior Choir Church
    Year Book.)

JUNIOR CHOIR ANTHEM COLLECTIONS

Anthems for the Junior Choir. Curry. Westminster Press. Vol. I, II, III.
Choral Gems from the Masters. Grant. Boston Music Co.
Eighteen Duets for soprano and alto. From the Bach Cantatas. 2-3. Drinker Li-
    brary, Westminster Choir College, Princeton, New Jersey.
Green Hill Treble Choir and Duet Book. Davis. E. C. Schirmer.
Junior Choir Church Year Book. Rutenbeck. Flammer.
Our First Songs to Sing with Descants. Krones. Kjos.
Rounds and Canons. Wilson. Hall and McCreary.
The Belfry Book. Davis. Gamble-Hinge.
The Treble Choir. Hall and McCreary.
Ten Sacred Songs from the Music of the Moravians. Mercury Press. (Unison with
    strings.
Twelve Motets for Two Equal Voices. Lassus. Music Press.
Two-part Anthem Book. Mueller. C. Fischer.
Songs of Praise with Music. Shaw and Vaughan Williams. Oxford University Press.

HYMNALS

Concord Hymnal. E. C. Schirmer.
Hymns for Children and Grown-ups. Friedell. Farrar, Straus and Young.
Hymns for Junior Worship. Westminster Press.
New Hymnal for American Youth. Appleton-Century.
Our Songs of Praise. Concordia.
The Junior Hymnal. Augustana Book Concern.

RECOMMENDED ANTHEMS FOR THE HIGH SCHOOL CHOIR

As It Fell upon a Night. Davis. Galaxy 1291. (SATB) (Effective Christmas number; not difficult; good range.)
Come Thou Almighty King. Whitehead. C. Fischer CM-602. (SATB) (A sturdy hymn-tune anthem; one that encourages active singing.)
Father of Heaven, Whose Love Profound. Willan. Concordia HA-2005. (Splendid text. Easy vocal range.)
For the Blessings of Our Day. Krone. Kjos 4218. (SA or TB) (Lower voices have melody in second stanza. Rhythm that strides.)
God Is My Shepherd. Dvorak. Birchard 949. (SATB) (Requires sensitive singing, and response to mood.)
I See His Blood Upon the Rose. Roberton. G. Schirmer 8597. (SSATB) (A favorite with many choirs.)
Let All Mortal Flesh Keep Silence. Holst. Galaxy. 5. (Mostly unison.)
Let Us Break Bread Together on Our Knees. Currie. (SAB) (A devotional setting of a Spiritual.)
Lord, We Cry to Thee. Dickinson. Gray 212. (SATB) (Prayer anthem. Sixteenth century melody. Interesting accompaniment.)
O God of Youth. Darst. Gray 2147. Unison. Challenging text. Range rather high for changing voices.)
On Christmas Night. Ehret. Volkwein. (SA or TB. Easy and effective.)
O Spirit Who from Jesus Came. Havey. G. Schirmer 9878. (SATB) (Devotional. In speech rhythm. Easy parts.)
Praise to the Lord. Whitehead. H. W. Gray CMR-2100. (Vigorous setting of fine chorale tune. Independent accompaniment.)
The Lord Is a Mighty God. Mendelssohn. Kjos 9. (SATB) (Much duplication of parts. Easy accompaniment. Paraphrase of Psalm 95.)
The Lord's My Shepherd. Mueller. C. Fischer CM-6616. (SATB) (Simple accompaniment. Much unison. Good range. Lovely melody.)
The Word Became Flesh. Brandon. Canyon Press. (Unison.)
What Shall I Render to My God. Lovelace. Canyon Press (SATB) (Actually only two parts. Good swing.)
What Strangers Are These. Purvis. Birchard 1447. (Question and answer anthem. Has character and mood.)
With a Voice of Singing. Shaw. G. Schirmer. SA-10227: SAB-10226. (Vitality and interplay of parts.)

EDUCATIONAL RECORDINGS

Christmas Carols of Many Lands. Vienna Choir Boys. Victor C-32.
Columbus Boy Choir. Box 350, Princeton, New Jersey.
No. 104. Familiar Christmas Carols. $3.00.
No. 105. I Wonder as I Wander, and Lullaby of the Christ Child.
Festival of Carols. Westminster Abbey Choir. His Master's Voice.
The King of Instruments, Vol. I. Aeolian-Skinner Organ Co.
Silver-Burdette Co.
Music for Young Listeners: blue, crimson and green albums.
Folkways Records and Service Corporation, New York City
PF5 Songs to Grow On: Vol. I.
Theodore Presser

Game Songs	Christmas Songs
Fairy Tales	Christmas Carols
Folk Songs	Party Game Songs
Favorite Songs	Folk Tunes

(Each set of four records)

Comstock Publishing Associates, 124 Roberts Place, Ithaca
Music and Bird Songs. (Unique Nature Study Record.) You may have heard this record on the Sunday afternoon New York Philharmonic broadcasts. It gives the song of familiar birds, and then cuts them down to half, and quarter speed, to reveal the amazing range and intricate intervals of the songs. 10-inch, 33 1/3 r.p.m. record; two sides, on vinylite.

Listening

Educational Records Boston Music Co., 116 Boylston St., Boston

CU 106—Tubby, the Tuba. Danny Kaye. $2.10.
DU 90022—Nutcracker Suite. Fred Waring. $2.10.
YPR 311—The Wonderful Violin (for ages 7 to 11). $1.45.
YPR 1007—The Emperor's New Clothes. Douglas Moore. $2.90.
YPR 409—The Chisholm Trail (for ages 7 to 11). $1.45.
YPR 407—Stravinsky (ages 7 to 11). $1.45.
YPR 710—The Bells of Calais (ages 2 to 6). $1.45.
YPR 713—Circus Comes to Town (ages 2 to 6). $1.45.
YPR 408—Music of Aaron Copeland (ages 7 to 11). $1.45.
Y 357—Why the Chimes Rang. $2.36.
Y 345—Peter and the Wolf. $2.36.
Y 344—Pee-Wee, the Piccolo. $2.36.
E 88—Christmas Album Lilla Belle Pitts and Gladys Tipton. $5.00.
   The Listening Program Lilla Belle Pitts and Gladys Tipton. Each album. $5.00.
      Primary Grades: E77, E78, E79.
      Upper Grades: E80, E81, E82.

Rhythms

YPR 317—Country Dances. Mozart. $1.45.
YPR 715—Waltzing Elephant (2 to 6). $1.45.
YPR 619—Little Indian Drum (2 to 6). $1.45.
E 89—Indian Album (elementary grades). Pitts and Tipton. $5.00.
   The Rhythm Program Pitts and Tipton, each album, $5.00.
      Primary Grades: E71, E72, E73.
      Upper Grades: E74, E75, E76.

Singing Games

RR4—Songs and Singing Games (5 to 8). $2.36.
E 87—Singing Games (primary grades). Pitts and Tipton. $5.00.
Y 335—Singing Games (6 to 12). $1.31.

Songs for Children

J 26—Nursery Songs. $2.36.
CU 100—Mother Goose Songs. $2.10.
CU 101—Nursery Rhymes. $2.10.
C.S. 4—Sleep, Baby, Sleep (quiet music). $2.36.
Y 337—Songs of the Zoo. $1.31.
YPR 404—Let's All Join In (American Folk Songs, ages 7 to 11). $1.45.
      The Singing Program. Pitts and Tipton. Each album, $5.00.

Rhythm Band Records

E 90—$5.00.

1. Amaryllis. Old French
   Minuet in G. Paderewski
2. The Secret. Gautier
   Pirouette. Finck
3. Gavotte. Thomas
   Rendezvous. Aletter

4. Rataplan—Donizetti
   Serenata—Moskowski
   Waltz No. 5—Koschat
   With castanets—Reinecke
   Shadows—Schytte

The House of Brason, 945-947 West George St., Chicago 14, Illinois
Young People's Records 10″ 78 r.p.m. Standard Speed Unbreakable Records, $1.25 each.

Age Group: 2-5

Dramatic Play

222	Hooray Today is Your Birthday	725	When I Grow Up
225	Twelve Days of Christmas	726	The Neighbor's Band
611	The Sleepy Family	728	Chugging Freight Engine
615	The Little Fireman	730	Singing in the Kitchen
619	Little Indian Drum	735	Little Grey Ponies
703	Little Brass Band	805	A Walk in the Forest
715	Waltzing Elephant	807	Happy Little Farmer
721	The Runaway Sheep	809	Three Little Trains

Activity Records

617	When the Sun Shines	714	Whoa Little Horses, Lie Down
701	Around the World	718	Winter Fun
705	Happy Birthday	722	Sing-Along
706	Trains and Planes	724	Out-of-Doors
712	Rainy Day	729	More Playtime Songs
713	Circus Comes to Town	802	Let's Play Zoo

Sound Records

501	The Magic Clock	609	Penny Whistle
601	Muffin in the City	710	Bells of Calais
603	Muffin in the Country	720	Music Listening Game

Age Group: 6-10

Fact and Folklore

403	Let's All Join In	435	Little Hawk, the Indian Boy
404	Birth of Paul Bunyan	438	Around the Campfire
410	Jazz Band	504	Timber-r-r
425	Adventures of Daniel Boone	508	Christopher Columbus

Music Masterpieces

313	Mozart Country Dances	432	Concerto for Toys and Orchestra
317	Everybody Dances—Mozart	1001	Haydn Toy Symphony
405	Folk Songs for Orchestra	1003	Summer Day
431	Round and Round	1009	Rondo for Bassoon and Orchestra

Instrumental Series

309	Lentil and His Harmonica	421	The Hunter's Horn
311	The Wonderful Violin	407	Igor Stravinsky
411	Said the Piano to the Harpsichord	408	Aaron Copeland

Magic-Tone Records 10″. 98c each. 545 Fifth Ave., New York 17, N. Y.

M6	Let's Go to the Circus	M23	Good Music Can Be Fun
M9	Children's Prayers—Children's Lullabies	M24	Children's Songs of France
		K113	Mexican Clap Hands Music
M15	Franz Schubert	M25	Children's Songs of America
M21	Chopin for Children	M26	Children's Songs of Italy

Record Guild of America 10″. 49c.
R124 Play Games—Activity Songs

Vox Records either 78 or 33 1/3 long-playing album—$4.00.
VL2590   Johann Strauss—His Story and Music.
VL2570   Tschaikowsky—His Story and Music.
VL2550   Schumann—His Story and Music
VL2540   Schubert—His Story and Music.
VL2520   Chopin—His Story and Music.
VL2510   Mozart—His Story and Music.

Haydn Society, Boston
HSC-I   Let's Listen to Haydn.

USEFUL AUDIO-VISUAL MATERIALS
Methodist Publishing House, Nashville

Primary

Children and their Homes around the World. Picture Set.
When Jesus was a Boy. 35mm filmstrip: color sale.
Mexican Children. 16mm film rental. Also 35mm filmstrip.
Sumo. 35mm filmstrip Story of an African Boy.
Nonebah of the Navajos. 35mm.
Your Family. 16mm rental.
Isaac of the Tents. 35mm.
Making Home a Happier Place. 35mm.
Boys of the Southern Mountains. 35mm.
Sammy. 17 slides color: Church of All Nations in New York.
Children at Worship Around the World. Picture Set.
Josie. 21 slides color: Church of All Nations in Los Angeles.

Junior

Two Thousand Years Ago Series: The Home, The Day's Work, the School.
One God. 16mm: The Catholic, The Protestant, The Jewish Way.
The Story of Dr. Carver. 16mm.
The Greenie. 16mm (an immigrant boy finds new friends in America).
Christmas Around the World. 40 frames. Sound.
Albert Schweitzer. 35mm.
An End to Darkness. 16mm sound (Son of an African Chief, and Christian Teaching).
People of the Congo. 16mm (Shows crafts and musical instruments).
Pygmies of Africa. 16mm.
Fire upon the Earth. 16mm Color (History of the Protestant Church).
The Story of the Christian Church. 35mm filmstrip. 53 frames.
Days of Wonder (full color nature film with sound).
A Journey through the Holy Land. (A sightseeing tour through Palestine.)
Jerusalem and Its Holy Places. 64 frames.
The Holy Land from Nazareth to Jericho. 45 frames.

Christmas

The Child of Bethlehem (presenting incidents from the stories of the birth of Christ and of His boyhood, as recorded in the Gospels). Sound motion picture. 22 minutes. Cathedral Films.
Holy Child of Bethlehem. Color film strip. Traditional Christmas story. Records use music and voices. 78 rpm sound and color filmstrip.
When the Littlest Camel Knelt (color film strip telling of the birth of Christ, in a new presentation). Color and sound filmstrip, 78 rpm.
Life of Christ. Elsie Adams Wood paintings. Set of six colored slides on birth and early life. Order from division of education, 79 E. Adams St., Chicago. (Other films available through your denominational headquarters.)

Church Film Service, 2595 Manderson St., Omaha, Nebraska
Merry Christmas. Sound film.
Shrine of a Nation. Westminster Abbey. Sound film. (Uses boy choir.)

Eastin Pictures, Davenport, Iowa
Instruments of the Orchestra. London Symphony, Malcolm Sargent. 16mm film.

Encyclopedia Brittanica Films, Inc., 20 N. Wacker Dr., Chicago
String Choir, Brass Choir, Woodwind Choir, Percussion. 10 minute films.
For other music films and films of countries and peoples, customs, and ways, consult Educational Film Guild Annual Edition (probably in your public library).

306

INDEX

309